MORE PRAISE FOR *SCARS OF THE SPIRIT*

"A certain kind of reading—end driven, moving toward the satisfaction of conclusion and resolution—is not the pleasure given by this text; and indeed were the text to give it, it would be in tension with its own mode of thinking, a mode of thinking we can weakly call dialectic, moving back and forth between the noting of appearance and fakery everywhere and the equally omnipresent desire for the real. In the experience it provides, this beautifully written book is truer to the lesson it would teach: the difficulty and necessity of the search for the authentic."

—Stanley Fish, Dean of the College
of Liberal Arts and Sciences,
University of Illinois at Chicago

"Hartman successfully recasts some of our basic questions—and it is perhaps through our questions that we understand our human predicament. Recommended."

—*Library Journal*

"This is a profound, learned, impassioned meditation on the role literary study can play in invigorating the imaginative life of our civilization—without which it is difficult to imagine having a civilization at all."

—Jonathan Rosen, author of
*The Talmud and the Internet:
A Journey Between Worlds*

The wounds made by the spirit leave no scars.

—Hegel

SCARS OF THE SPIRIT

THE STRUGGLE AGAINST INAUTHENTICITY

GEOFFREY HARTMAN

For Joanna and Daniel Rose

First published in hardcover in 2002 by Palgrave Macmillan
First PALGRAVE MACMILLAN™ paperback edition: August 2004
175 Fifth Avenue, New York, N.Y. 10010 and
Houndmills, Basingstoke, Hampshire, England RG21 6XS.
Companies and representatives throughout the world.

PALGRAVE MACMILLAN is the global academic imprint of the Palgrave Macmillan division of St. Martin's Press, LLC and of Palgrave Macmillan Ltd. Macmillan® is a registered trademark in the United States, United Kingdom and other countries. Palgrave is a registered trademark in the European Union and other countries.

ISBN 1-4039-6558-7

Library of Congress Cataloging-in-Publication Data

Scars of the spirit : the struggle against inauthenticity / by Geoffrey H. Hartman.
    p. cm.
Includes bibliographical references and index.
Cloth ISBN 0-312-29569-3
Paperback ISBN 1-4039-6558-7
1. Authenticity (Philosophy)   I. Title.

B105.A8 .H37 2002
128—dc21

2002020727

A catalogue record of the book is available from the British Library.

Design by Letra Libre.

First PALGRAVE MACMILLAN paperback edition: August 2004

10 9 8 7 6 5 4 3 2 1

Printed in the United States of America.

CONTENTS

ACKNOWLEDGEMENTS

I have had the pleasure of discussing portions of this book with Leslie and Susan Brisman, Tom and Lilian Greene, Richard and Carol Bernstein, Heinz-Karl Barck, Henri Raczymow, Annette Wieviorka, Mark Krupnik, Lawrence Langer, Helen Elam, Cathy Caruth, Richard Weisberg, Martin Jay, and Vivian Liska. My wife, Renée, was a sounding board at every stage. Earlier versions of five of the thirteen chapters have appeared in *Partisan Review*, *Raritan*, the Tanner Lectures on Human Values (vol. 21, 2000), the Emory Humanities Lecture Series, and *Aufmerksamkeiten*, edited by Aleida and Jan Assmann. I also wish to thank Allison Weiner and Martina Kolb for checking and researching help, and Kristi Long, my editor, for good advice and encouragement.

FOREWORD

Those who put their thoughts into writing often remark that even when they believe they are expressing something original (or "ahead of their time"), they suddenly notice the same concerns all around them. So the very week I sent a draft of this book to publishers, the Sunday *New York Times* carried an article on the controversial rapper Eminem's "intricate and sophisticated identity assaults" as well as a Book Review end piece that linked the identity issue to the theme of authenticity by evoking the continued prevalence of national/ethnic/religious profiling. Critics who indulge in the latter, the author suggests, act as their "culture's power brokers."[1] This year also, several cogent analyses of Binjamin Wilkomirski's Holocaust fabrication and the (Vietnam) False Witness Syndrome have appeared.

The concerns broached in these essays are, then, far from unusual. They sprout everywhere and disturb everyone. But the personal essay does not have to be original or jazzy, and can even bear some academic ballast. I try to observe, without stereotyping or forcible yoking, the way life and art interact.

❏   ❏   ❏

"Dangerous Good Words," chapter 1, is aware of the etymology of "authenticity." But its meaning has broadened beyond the Greek word linked in antiquity to the Latin "auctoritas," which defined authority as the power, legal or moral, vested in those who founded an institution or claimed they were transmitting vital truths from an ancient source. Although an aura of this meaning lingers, the allusion to presumed origins, except when it involves documents that need to be authenticated, has disappeared into its obverse: In nontheocratic societies, authenticity now signifies a moral strength *not* based primarily on formal or institutional authority.

In my first book, *The Unmediated Vision* (1954), I described the modern poet as rejecting traditional mediations in order to attain a more direct relation to experience. Like a new Perseus he faced the Gorgon of reality without a protective mirror. Youthful optimism made me write at the end of that book: "The experiment has only started which, clearing the mind for the shock of life, would in time overcome every arbitrary god of the intellect." Understood this way, the search for authenticity and for experience coincide.

The New Perseus, I also wrote, had to draw a mediating mirror out of the very elements that threatened him. Today these elements include likenesses more numerous, artificial, and tricky than any Renaissance or Christian Platonist discourse imagined, when it speculated on similitudes, simulacra, and resemblances that draw seekers toward the true image of things. "Good Men . . . find every Creature pointing out to that Being whose image and superscription it bears, and climb up from those darker resemblances of the Divine Wisdom and Goodness . . . till they sweetly repose themselves in the bosom of the Divinity."[2]

But it is not clear whether our new knowledge-mirrors, our semiotics, or other interpretive and filtering mechanisms, can deal with either raw experience or its excess of replica. From the film *Blade Runner*, inspired by Philip Dick, to Steven Spielberg's *A.I.*, technological fantasies express something of the terror as well as the complexity of dealing with the growing resemblance of natural and simulated. In his poem "The Garden," Andrew Marvell calls the mind "that Ocean where all kind/Does straight its own resemblance find," but the French critic Maurice Blanchot is haunted today by resemblances without prototype or archetype, by appearances that are the reality they seem to mask.

I do not give more than a sketchy historical overview of this development. Only contemporary history enters as a matter of cultural and political urgency. With respect to simulacra, I take it for granted that imitation, as *homo faber*'s deceptive, or at least playful manufacture of images and semblances has always existed. "As if his whole vocation/Were endless imitation," Wordsworth writes of the infant's attempts to con adult roles in the "Intimations Ode." Role theory extends this child-centered model into an always incomplete maturity.[3] Why does Rimbaud say "Love must be reinvented"? Is it because we want to retain a childlike freedom, or is it because we discover that even love is dominated by convention and role-playing?

One of the oldest allegorical figures is the "Faux Semblant" or Dissembler. Since malevolence can simulate normality or even goodness, a part of our mind always fears to find a suspect identity. But dissimulations of a more innocent kind also exist. By the fatality of a natural deformation no one avoids conformity, or its pretense. Mozart, in *Cosi Fan Tutte*, despite his scenario's conspicuously insincere clichés about women's liberation, shows how hard it is—for both men and women—to get beyond the simulation of emotions. The arias of this joky opera reach a depth the twists of an infantile plot only emphasize.

While this aspect of the human condition seems to me universal, the specifically contemporary problem is, as I have indicated, how we should deal with the proliferation of replica. The distinction—or indistinction—of appearances and reality enters a new phase. The omnipresence of video, for instance, has altered our sense of the everyday. To engage fully with daily life could be a mark of the authentic. Yet, at any point, as we direct the movie camera toward even the most trivial event, there is an insidious expectation, an excitement not unmixed with fear, that the filmed nonevent may become eventful. Don DeLillo, the novelist, captures this perfectly in a scene from *Underworld* in which a twelve-year-old records a random murder on tape.[4] Reruns of amateur video sequences that have become famous—of Kennedy's assassination, for instance, or the LAPD's savaging of Rodney King—do not cease to fascinate: Something has tainted our eyes, made them more anxious.

How deep, how automatic, is this apprehensiveness? Are nerves now wired to the stale, revelatory glow of the TV set? If so, could the media's reality effect, its simulacra, undermine the pleasure we once took in artistic forms of imitation? Such forms used to provide closure, moderating (if only by art's ritual devices) an anxiety that arose from the open-ended narrative of life.

It is ironic, but the empowerment that comes with being able to make home movies about the simplest stuff actually enhances a taste for artifice—although not always for art. The reason is that Hollywood films, for example, are in many ways more predictable—more comforting because of their conventional limits—than randomly operating, liberated camcorders. This conventionality also affects the imaging of character. Unconventional roles become role models through constant exposure by movies and MTV. As for the everyday realism that crowds into DeLillo's novel, it seems less real now than what is seen on any amateur tape. DeLillo: "There's something about the nature of the tape, the grain of the image, the sputtering black-and-white tones, the starkness—you think this is more real, truer-to-life than anything around you. The things around you have a rehearsed and layered and cosmetic look."[5]

The question that arises, beyond whether realism as a style has reached its term, concerns interpersonal relations as well as the future of sensibility. Those equivocal simulacra, so real and yet unreal, can be playful as long as they leave the normative world untouched. If that world is not in question, the anxiety I have talked about remains manageable. Yet our present, immense, pixelish capacity for technological reproduction, including biological cloning, opens an alarming vista that extends Freud's discovery of the psyche as terra incognita with uncanny mechanisms and drives.

Moral issues surface here because sense perceptions cannot be totally separated from the sphere of the interpersonal. To influence the "gaze" is also to influence the "face" of things. A comic but tense episode in *Underworld* depicts how a casual window-shopping look becomes dangerous when interpreted by a combative stranger as "the look." A glance without ulterior motive arouses territorial instincts. The absurd encounter suggests that ideology can intersect a totally harmless gesture. When an identity politics as naïve as in the scene from DeLillo takes over eyes and ears, it means that marginal differentiation is usurping interpersonal space. Otherness, so central an issue in contemporary moral philosophy, becomes even more of a problem because of that usurpation. When the space between persons (the *inter-esse*) is not respected, dialogue disappears.

If, as I think, the trouble arises from a visceral feeling of identity lack, of being a mere phantom, a simulated person ("android" or "replicant"), rather than "the single one" (Martin Buber, modifying

Kierkegaard, uses that term to characterize the individuality of the authentic individual),[6] then self-legitimation is obliged to depend on absurd acts of assertiveness. The inventive heraldry of conversation is bypassed and signifying turns into an escalating mode of violent address, a demand on the other that is impossible to meet. This manner of resisting sameness—the individual's wish to achieve difference through self-assertion—is soon exhausted, however. It wearies us out, the paradox that resistance to sameness must come through an insistence on self-identity. In this battle, force majeure gains the upper hand by offering an orgiastic communal merging, the prefabricated likeness and absolution of a group identity.

Let me mention, finally, Jean Baudrillard's view that differentiates simulacrum and simulation. The simulacrum is said to be an indistinguishably true simulation, a "hyperreal" model that is its own reality referent.[7] Baudrillard, a French culture critic, suggests what may always have prompted not only the concept of absolute immanence but also that of absolute transcendence: of the One who exists beyond imitation, and so both inspires and defeats all copies. The "scars of the spirit" referred to in my title are suffered in the pursuit—and imposition on others—of a transcendent ideal beyond earthly realization. A commonplace epistemological issue, how to be more discerning in an environment of replica, how to distinguish the true copy, the authentic imitation, betrays here its undercover theological aspect.

Returning to the sphere of ethics: Decisions must be made, yet how can they be made if not only a streaming knowledge but also a radical indeterminacy thwart the critical edge of decision-making? We have confused documentation with the Book, Emmanuel Levinas, the French philosopher, writes. The gap widens between information and wisdom, between the cumulus of fact and the approach to truth. When archive fever, as it has been called, and its surplus of artificially conserved historical memories, lead to the anticipatory exhaustion of all potential ideals (Baudrillard talks of the "divine irreference of images"), an indifference close to nihilism can ensue.[8]

That my treatment of the counterfeit (the faux real) on the way to understanding authenticity remains more tentative than Baudrillard's, and my discussion of the relevance of art and the aesthetic less assertive than that of a French philosopher like Lyotard (item: "Aesthetics is the mode taken by a civilization that has been deserted by its ideals"), is a fault I cannot excuse by a further reflection on style. I have responded to the urgency of these issues without the megaphone of a more assured thesis.

This book is dedicated to friends whom I do not hesitate to call authentic and whose engaged personal support of so many communal, intellectual, and art-centered activities I admire.

Geoffrey Hartman
August 2001

PART I

TRIPLE OVERTURE

CHAPTER 1

DANGEROUS GOOD WORDS

"Spirit" and "authenticity" are word concepts that cannot be saved from their own pathos. Perhaps we should not even try to sober them up. The impression they leave is clear enough. As in paintings from earlier centuries that do not disdain the language of gesture, where the figures portrayed point upward to a cynosure even as it is about to be taken from sight, so "spirit" marks that vanishing point; while "authenticity" evokes something more solid and steady, more in-itself than transcendent. Like "integrity," it suggests an earthy quintessence, firmly local, and with a constancy that, in Shakespeare's words, will not "bend with the remover to remove."

Both qualities express dissatisfaction with the human condition, either by attempting to rise above it (spirit) or to be more fully of it (authenticity). What will convince us that we are real, or that our being here has a reason? That we can infuse existence with an authentic or spiritual rather than contrived and self-deceiving purpose? The dramas in which we are enmeshed, whether at home or in the public sphere; the sense, often, that life is somewhere else ("over there—/Behind the shelf/The Sexton keeps the key to—"[1]); that personal autonomy is a sham and some great endeavor is needed to justify our life: Such feelings come on more strongly when the *previous* generation has passed through a cataclysmic historical event. The burden of such an event is transmitted in conscious or unconscious form to the third generation and beyond. Not necessarily as a curse (the dark legacy of genocide, for instance) but as a haunting, ambiguous sense of living in the aftermath, of having missed a fateful, defining moment.

A canon or authoritative tradition is, in this light, the active residue of such moments. It remains somewhat abstract, though, a merely suggestive set of themes and molds, an intriguing subject for imaginative exploration that helps to articulate thoughts and feelings and prepares the inexperienced for what may come. Nothing, of course, can fully immunize us to what life will bring. And should catastrophe or crisis supervene, earlier forms of containment are often sorely tested, if not shattered. So Jean-François Lyotard has said that the Holocaust is like an earthquake whose force destroyed the seismic instruments.

The records gathered under the name of science, history, or art nonetheless remind us of what has survived previous tremors. Even in the absence of a personally experienced *tremendum* (whether catastrophe or ecstasy), these survivals challenge the imagination: There is no need to undergo a renewed violent testing to prove that humanity has confronted what threatens to exceed its capacity or understanding. Other survivals, too, supplement canonical tradition or even challenge its relevance. For while the modern diaspora is characterized by extreme social mobility, especially in North America, so that it is not unusual to find someone in a family with illiterate grandparents who has become an artist, intellectual, or articulate professional, the eventual result is a rediscovery of roots, of a "grounding" genealogy. Old photos, in this context, often seem like icons or sacred relics: not only images of authenticity but authentic images.

Through oral history, moreover, now systematically pursued, there is an attempt to honor the life stories of ancestors who bear on their faces and in their demeanor the travails of the past and appear to be close to their traditions and even the soil they once cultivated. The American ethos of total assimilation, the so-called melting-pot pattern of acculturation, is questioned by these contrary strains. A multiculturalism emerges that seeks an alternate theory, one that would respect rather than neutralize dissimilar ways of life.

❑   ❑   ❑

Concerning "authenticity," in particular, it has often been observed that words themselves, however needful in expressing or sustaining such ideals, also subvert them. The words evoked too often and explicitly become jargon. Theodore Adorno, in Germany, criticized Martin Heidegger's "jargon of authenticity," and Kenneth Burke, in America, talked skeptically of "god-terms." (Burke cites the oratory of a politician who modulated effortlessly from "gold" to "God.") There is a temptation to use these charged phrases for trivial or masked purposes. Except for "spiritual" itself, "authentic" may be the most inauthentic word around.

The authentic person should not have to trumpet identity statements attesting to genealogy, background, faith, integrity, public achievement. One gets tired hearing politicians vaunt their birthplace, their roots (the more folksy the better), their undiminished belief in human goodness and the country's destiny—while lambasting the decadence and corruption around them. Nor does being an intellectual and qualifying one's opinions help: Most people seem to go for the rah-rah, give-them-hell orator, not because they necessarily trust such rhetoric but because they trust intellectual politics still less. (Politics should be fun: Although nothing changes, everything can be challenged.) We know too well, moreover, that ideas in the hands of ideologues kill.

Two barely compatible images connect speech and character. There is the quiet, even taciturn person, solid as rock, a doer who gets things done by an inner and unostentatious strength. We are impressed by signs of a tacit knowledge, a prereflective (or postreflective?) understanding. But we also applaud charismatic leaders whose eloquence persuades people that destiny is on their side and everything can be changed for the better, even transformed into a new order. In both leader types "their word is their bond," but in the first the words are few, and a sense of dignity, of power in reserve, is what actually persuades; in the other, the words are many and seem to flow from the manifest destiny the speaker proclaims.

Very rarely, of course, does political theater (or any other kind) exhibit so sharply these contrasting types. Most clashes, moreover, in democratic, TV-fueled elections, rely on personal showmanship and deceptive or highly selective ads. But there can be no political contest without a judgment of character that turns on whose word is good. Who is credible and how do we estimate the promissory notes called words? "The record" is never entirely self-evident: Actions have to be brought forward, reassessed; they are vulnerable, then, to insinuation or misrepresentation. Nor, since voting means anticipating the future—luckily, in democracies, only a delimited portion of it, usually from two to five years—can past behavior stand as a total guarantee.[2] Future actions are not to be deduced entirely from a person's worldly success or failure, because the goddess Fortuna or some other quirky factor may intervene. The resilience of the reformed ("born again") sinner-politician is the wild card in many a political contest.

❐ ❐ ❐

Literature plays out the dilemmas just sketched at every level of existence, not only the political. You might immediately object that "play" is the operative phrase and that, in the political arena, however much of a show is put on, the clock is ticking, so that a vicarious, playful exemplification has no place. I am sure that is too fatalistic a view of politics and too slighting a view of art. Besides, time in art *is* often put into play as timing: Fiction has to rouse and resolve suspense, for example, and tries not to cheapen the process of discovery by excessive foreshadowing. The Dutch historian Johan Huizinga was motivated to write his famous book *Homo Ludens* (about the play element in culture) in part because he saw how Nazism was removing serious play from politics and substituting a totally controlled, ritualistic spectacle. Thomas Mann's brother, Heinrich, writes in 1934 about the Nazi regime: "Everything is prefabricated, arranged in advance, dissimulated" (Alles gestellt, alles bestellt, alles verstellt).[3]

The relation between play and reality affects all of life. It is not just a temporary factor in growing up. As D. W. Winnicott has shown, it shapes mature decision making and the well being of individuals and polities. If "the battle of Waterloo was won on the playing fields of Eton," the reason must have been an ability both to fight and to play, to flexibly leave and reenter a safe transitional space that allows for growth, speculation, imaginative options.[4]

Our civic culture too is directly dependent on tolerating close calls, peacefully negotiating rules, and mocking powerful pretensions. It is a sad mistake to relegate art to the expendable margins of schooling or public priorities. The German poet-philosopher Friedrich

Schiller argued at length for what he called "aesthetic education" as an extension of the play instinct and a distinct phase in humanity's progress toward removing a twofold dependency: one that comes from "above" as well as from "below," from coercive ideologies as well as from instinctual drives.[5] Yet Schiller knew that the autonomy enabling the freedom of individual or nation was an ideal, that personal and political liberty would never be attained once and for all through the intermediate development of an aesthetic sensibility. As art produces permanent transitional objects, so the concept of aesthetic education suggests not so much an end state or utopia as its continual re-envisioning.

❑   ❑   ❑

I do not intend to offer a systematic defense of art. In fact, I sometimes wonder what claim still can be made for its contribution to authentic existence. For the complicity of art in the realities of its time, a complicity that has become the dominant theme of contemporary criticism, makes it harder to look beyond a demystification that justifies it only as an instrument involved in the social or political struggle. Although this view does not inevitably condemn authors who are not overtly engaged, it insists on uncovering their "political unconscious." But would we bother with art if it were unable to encourage some ideality or imaginative license? Obversely, and despite appearances to the contrary, the nervous realism of the news channels, always trying to be ahead of the curve, is no less fallible than the predictive potential of art. "The entrails of the fish have become cold in the wind," Ingeborg Bachmann writes, anticipating hard times and hardened sensibilities. "Throw them back into the sea."[6] "There is no history: only the weather," we read in Derek Walcott's *Tiepolo's Hound*—though he immediately leavens the prosaic dictum with lyric evocations of that weather.

Valued only as exemplary fodder for the politically savvy mind, many works would have to be dismissed as morally inauthentic, a self-deluding species of consciousness or a counterfeit *promesse de bonheur*. Purely realistic social portraiture, moreover—its intoxication with disintoxication, with the "desolation of reality" mimicked by extreme performers of the movie or popular music industry—easily succumbs to caricature or cathartic entertainment, to a competitive marketing of its power to shock or shame.

Literary theory, despite present trends, need not accept a reductive view of the relation between art and politics. It should keep the use and abuse of speech, the justness and scrutinizing power of words as well as their deceitful or deceptive character, constantly in mind. It can recall how thought is deeply, and not always consciously, verbal, how the common tender of words enters every aspect of culture. Here and there a significant book refounds language: That glimmers again, the crust of accretions is subverted, each word carries a depth charge. A negotiation occurs between Keats's "all the dead whose names are in our lips" and Rilke's challenge to taste the fruit as well as the name by letting inadequate voicings melt away: "Is your mouth, at last, slowly losing all its namings?"

Most of the time, unfortunately, we remain unaware of the lava of petrified metaphors that constitutes so much of daily language. Perhaps because words on the page, although meant for thoughtful absorption and reconsideration, must always reenter the pressured marketplace of ideas: chaotic debates where force of personality is often decisive. Too much air or constant public exposure asphyxiates those words, so they become fish gasping on the strand. In literature they refresh and move as quick as in the sea.

❏   ❏   ❏

Let me turn to what may seem to be an entirely different and nonpolitical issue: the link between authenticity and attribution. Correct attribution, the standard of authenticity for connoisseurship in the pictorial and occasionally the other arts, is important where there is a distinction between master and disciple in a workshop setting or where anonymity and historical distance have made authorship uncertain. Authenticity through authentification becomes an essential ingredient of value, although primarily of market value.

More crucial, however, is another motive for authentification: the fear of being taken in by a counterfeit or the work of a lesser hand; and this betrays an uncertainty about the internal features of valuation. The identity of the artist matters as a guarantee of a direct correspondence between the mind of the maker and the attributed work. As if divine truth or the expulsion of any kind of treachery or trickery from so high a sphere were at stake, we want no shadow falling between maker and artifact, nothing that might resemble the hand of demiurge, forger, or printer's devil.

Jane Tompkins, whose memoir I comment on in chapter 4, goes wrong in one respect.[7] Her attack on the New Criticism (an influential mode of literary study from the 1930s into the 1960s) is simplistic. The movement did indeed reject the bearing of canned historical knowledge on the understanding or valuation of the work of art and denounced certain notorious "fallacies" (genetic, intentional, affective) commonly used to determine artistic meaning. But this purism was not caused, as she claims, by a wish to remain within a life-distancing, aesthetic realm. Rather, the scholar-teachers associated with the movement felt that students were unable to cope with an increasing information load threatening to replace the textual integrity or immanent qualities of the literary work. The very sense of fraudulence that invades Tompkins the teacher is also what the New Critics sought to prevent by freeing art from false standards of appreciation. Whether they succeeded in finding internal criteria of authenticity is another issue.

The struggle of the individual against inauthenticity leads to a distinct increase in autobiographical reflection. A memoir like that of Tompkins strives for transparency. It presumes a convergence, even coincidence, of first-person narrator and the self being portrayed. Authenticity through sincerity (a kind of self-authentification) is certainly a powerful motive. But the new biographical culture, in which life stories like Tompkins's participate, is also prompted, not always consciously, by the wish to find a less intellectualized probity, one more in touch with a people source and retrievable through a reflection that bends back to toiler and folk artist.

Concerning the striving for self-transparence, no one is so naive as to think all masks can be removed, all memories unified, all shadows dissolved. Shadows may be deliberately added, in fact, and often to reveal rather than conceal. The deeper they are, the more shameful or painful, the realer the life depicted. What Michel Leiris, an important French writer, calls introducing the "shadow of a bull's horn"—that is, courting in an autobiography the psychological equivalent to a matador's dangerous self-exposure, precisely because one's life has not been tested (in Leiris's case) by two world wars— shows once again the difficulty of claiming authenticity.[8] Recently, moreover, a "false memory syndrome" has emerged as the malign counterpart of a true quest romance.

The inflation of autobiographical writing, a relatively minor genre in literary history, previously limited to individuals caught up in exceptional happenings, is also related to the mounting number of refugees in the world and our awareness of their ordinary yet extraordinary situation. Diaspora and displacement, or other disruptive forms of mobility, have become a common fate. The stranger has moved from beyond the border into our midst without lessening an easily inflamed vein of suspicion that turns to xenophobia. Facing that strangeness in others, we become more aware of the other in ourselves: of what within remains ambivalent, unintegrated, in between. Ottavio Paz's "brief vertigo of the inbetween" is not so brief, because it keeps recurring. Ancestral avatars, at the same time, in the form of images and voices relayed from an older world by the reliquary magic of mechanical reproduction, by a distinctly human photo-synthesis, tease the imagination with hopes of a less fragmented personal continuity.

Is not irony, then, more appropriate than authenticity as stance or standard when we read an autobiographical account that calls itself *False Papers?* Reviewing André Aciman's memory pieces with that title, Wendy Lesser says the author "achieves his clearest note of authenticity" when describing an invasive feeling of displacement, "the loop and interminable traffic" between several countries. Yet life, as Aciman writes, is "little else than a collection of close calls and near-misses," and his love for Paris or New York or the forever lost, forever desired Alexandria, cannot be contained by the one or the other concrete city, by any here-and-now. All are "shadow cities," habitations of the mind, lost and found and lost again.[9]

Even without being a refugee, almost everybody claims a tale of loss, alienation, and, sometimes, resilience. A Babel of vernaculars, moreover, and politicized conflicts like that over bilingual education make it difficult to focus on speech as a potentially unifying *logos*. Yet new expressive genres do arise, and the field of cultural studies is currently full of memoirs featuring encounters with social suffering.

❏   ❏   ❏

In the past, these parables of a "Stygian authenticity"[10] did not always take the form of confession or autobiography: Joseph Conrad's *Heart of Darkness*, perhaps the classic instance, shows how powerfully atrocity can be dealt with in fiction. Conrad invents a narrator both distinct from and contemporary with the "I" of the author. Authorial intimacy or omniscience is replaced by this hearsay distance; and the reflective, unhurried story helps to prepare for horror without lessening the burden of having to judge Kurtz's descent into savagery. The darkness toward which readers are relentlessly if gradually conveyed reveals a potential complicity.

A similar, less exotic instance of this Stygian structure is William Wordsworth's "The Ruined Cottage," a narrative of common life among the rural poor in the 1790s. It depicts successive vignettes of Margaret, abandoned by a husband unable to look upon his starving wife and baby. Robert sells himself for conscription money in a year of famine during England's war with France. Wordsworth calls his poem "a tale of silent suffering," and to respect that silence—to find a mode of expression that would rescue it from inexpressiveness without becoming exploitative or ventriloquizing—is the creative challenge.

To that end a hearsay frame, like Conrad's, links the writer to an oral mode of transmission, now dying out. The poet learns the story of Margaret from a Pedlar who had visited the abandoned woman's cottage in his rounds. But instead of exploiting the oral literature of his time—in particular, the traditional ballad with its sensational or supernatural incidents—the Pedlar, a wisdom figure taught by Nature, depicts Margaret's mounting despair and destitution with a maximum of realism and a minimum of voyeurism. While Wordsworth turns to relics of medieval ballads in order to "redeem" the course of English poetry, his understanding of their greater authenticity is highly qualified. He produces a new, "lyrical" ballad, in which the interest in narrative, in telling a rousing story, gives way to depicting very ordinary, often minimal incidents. (Yes, in that respect, Wordsworth is a minimalist.) What matters to him is expanding the sympathetic imagination and revising the concept of news, of eventfulness. The sympathetic imagination enters crucially since almost nothing of Margaret's cottage and garden remains. The Pedlar's eye resurrects traces of human life from what has become a wilderness, without overlooking the obliterations of time and nature.

Wordsworth's poet-listener, then, stands at a significant remove from his tragic tale. He cannot (as yet) see through the landscape to what is ruined but is taught by the Pedlar whose narrative has no single epiphany, shock, or revelation. The old man's account of his repeated visits slows rather than hastens time, slows it to beyond our nervous desire to see the worst. The focus, consequently, shifts from the original incidents to their reflectors: the character of this storyteller who filters their impact and the poet-listener's response. Conrad's "heart of darkness" and Wordsworth's "still sad music of humanity" get through (*de te fabula narratur*) because the incidents are embedded in a responsive human milieu by a structured ethics of narrative. Both authors know that the reception and transmission of traumatic knowledge is like handling fire.

□   □   □

As I have mentioned, the resource of fictional treatment has given way—not entirely, of course—to biography and autobiography. This development may be reinforced by a further historical change: in the means of representation. Though the connoisseur's anxiety of being in touch with the real thing remains invariant, as does a wish for what is called, especially in the political domain, transparency (a standard of honesty that would allow us to discern truth freed of manipulation and deception), the circumstances surrounding the quest for authenticity are altering fast.

Most literary criticism of the intensive kind, marked by forbidding names such as narratology, semiotics, poststructuralism, postmodernism, French Freud, and deconstruction, has emphasized for the last forty years a radical ambiguity that complicates the act of communication. Previously a rich but resolvable kind of ambiguity (also identified as paradox, irony, polysemy, organic or dramatistic form) had been popularized by the New Criticism. For these thinkers, the obliquity and density of literary language served as a humane antidote to the rising tide of media instrumentalism: to propagandistic—commercial, ideological—simplification. It also countered a coherence theory of truth coming from a logical positivism that tried to purify ordinary as well as literary language in order to produce a relatively transparent medium. The New Critics held that literary complexity (like fiber in the digestive system!) stimulated a slower, absorptive kind of reading and a larger resonance of imaginative positions.

The value of an ultimate unification of that complexity was never questioned, however. The "darkness" of art for these critics was also, it turns out, means to an end: an improved capacity to integrate the diversity of modern experience. But after the New Critics, and under the impact of continental European theories, this strategic view of a darkness that would lead to greater linguistic control and transparency was undermined. Also affected were notions of "subject" or self, its integral character, its authenticity.

The most important factor, though, that alters the conditions under which we think about authenticity, is—in conjunction with the linguistic turn just described—an invasion of simulacra, or the media-turn: the rapidly growing influence of film, TV, Internet, and even deliberately inauthentic pictorial constructs.[11] The spoken or written word does not lose its central place in communication yet its reception is increasingly dependent on other media. An era of mechanical reproduction is in full swing, and we can observe more of its impact than Walter Benjamin could in his justly famous essay of 1936.[12]

◻   ◻   ◻

It is quite obvious that technology has created a new vein of gothic darkness, of *noir*. Paradoxically, this is woven from the very "film" of transparency. Augmented techniques of fictional deception, of entangling us in illusions, produce a strange mental indulgence. Movies like *The Matrix* and *The Thirteenth Floor* make us enjoy, or at least tolerate, an environment full of simulacra, where the giddiness of simulation within simulation rivals the story-within-story format.

Correlatively, the distinction between original and copy becomes at once crucial and unimportant: crucial from the perspective of the market, unimportant from the consumer's point of view. Yet the psychology of art continues to reflect a spiritual pursuit: for "the One," the just, chosen, authentic work or individual on which everything depends. Our quest to find the distinguishing characteristics of that One, by trials that would get rid of pretenders or false copies and reveal the truth of something great without pretense, nourishes fiction as it always has. At the same time, the emergence of a liquid art (protean in its variety), including "self-consuming artifacts," threatens not only the distinction between art and entertainment held to by Adorno and the Critical Theory movement but also the distinction between work (resulting in durational and even monumental products) and labor (transient products for consumption) that Hannah Arendt sought to establish.[13]

While attribution itself, given the glare of publicity, is rarely an issue today, since the collective character of an art like film necessarily results in hybrid or cooperative work,[14] authenticity in this new climate does face a special challenge from techniques of self-legitimation fostered by autobiography and testimonial literature. It may be that the only solution to system failure—to the increasingly inevitable knowledge that there are no across-the-board solutions, that the very idea of a solution harbors an illusion—is biographical. "This is simply what I do."[15] We are confronted, therefore, not only by identity statements of all kinds but also by a number of identity thefts, of forgeries or fabricated memoirs.

Asymptotically, at least, we seem to be approaching the condition described in Baudrillard's *Simulacra and Simulation*. Insofar as signs of the real substitute for the real, historicity itself is preserved only as a sort of artificial or frozen memory. This development would constitute, writes Baudrillard, the "veritable final solution of the historicity of all event."[16] The Holocaust, as Baudrillard's phrasing makes clear, is not spared (consider Binjamin Wilkomirski's *Fragments*[17]), and there are even more peculiar simulations, as when a white man, an avowed racist, authors the self-affirming autobiography of an Australian aborigine woman.

An especially sophisticated case is that of the French artist Christian Boltanski. He is haunted by the reality claim of photographs and other simulacra. In his installations and writings, he makes us wonder whether authentic images exist any more than authentic life-stories. But even his deliberate toying with replica, his rephotographing of photographs, does not diminish a persistent visual desire, the wish to penetrate beyond surfaces and silhouettes, either to the skull beneath the flesh or to the lost body of empty, unholy relics. Each of his portrait galleries, shadowed by the Holocaust, is a makeshift mausoleum.

❑   ❑   ❑

Mimesis, or imitation, has been at the center of reflections on art since Aristotle. He declared not only that it was a universal source of delight but that it played a role even in the pleasure gained from the representation of tragic events. The pleasure came, he speculated, from "catharsis," a quasi-medical purging or purification of pity and terror. These feelings were roused by Greek tragedy and so eliminated, or recreated in a more noble form.

The debate about the sources of the delight derived from imitation—particularly artistic imitation—of painful events has changed since the eighteenth century into a debate about the nature of human imitation generally and its relation, however archaic, to magical practices and effects. "Simulation puts into question the difference of 'true' and 'false,' of 'real' and imaginary.' The one who simulates, is he ill or not, since he exhibits 'true' symptoms?"[18] At present, the medical, artistic, and moral issues surrounding mimesis come together and raise an acute moral question. If catharsis matters, because it alleviates pain and leads to reconciliation, is that effect counterproductive insofar as it is the outcome of simulation, of role playing? Does its origin in deceit throw doubt on any ensuing psychological or social remedy? Alternatively, is such playing with fire not fraught with psychic danger, when it ceases to be deliberate and lapses into a mimetic-traumatic identification with the source of pity or terror?[19] The cathartic cure, in that case, the acting out, might become a psychological defense worse than what it seeks to cure and could continue a vicious cycle.[20]

In an age of simulacra (where the difference between original and imitation tends toward zero), the dimensions of this dilemma increase. "Authentic" becomes an overused, vague term of praise, revealing the increased difficulty of finding and applying criteria of criticism. (See chapter 12.) The cultural atmosphere is soaked in cool simulations of the idiom of ecstasy, extremity, and compassion: "Many Mourned the Death of the Cybersweetheart Who Never Was."[21] The counterfeit turns practically into a medium. How strong must artists be to overcome an anxiety—about self-construction or simulation—they often do not know they have? To be sensitive to that anxiety is to pose the question of authenticity.

❑   ❑   ❑

Novalis held that the first true philosophical act was that of annihilating the self (*Selbsttötung*). The second, I am tempted to add, and it may come to the same, is the comic catharsis of parody and persona hopping. Philip Roth is the assassin of the autobiographical impulse and its vaunted sincerity. His extraordinary, intrusive rendition of the inner life of all his personae—in *The Human Stain* the author's intense, vacillating sympathy turns minor characters into major ones—together with a savage reality check that undoes every vestige of self-deception, however idealistic, fortifies the reader's longing to get beyond a counterfeit, culturally deformed self. But while Roth expertly dispatches the egomania and talk-show quality of America's "dopey culture," he cannot himself entirely avoid its "hyperdramatization," the "Yap, yap, yap" his brutally eloquent profanity excoriates. (It is an anonymous teacher who speaks in the following passage from chapter 3.)

> If Clinton had fucked her in the ass, she might have shut her mouth. . . .
>
> Yap, yap, yap. . . . The sincere performance is everything. Sincere and empty, totally empty. . . . The sincerity that is worse than falseness, and the innocence that is worse than corruption. All the rapacity hidden under the sincerity. And under the lingo. This wonderful language they all have. . . . Their shamelessness they call lovingness, and the ruthlessness is camouflaged as lost "self-esteem." . . . The hyper-dramatization of the pettiest emotions.
>
> Relationship. Clarify my relationship. They open their mouths and they send me up the wall. Their whole language is a summation

of the stupidity of the last forty years. Closure. *There's* one. My students cannot stay in that place where thinking must occur. Closure! They fix on the conventionalized narrative, with its beginning, middle and end—every experience, however ambiguous, no mattter how knotty or mysterious, must lend itself to this normalizing, conventionalizing, anchorman cliché.[22]

Despite Roth's gender-inflected send up of academic theorists, such as *The Human Stain*'s Delphine Roux, a Ph.D. from Yale's French Department, the fact that authenticity cannot be presumed of autobiographical writing has been fully recognized in literary scholarship. There is a general insistence, even when personality counts, on the separation of the empirical self and the writer's self. Among modern writers or theorists, Marcel Proust, Paul Valéry, T. S. Eliot, Roland Barthes, Paul de Man and Maurice Blanchot specifically connect art and impersonality.[23] Denis Diderot's *Paradox of the Actor* and fiction's renewed interest in confidence men, counterfeits and picaros, from Melville through André Gide, Thomas Mann and Saul Bellow, undermine an astringent sincerity. Moreover, as Mikhail Bakhtin pointed out, private life first becomes visible in the public sphere through the representation of criminal or socially trangressive acts, and institutions like the trial.[24]

Literature is touched by a taint of illegitimacy because of that content. The very thing that gives it a modern interest also marginalizes it. Add to this a more intrinsic objection, for art is always a copy, as Plato saw, always at a remove that coincides with its counterfeiting, always an unauthorized stealing from life by outmaneuvering taboos placed on the imitation of reality.

Thus autobiography, whether it deals with private acts and feelings or a life of public service, cannot escape suspicion. Bakhtin, who describes its ancient link to embedded social practices as well as narratives of conversion and transfiguration, shows that from early on both autobiography and biography belong to the same universe of discourse. Stories about oneself, whether performed within the "public square" of encomium, funeral oration, and sanctioned self-praise, or outside of it, never quite detach from narrative fiction. Like fiction, they expand the reality claim of what is, or appears to be, excluded.

The novel depicts with comic or serious realism adventurers, rogues, tricksters, criminals, parvenus; and self-biography too cannot shake off the charge of illicit or tricky behavior.[25]

In early modernity, the struggle against inauthenticity involved the great humanist editors who questioned the integrity of certain ancient texts or sought to restore those that had become corrupt. For how could authority be justified if based on false papers? The rise of a new source of authority, that of "reason" or "inner light,"[26] is not, however, an entirely liberating development. The Protestant examination of conscience, together with its instrument of spiritual autobiography, and the exploration of what Samuel Taylor Coleridge called the underconscious, make melancholia and depression, or a guilt arising from secret fantasies and a fear concerning the omnipotence of thoughts, burdens hard to shake off.

In general, good works in the public realm can no longer claim the clarity of a legacy immune to revisionary thoughts. Yet the right to value private life also may not be taken for granted, even today. Quite often privacy issues must still be represented—in the sense of seconded—by a literary and quasi-performative act. Starting with the Greek romances, novelists employ what Bakhtin calls "third person" representatives of private life. (He cites a long list of them: a man trapped in the body of an ass, a rogue, a tramp, a servant, an adventurer, courtesans, prostitutes, pimps, clerks, pawnbrokers, would-be doctors.) These become typical literary devices for spying and eavesdropping on covert, intimate goings-on. Yet, paradoxically, because of their lowly status the life of these marginal people is not valued: If not actually outlawed or assigned to a demi-monde, such characters are treated as if invisible. Precisely that allows them unusual access to the scandalous underside of the master class.

Bakhtin's account is brilliant and indispensable. In the new biographical culture, however, (see chapter 4) the autobiographer is more than a third-person observer to himself who speaks in the first person so as to disclose a life judged to be beyond the pale and that, in its subversive triviality or extremity, cannot be integrated into a public realm of values. The difference is especially clear when we consider testimony narratives.

As Paul Celan (perhaps the greatest post-Holocaust poet writing in German) reminds us: "Niemand zeugt für den Zeugen" (No one is a witness for [i.e., authenticates] the witness). This remark is not just directed to others but to the witnesses as other than themselves: as utterly changed, dispossessed, by what they have gone through. Historical evidence for the Holocaust is overwhelming, so Celan is not—or not only—expressing a feeling of isolation shared by many survivors. Nor does he refer to the dilemma of proving the truth of something that is invisible except for those in the faith. And the first-person narrator of Holocaust testimony certainly differs from the Bakhtinian extra or *figurant*, who is promoted from marginality to tell a story in the first person, or acts as the porte-parole of writers who outwit constraints on the representation of reality.

A more radical challenge faces the Holocaust survivor: It is to go from having been a nonperson, even a dead (or zero) person, to a *kakangelos*, a bad-news-angel harrowed from the living dead of the camps or hiding places. Hence the extraordinary recent emphasis on what in camp slang was called a "muselman." (See chapter 6.) If authenticity is to prevail, the survivor as witness to the traumatic event will be at once a first person and a second person: one who is able, despite everything, to say "you" to the self that has remained, one who seeks an "I-Thou" relationship with a disappeared or damaged self.[27]

□   □   □

I come back, then, to the "One" beyond all imitations. (See also chapter 5.) In order to distinguish between icons in a celebrity culture, critics attribute star quality to some and not others, and it is hard to determine how much is hype orchestrated by the marketeers. Memoirs, whether ghostwritten or not, are habitually used to enhance the popularity of a career. Still, the problem with authenticity does not arise so much in this limelight as in the permanent twilight of ordinary lives, where more and more are emerging from privacy and anonymity to tell their stories.

Why do so many leave the shelter of family or home to grasp at public exposure? Do we need to hold up the mirror of television to our individual lives? What kind of judgment or justification can come from the (directed) applause of audiences? There is an increasingly frenetic movement into the public sphere that implies a quasi-religious desire to be justified, or at least to be heard. How different and urbane is Prospero's epilogue to *The Tempest.* "Release me from my bands," this master of the revels says in his appeal,

> With the help of your good hands.
> Gentle breath of yours my sails
> Must fill, or else my project fails.

Prospero suggests that the theater audience, which has conspired with him during the play to sustain an illusion, is still needed to complete his project, although the play is over and he has renounced his magic.

However provisional and disillusioning media minutes of fame may be, and whatever psychic or moral stance motivates those who come forward on TV to complain or boast of their lives, such painful bravado exhibits a total reversal of a previous decorum: the struggle against the self and for a deeper inner life. In Emily Dickinson, an extreme example to be sure, that active struggle to subdue the ego by the ego was not satisfied by anything but intimations of eternity—intimations as fugitive and spasmodic as her poems. She wished to attain immortality, not publicity. Supremely self-aware, and never giving up her resistance to the limelight, she even mocks the vanity of her withdrawal from a modern fatality:

> I'm Nobody! Who are you?
> Are you—Nobody—Too?
> Then there's a pair of us?
> Don't tell! They'd banish us—you know!
>
> How dreary—to be—Somebody!
> How public—like a Frog—
> To tell your name—the livelong June—
> To an admiring Bog![28]

Matters become messy, however, when one tries to discriminate between such closely related activities as the play instinct, acting, acting out, mimesis, repetition-compulsion, showing off, over-identification with role models or fictive personalities, and a necessary empathy, that "visiting" of other positions Hannah Arendt saw as essential to a pluralistic politics.

Even if Dickinson's aversion to publicity was influenced by a Puritan distrust of the unlicensed or exhibitionistic spectacle, she goes further and turns against religion's own ritualized performances. She contrasts these with a nonanthropocentric nature's spontaneous, as if unselfconscious, mode of being, and praises birdsong's "independent Ecstasy"— independent of the applause of "Deity and Men." She prefers a miracle "forgotten, as fulfilled" to the Book of Revelations' revelations.

❐   ❐   ❐

The independent nature Dickinson describes has always been perceived as revelatory. The problem is how to interpret its signs. A hermeneutics must be found to open that second, autotelic or atelic, "book" of God. How can we read nature in order to master or follow it and so achieve a concordance of the two divine volumes? Vico, the early eighteenth-century Italian philosopher, thought there was a better chance of understanding history than nature, because the former was created by mankind and only a creator understands what he has made. But with the progress of science culminating in a technological age, the fundamental building blocks of the cosmos have become known and are beginning to be cloned.

The advance of artificial intelligence has made a "second nature" appear, in which human reproductive power competes with the cosmos and the role of artifice grows to such an extent that authenticity cannot be aligned simply with qualities in opposition to artifice. The complex polar distinction of "nature" and "art," inspiring Shakespeare's *Winter's Tale*, blurs even more. The magus figure, or the author himself, equipped in Shakespeare's romantic comedies with a device to make things good again, to undo the hurt and confusion he has so cleverly devised in the first place, still hopes for a *natural* magic that would make his art unnecessary. How probable is it, however, that a modern-day Prospero would break his staff and renounce his powers? Maybe that is the moral motif undergirding Foucault's untiring emphasis on interested knowledge, its problematic link to power institutions.

Of the reality-revel "Big Brother," it was remarked by an organizer that the participants, all nonprofessionals, began to "produce themselves" as soon as they were on stage. Whether this was instinctive or a reflex of our Society of the Spectacle, it indicates, as I will argue, that the rise of fakery facilitated by the media's production of simulacra does not make the issue of authenticity or moral discrimination easier. Critique itself becomes uncertain, concentrating on "uncovering the device" (a technique of the formalist school of literary analysis) or playing like Nabokov, the modern novelist, with "pale fire." Indeed, the great contemporary sin seems to have become the cover-up itself, rather than lying or dissimulation: the dissimulation of the dissimulation. *New York Times* journalist Frank Rich has called this the "Survival of the Fakest."[29]

In such a climate, the biggest challenge by far is whether an antidote to the media and their increasingly unreal realism can be found. The attractive technical gloss of cinematic photography, as well as the daily opium of TV, fosters a low-grade but addictive idolatry of the image. How to break through, without a counterproductive reliance on additional visual shock, terror, trauma?

"Tele-Suffering and Testimony" (see chapter 5) takes up issues of sensibility and pedagogy raised by our technological mastery of the faux real. Whereas even small breaches of public decorum or artistic convention used to provoke comment, today the threshold at which outrage makes a *thoughtful* difference has been raised to so high a level by real-time news and illusionistic reproduction that a blunting of empathy, and even of our capacity to respond, may occur at a moment in time when that response is, more than ever, called for.

That the testimony of the victims of injustice or violence can now be gathered and publicized is a significant advance that could lead to deterrence. Yet traumatic realism often produces an unreality effect; and although this reaction is clearly a psychological defense, it may induce a weakening of the reality principle and lead to the delusion that all the world's a movie or, obversely, to a radical distrust of the media, as if the latter were always being manipulated. We ask constantly, "What is authentic?" but do we stay long enough for the answer?

Maurice Blanchot claims that writing is unable to reference its own authenticity.[30] Hence the need for a critical reading of literature and the media. Since reading of this intensive kind, however, inevitably turns into writing (in Thoreau's *Walden*, Stanley Cavell remarks, "reading is not merely the other side of writing, its eventual fate; it is another metaphor of writing itself"[31]), the issue of finding criteria for not only an empathic but also a valid interpretation remains part of a commentary that augments the presentations of art. That intergenerational conversation, together with the art enfolded by it, is the nearest we may ever come to moderating an impatience bound up with our sense of the intense brevity of life, with the multiplication of partial or illusory identities, and with passions that turn the quest for a grounding authority or a spiritual purpose into a ferocious weapon, a transcendental violence.

CHAPTER 2

A SHORT HISTORY OF THE UNREAL

Value words with complex associations, such as authenticity and spirit, gather about them a swarm of synonyms and antonyms. Authenticity contrasts with imitation, simulation, dissimulation, impersonation, imposture, fakery, forgery, inauthenticity, the counterfeit, lack of character or integrity; spirit with letter, legalism, matter, materialism, deadness, flesh, body, embodiment, carnality, incarnation. Some of these antonyms may accrue a positive or antinomian meaning. Deadness signifies the opposite of spirit, but death, in cultures that encourage it as a cult or ideology, is not the denial of life (except for an "unreal" life) but the gateway to spiritual fulfillment.

Commonly employed words, then, are not indivisible atomic units: They are charged, recharged, by historical usage and contextual inventiveness. Terms like "real"/"reality" have become so honorific that even their contraries benefit. "Abstract" or "unreal" can be pejorative, but context may overturn accepted connotations. To classify certain paintings as "abstract" does not always involve a negative judgment. While one might think the real is what is actual or possible, Maurice Blanchot talks of "the impossible real."[1]

In art, since "realism" is inevitably a stylized form of what is deemed to be real, it allows room for ellipsis, license, and illusion. And, however real the unreal is as a feeling or an effect of art, our hunger for reality, or else for the fulfillment implied by "spirit," never diminishes. "We crave only reality," according to Thoreau. That same craving (not unmixed with bouts of revulsion) also helps to motivate the recent upsurge of confessions, memoirs, autobiographies, testimonies, journals, and biographies.

Even the early novel's adventures were often supported by the pretended discovery of a journal or first-person narrative claiming to be an "authentic narrative." Whether this device was believed or not, it soon became unnecessary, since fictive realism was enjoyed for its own sake, and indiscretion or even counterfeit reportage was not felt to stand in the way of a more basic veracity.

By now both personal memoirs and biographies have come to be looked at as an instructive and expressive literature rather than strictly historical ("factographic") documents. A biographer, it has been said, is a novelist under oath. The recent term "faction" points to a radical shift in sensibility we are still sorting out. History, especially contemporary history, becomes very quickly the subject of a re-creation that reads like reportage. It is notorious that Edmund Morris, the biographer of *Dutch*, a life of Ronald Reagan, gives himself a counterfeit eyewitness presence, like Woody Allen's Zelig (in the film of the same name), in order to describe Reagan's life before 1985, the year Morris gained access to the president. Self-inserted into prior historical events, he acquires a fake yet effective presentational intimacy.[2] Philip Roth has the parallel and disconcerting habit of inserting his authorial double into novels still under construction.

With real-time news being broadcast around the clock, public taste validates the saying that truth is stranger than fiction. Unfortunately, it tends to go for that truth-clone rather than for a more discreet, complex, and often indirect imitation of reality. No doubt the immediacy of photographic transmission, changing us into observers of events transpiring anywhere in the world, provides the pattern if not excuse for this development.[3]

Think of the difference between this immediacy and having to communicate by older modes of action-at-a-distance, such as Morse code or semaphore. Information carried by the audiovisual media seems far less encoded. In what has been called a "society of communication" a fallacious sense arises, quite routinely, and despite an underlying awareness of the complexity of computer codes, that the media are not mediations but "transparent": in the sense that nothing intervenes between sender and receiver, or that something has been transmitted in direct, undistorted fashion. "We distrust our instruments," Emerson declared; but we often distrust ourselves and compensate by wishfully putting a lot of faith in media machines.

Consequently, that "suspension of disbelief" commended by S. T. Coleridge as a legitimate effect of art's power, or as a state of mind critics should bring to art, becomes too easily a second nature. A media-inspired confusion between fake and real is often tolerated. Mankind wants to be deceived, an old saying goes: Has the era of the authentic fake arrived? The fake becomes a genre delighting in the antinatural, the phony, the cosmetic, the transvestite, the falsie of the self-made man or woman—forgeries often so skillful they cannot be discovered unless they unmask themselves. An ad for the MTV movie awards (June 8, 2000) runs: "AN EVENT SO HOLLY-WOOD EVEN THE POPCORN IS FAKE."

This, then, is the atmosphere in which we live and breathe and have our being. One is not surprised that the Green movement is growing rapidly and that many are thinking also about an "ecology" of the emotions. Nowhere is the suspicion of fakery or hypocrisy more disturbing than in our presumed feeling for others, in our capacity for sympathy.

The sympathetic imagination, as Adam Smith, the eighteenth-century economist and man of letters pointed out in *Moral Sentiments*, is the scarcest of goods. The sense that especially in modern society the living has become abstract, that artificial, bureaucratic, or secondary mechanisms are blocking sources of vitality or dangerously simulating them, becomes unbearable. New dichotomies spring up as a reaction to controlling schemes, especially by governments. Among these dichotomies is an invigorated opposition of local and global, which goes back to a contrast between cosmopolitanism and what was called "local attachment" in the later eighteenth century. The progressive liberalism of the former clashes with the nostalgic "small-world" conservatism of the latter.

❏   ❏   ❏

Historically, nationalism often usurped a fidelity associated with local attachment. Moreover, with the gradual disappearance of the leafy city (the *rus in urbe*), the countryside is sentimentalized as idyllic, so that rural and authentic merge in such concepts as Rousseau's "sentiment of being." Yet crucial exceptions modify, without quite neutralizing, an explosive dichotomy. So Wordsworth's nature poetry is patriotic rather than nationalistic and the direct outgrowth of a felt need to preserve England's rural character. National and ecological considerations combine to maintain the outdoor room of nature as a green belt for the mind amid rising encroachments and pressures. Wordsworth defined the latter as industrialization, urbanization, and the ever-growing dependence of the imagination on sensational stimulants, including "frantic novels" (his phrase in the preface to *Lyrical Ballads*) and the speeded-up transmission of news. In the following century, the countryside *promeneur* strives to turn into the urban *flâneur* and rural virtue continues to project an influential image of authenticity.

Thoreau begins *Walden* by saying that he requires of every writer, hence also of himself, "a simple and sincere account of his own life." Sincerity, however, which is certainly an aim of the genre of autobiography, cannot be taken for granted just because first-person discourse implies it: Thoreau strengthens his claim for, so to say, an authentic sincerity, by linking it to the simple life in rural nature. When he writes, after more than two years of living in solitude and by the labor of his hands, that he became "a sojourner in civilized life again," this quiet phrase begins a savagely ironic attack on an "economy" (the title of his opening chapter) that compels the mass of men to contract themselves into "a nutshell of civility." [4]

In the previous century, Diderot had mocked Rousseau's pre-Thoreauvian claim to be a "citizen." That word trailed a cloud of glory from the Athenian city-state, and Diderot thought it was incongruous to be both a self-styled hermit (Rousseau called his country retreat a "hermitage") and a citizen. Though Diderot's objection, in the name of civic activism, to a country life of self-reflection seems to have as little bearing on the blood of Cambodia as Thoreau's pastoral revision of the concept of citizenship, the myth of rural virtue in Cambodia, associated with the peasant class and the creation of an authentically productive society, becomes ideologically virulent and devastates a nation.

The schism, it appears, between country and town, or peasant and burgher (bourgeois), conceals seeds of a potentially fatal desire for a more innocent or unified mode of existence. Rural nostalgia, euphemized and sanitizing its relation to "pig earth," also became politically potent in Vichy France. In the United States, the myth of rural redemption still masquerades as pop art: Superman, saved as a baby from the exploding planet Krypton, lands somewhere on a farm in mid-America. He eventually becomes urbanized—but as a supranatural fighter against urban crime. It is telling that the quasi-apocalyptic vision climaxing the movie *The Thirteenth Floor* consists of a computer-green field, an electrical maze or grid (more screen saver than mirage) not hidden away in an office tower but located beyond the end of an infinite rural road leading from Tucson, Arizona, into the heart of a monochrome desert.

❐   ❐   ❐

No doubt every moment in history is marked by some deceitfulness and the marketing of illusions. In *The Golden Bowl*, Henry James invents a "perfect fake" that is not "the real thing" yet proves to be the touchstone device opening innocent eyes to the at-once noble and sordid depths of human deceit. Artistic illusions, even in this symbolic form, seem less innocent than before.

George Orwell is the keenest prophet against this development in the political sphere. The triumph of manufactured, media-disseminated propaganda over whatever the facts might be was brought home by a Yugoslav's cynical remark, some years ago, about the political scene in his country: "To influence us, it does not matter whether something is true or false, it must only be clear." The consistent lie, in such an atmosphere, is more important than the possibility to speak truth, and it creates a mock transparency. This opium for the people is reinforced by a state-dominated news system that poisons everything. All inner life, then, becomes suspect, and the ruling elite guards against independent thought by hypocritical rituals enforcing a collective complicity, such as show trials, loyalty oaths, forced confessions, and staged demonstrations.

A scruple has always existed, of course, concerning one's innermost thoughts, because they may not be accessible even to oneself. Purify me, the psalmist cries to God, clear me of hidden faults. Popular fiction is full of unsuspected (as well as obvious) evildoers, and many people, although innocent, are tormented by the idea they have sinned unconsciously.

A repressive regime will not rest before the unknown sinner is identified by the thought police. In some of the worst days of the Stalinist terror, the KGB was given a quota to fill, like the police in our cities when a municipality wishes to raise money from traffic tickets. But the KGB quota was the human flesh of subversives. Its operatives had to bring in and incriminate a set number of Soviet citizens, whether there were grounds for suspicion or not, whether proof was found or had to be fabricated.

And we have learned from contemporary inquisitorial methods how easily the simplest answers can be twisted into that proof. Anything you say can be held against you. Ultimately, there is the resort of torture, a questioning by other means. Put Nature to the question, Francis Bacon advised the scientist. He was using a sinister as well as witty metaphor, since "question" could also mean bringing torture to bear so that the suspect would confess. Jacobo Timmerman, who suffered under the Argentine military regime, remarks bitterly in *Prisoner without a Name* that hope is something that belongs to the interrogator rather than to his prisoners. "The interrogator always seems to feel that he can succeed in modifying the will of the interrogated."[5]

I remember being haunted in early childhood by a weekly cartoon whose protagonist was a man in a mask. What haunted me was that when finally unmasked, he had no face. The torturer assumes not only that everyone has a mask that can be stripped away, so that nakedness or transparence can be achieved, but also that it is finally unbearable for the victim to remain faceless, to refuse an identity, however incriminating. The technique, similarly, of propagandistic caricature is always directed against the face as if it were a mask: The caricature presumes to lay bare sinister hidden features.

❑   ❑   ❑

Let me add a less-cruel thought about the unreal real. I have already suggested that what distinguishes those who escape direct participation in a cataclysmic and encompassing event, such as the Great Depression, the Second World War, the Holocaust, the Vietnam war, the civil rights struggle, or other *collective* trauma, is a troubling mood that they are functioning in a vacuum, however active and generous their lives may actually be. Not that I wish to deny the traumatizing role played by everyday incidents. But as a constant, these do not have a distinctive, generation-specific effect. Although the spreading use of the word "trauma" is an important interpretive magnification that does mark today's social and humanitarian thinking, and so constitutes a difference with generational implication, that very fact—the rise of posttraumatic stress diagnoses—is probably a reaction to the absence of something more collectively defining. Jorge Semprun, a communist resistance fighter who spent sixteen months in the hell of Buchenwald, writes in *Literature or Life* that he "lived the experience of death as a collective and even fraternal experience." How to live death as a fraternal experience (Semprun took many years to recover the will to write about it) is unimaginable to most of us.[6]

Consider, then, an autobiographical writer of the postwar generation without losses connected to the Holocaust or World War II. Joyce Maynard's account of her affair with J. D. Salinger, lasting about a year, although with a life sequel that took decades to resolve, has the strange title *At Home in the World.*[7] Strange, because the entire book shows how much she is *not* at home in the world. Her memoir strikes one as an effort to achieve normalcy after the authoritative, determining, demanding encounter with Salinger. There is nothing wrong with that effort except that it contradicts what drew her to Salinger in the first place and then assured his hold over her: the wish to be justified as a writer.

Maynard fills up the void left in her life by Salinger's abandonment and the resulting loss of self-esteem. Her sensitively recorded later activities impinge like ads for her brave demeanor, productiveness, normalcy. If this is normal, one thinks, this endless engagement with the business of socializing, publishing, child rearing, and a not-untumultuous set of marriages, if this is as American as Apple Pie, what is abnormal?

But loneliness and a feeling of inadequacy always seep back. There is a leak in the self-publicity pump. For Maynard really is the opposite of Salinger in her determination to funnel everything that happens to her (with a disarming confidence in its transparency and self-evidence) into writing for an immediate public. She becomes the apotheosis of middle-brow journalism. The richness of all that detail, all that perceptiveness, that insight and pathos, goes . . . where?

Why should it have a direction or a role model to define itself against? But it does: Maynard's story begins and ends with Salinger. Since she lacks the resource—and pressure—of other kinds of literary guidance, he is the authority she must, she cannot evade. Even if, at the end of the book, she confronts Salinger in his retreat and affirms her contrary identity, claiming that, unlike him, she is "at home in the world."

Salinger has become a classic, and his reclusiveness over the years gives him mythic status. His portrait of Holden Caulfield in *Catcher in the Rye* swept away, like Hemingway's fiction—but aiming at an emerging youth culture—a load of phony sentiment.[8] Thirty years ago, fresh at Yale, Maynard fell under Salinger's spell, at first through his letters and personality rather than his famous book. We glimpse something in their relationship that is typical of Americans born after World War II who experienced Korea and Vietnam from a distance or only through the turmoil of the late 1960s.

Today, in fact, we think in foreshortened generational terms and try to define each new, youthful wave: Baby Boomers, Yuppies, Gen X, Millennials. Every decade or two a new identity quest is proclaimed, divined by the media and its gurus from the chaos of teenage aspirations. Is not Maynard's candor about her life—a journalistic realism that refuses to draw the line between intimate personal details and public reportage, and seems to have no purpose beyond her desire to become real through writing—is this not the logical culmination of her career as an *enfant du siècle?* It started at the tender age of eighteen when she represented her "generation" in the *New York Times Magazine* of April 21, 1972, which also put her picture on its cover. Salinger writes to her and praises her essay but warns her against the media, and the affair begins.

Salinger failed totally in saving Maynard from the tyranny of publicity. What greater contrast can there be than between her statement "For over thirty years, Jerry Salinger has sought his protection in privacy and silence. I have come to believe that my greatest protection comes in self-disclosure. It's shame, not exposure I can't endure. . . . If I tell what I do, nobody else can expose me," and Salinger's words after she confronts him in November 1997 with the question "What was my purpose in your life?" By her own avowed standard, she has to endure his answer, which rejects her kind of personality-centered and publicitarian testimony: "You have spent your career writing gossip. . . . You write empty, meaningless, offensive, putrid gossip. You live your life as a pathetic, parasitic gossip."[9]

Maynard's example suggests that, despite an unchastened vitality, each generation, while overthrowing past exemplars, still needs mentors or heroes. What certainly contributed to Salinger's influence is that he writes from the perspective of having passed through the terrifying initiation of war without actually depicting it. His authority, in that sense, is purely literary rather than confessional. He is no longer, if he ever was, at home in the world; but his observations of how young people cope—or don't—with trauma, and the lack of a great, collective purpose, and how one should preserve purity of feeling and honest speech despite the publicity machine, are all the more compelling.

❏   ❏   ❏

Salinger revives an image of the writer's authenticity at a time when a new and freer ideal emerges: the right to self-expression, even self-exposure, based on a belief in its representative or "generational" value, as against an earlier, more demanding ethos of self-fashioning—defined by Coleridge, in reference to Shakespeare, as "the power of working creatively under laws of one's own origination."[10] But is the new ideal truly liberating? Does it not lead to a restless identity search, or to identity reversals, conversions that could be a form of identification with the aggressor? What is terrifying in one's own environment may produce an involuntary adherence. The most that can be claimed for identity politics is that, in pursuit of authenticity, exceptional individuals come to incorporate a truth whose validity is sociologic and can be appreciated only with the passage of time.

In that light, my judgment of Joyce Maynard could be accused of underestimating the situation of the woman writer. If Hemingway and Salinger aspire to a macho kind of style, lean, cool, colloquial—and, in Salinger, sassy—is there not also a rebellious ideal of authenticity in Maynard's frank, verbacious picture of her peculiar apprenticeship and its betrayal by a seductive mentor? Or does Salinger's vituperative claim in their last interview, that she is exploiting her relationship with him by writing this memoir, have any merit?

Maynard leaves unresolved the issue of who has exploited whom. But Salinger's accusation clarifies one thing in her as she confronts him. "'I'm always writing. . . . I'm a *writer*.'" She alleges to "have never called myself that, before. I have always left it that I write."[11] The question for the reader becomes what that identity statement affirms, since Salinger's concept of what a writer is could not be more different.

After an interview in which she stayed composed but which must have been searing, Maynard, like a professional reporter, notes down everything as soon as possible, proving indeed not that she is a writer but that she is always writing. "I climb into the cab. Turn on the ignition. I head very slowly down the hill. When I get to the main road, I pull the truck over and take out my notebook. I write down everything that just happened." A minute later "the storm finally breaks."[12] Because of the rain obscuring the windshield and her own clouded eyes, she crashes the truck. This synchronization of outer and inner weather is one of the oldest moves in a writer's craft. But what follows is remarkable, for a lost memory hits her that she recounts in dramatic detail and reveals how much verbal abuse, how much shaming, she had repressed.

❑   ❑   ❑

The quest to become real as a writer, through the very act of writing and in the absence of great, if often tragic, experiences, is partly the superego heritage of the High Modernist tradition, or that branch of it associated with the work of Mallarmé, Flaubert, and Proust, and partly an attempt to find an authentic way of portraying a life of private traumas in the aftermath of the extraordinary period between 1914 and 1945 that involved many Americans in Europe's turmoil. There is something of Mallarmé's Hamlet, "the latent Lord who cannot develop" ("le Seigneur latent qui ne peut devenir"), in every modernist. To this day the figure of the artist has retained that glow, that imperfect halo, despite some fading in the postmodernist years.

But first the American pastoral was given its coup de grâce. It was never a pastoral, as Philip Roth's *American Pastoral* and such minor films as *Pleasantville* or *The Stepford Wives* bear out. More than a touch of gothic darkened it. Henry James's and Edith Wharton's portrayal of the invincible workings of social convention in the New as in the Old World, and the often-noble sacrifice society exacted when contravened, yields to outright satire or desperately funny critiques. The brave-new-world attitude, the hypocrisy of its assumed virginity, and a resolute neglect of all that was richly corrupt in its everyday texture led after the war and its "Great Generation" to a remarkable spate of comedic as well as disillusioned novels. Roth's *American Pastoral*, while providing a stunningly detailed and compassionate portrait of two fathers from the "World of our Fathers," also immerses the reader in a painful depiction of the generation gap between the postwar Arcadian dreams of Seymour Levov, the Jewish "Swede," and the career of beloved daughter Merry, who turns radical and pathologically homicidal during the 1960s.

A parallel generation gap opens up when we consider the image of the artist. Roth's "Zuckerman" or "Philip Roth" is anything but the heroic (Proustian) writer fathered by modernism. The decline of that myth did not make it disappear, however: Salinger remains a puritan modernist. His art fights gossip, journalism, and distraction with quasi-religious rigor. Yet the modernist's religion of art failed to provide a central, subsuming event for the imagination. The drama of Sinai or Golgotha, of Wallace Stevens's "master folded in his fire," loses its hold and neither illuminates nor devalues events in the light of sacred time.

T. S. Eliot's *The Waste Land* still echoes a central revelation. Or rather, the very absence of revelation becomes the central event. Eliot depicts a disheartening vista of intolerably trivial, if traumatic, episodes, set off by powerful literary memories. André Aciman's "shadow cities," in comparison, ghostly as they are, differ utterly from *The Waste Land*'s deathscapes, evoked in a breaking and fading voice against a resonant backdrop:

Jerusalem Athens Alexandria
Vienna London
Unreal

The unreal does not arouse religious pathos in Aciman. His memory perspective, displacing the present in favor of past or future perfect, remains totally secular: He abides it without disparaging a life on which it casts luminous shadows. Eliot, nonetheless, may be the more subversive writer. He is an agent provocateur. Through the haunting pessimism of his "ragging," his parodic montage of high literary reminiscence and colloquial stammering, he mocks the degraded condition of language while keeping alive the dream of a purification. The Holy Word, or logos, is the grail motivating Eliot's surreptitious questromance like a Freudian lost object.

Charismatic religious and political movements are not disappearing: Indeed, they have demonstrated a nostalgic purity's staying power, its potential to relive the illusion of real presence. The manic intensity of this reality craving also shows up in the last pages of Roth's *The Human Stain*. Its final chapter, "The Purifying Ritual," portrays the dead end and white-out of all such rituals in a bewildering American and macho context. It is as if Roth, having finished his long parabolic story about a distorted ideal as it affects race relations (although not only these), was rewriting Thoreau's eulogy of White Pond and Walden, those absolute places of peace and purity. Roth stages an encounter of Zuckerman and Farley (the Vietnam veteran with PTSD, and possibly a murderer) as the latter is ice fishing on a desolate mountain lake "Away from man, close to God." The atmosphere of their ominous encounter is utterly different from anything in *Walden*. Is Roth considering finishing off his narrator and alter ego?

For Zuckerman is, in his own way, an embarrassment, being almost as obsessive as Farley, and with his own "rapturous drive." All roads, therefore, lead to this tense finale. The reader senses a precarious autobiographical convergence. The face-off is magnified by its fixation on one spot and on a hard, natural artifact (an ice-breaking auger). Roth's peculiar ending, moving from human stain to a rhetorical focus on the nonhuman, evokes a pastoral scene of yearning and purgation that recalls Thoreau in its very incongruity:

> [Farley] came up to me and raised the auger's long bright bit right up to my face.

Here. Here was the origin. Here was the essence. Here.

... Just facing him I could feel the terror of the auger—even with him already seated on the bucket: the icy white of the lake encircling a tiny spot that was a man, the only human marker in all of nature.... Only rarely, at the end of our century, does life offer up a vision as pure and peaceful as this one: a solitary man on a bucket, fishing through eighteen inches of ice in a lake that's constantly turning over its water atop an arcadian mountain in America.[13]

Phyllis Rose's *The Year of Reading Proust: A Memoir in Real Time*[14] bears comparison with Maynard's book: It is a writer's autobiography that compensates for the relatively insignificant (from a public point of view) incidents of her daily life. Rose seems to have no mentor or deliberately avoids having one. Instead, she chooses Proust's masterpiece to be her conscience and to monitor her work by promoting its greater inwardness even as she fights her sense of being a fake—not socially, but in terms of art. She searches for a way to magnify daily life despite the entropic flow of time. Calling her book "A Memoir in Real Time" contrasts it with Proust's "recovered time," which proved more real when found again through the act of writing about it. The existential question focuses on the relation of writing and reality.

Rose intends to make the best of a diminished thing: to value what she lives as she lives it, despite intermittent feelings of trivial pursuit. Her life, in its happening, its impressionistic momentum, must feed her art: She uses her awareness of the moment as it passes, not deepened by time, loss, or memory. There is, of course, the memory of Proust's great oeuvre. But does that lead, in Rose, to a redemption through style or simply to stylishness? At times her hyperboles are reminiscent of the quirky, passionate flights of fancy in the speech of Fitzgerald's women, such as *The Great Gatsby*'s Daisy. She remains haunted by the modernist antinomy expressed memorably by Yeats, who said we had to chose "perfection of the life or of the work."

That the elevator word "real" is also at the core of Maynard's memoir is confirmed by her epigraph. It comes from a children's story for adults, Margery Williams's *The Velveteen Rabbit*. Here is most of the epigraph:

"Real isn't how you are made," said the Skin Horse. "It's a thing that happens to you. When a child loves you for a long, long time, not just to play with, but REALLY loves you, then you become Real."

"Does it hurt?" asked the Rabbit. "Sometimes," said the Skin Horse, for he was always truthful. . . . "Generally, by the time you are Real, most of your hair has been loved off, and your eyes drop out and you get loose in the joints and very shabby. But these things don't matter at all, because once you are Real you can't be ugly, except to people who don't understand."

Despite that final, consoling sentiment, the hurt of the real is real enough. And it is strange that the unreal of fiction should be needed to convey the wound of the real.

Michael Cunningham's *The Hours* accentuates the issue. Inspired by the diva of High Modernism, Virginia Woolf—who is to Cunningham what Proust is to Rose—his novel epitomizes the life of three women.[15] Four, if we count, as we should, Clarissa Dalloway, since Woolf's fiction has as much presence, in the *The Hours*, as Woolf herself or the other principal figures. Several "hours" are made to link up: a moving re-creation of Woolf's suicide early in the Second World War, together with vignettes from the time *Mrs. Dalloway* is being composed, and which imply the return from the trauma of the First World War to the rituals of ordinary life. These portrayals of Woolf merge with the fictive lives of other semidomesticated women, one married to a veteran of World War II, another who faces the wastage by AIDS of her closest male friend.

Both women, like Woolf herself, are subject to feelings of unreality (the "nowhere feeling") as well as ecstatic if fleeting moments of embodiment. They are surprised, Cunningham writes, by the presence of their own ghost, and have to work to stay "in character." All need a second, fictive personality: "Sanity involves a certain measure of impersonation," as Woolf is made to say. What both defeats and lends them their aura is a missed (personal) opportunity or a great (public) event that passed them by. They seem to come too late for heroism. Yet, as with Mme Bovary, the real unreal in their life refuses to subside, and they will not give up the seduction of reading and imagining. "The trick," Cunningham's Woolf reflects, "will be to render intact the magnitude of Clarissa's miniature but very real desperation. . . ."

This insight applies equally to the women Cunningham invents. One of them is also called Clarissa, and the honorific "Dalloway" is bestowed on her by the AIDS-stricken writer whose own novel is said to take more than fifty pages to depict a fictionalized Clarissa "shopping for nail polish which she decides against!" (Those "pure nails" recall a Mallarmean theme.) Cunningham captures the gender trouble, the fugitive extreme emotions, and generally the vanity and waste of the consumer's life, but what can "render intact" (an ambiguous phrase) mean in a situation that so easily parodies itself?

Erich Auerbach's *Mimesis* (1946), in a famous chapter on Virginia Woolf, understands the realism of her excursive, accidented, deeply distracted stream of consciousness as the culmination of the serious representation of reality in Western literature. His thesis, enlarging the reality quest of the modernist writer, is underwritten by Hegel's *grand récit*, a quasi-historical vision of the unreal becoming real through the travails of humanity's self-realization, a story accepted, although revised, by Marxism. Is philosophy too, then, at least in this narrative format, a fairy tale for adults, or the overelaboration of rare moments of real presence strung out as an antidote to the nonintact or inauthentic?

CHAPTER 3

REMNANTS OF HEGEL

"The wounds made by the spirit leave no scars." Hegel's famous pronouncement in the *Phenomenology of Mind* (1807), which suggested the title for my book, comes during a knotty discussion of how conscience, despite its private nature, emerges to make a truth claim in the public sphere. Hegel describes an acute consciousness of self that joins with doctrines of inner light (a personally vouchsafed and accepted illumination) to achieve absolute certainty, but runs up against the same assertive confidence in others. The worldly result is defeat, impasse, religious and political strife.

Yet Hegel's dialectical vision of the workings of the spirit turns such collisions into a viable and ultimately seamless progress. This is the context in which the wounds inflicted by the spirit are said to leave no scars. (They are absorbed into a philosophic stream of consciousness; what is later called the free indirect style, which intuits and replicates the inner speech of the individual mind, here claims to capture a dynamic and collective advance.) When Emerson confides to his Journal, "I am defeated all the time yet to victory I am born," he expresses a similar sentiment, without Hegel's massive dialectical machinery.

The spirit does leave scars, however, both evident and eloquent. Nor do the wounds beneath always heal. One is tempted to turn Hegel's axiom on its head and identify those scars collectively with history's uncertain moral progress or individually with works of art that dress, encompass, even draw strength from, traumatic encounters described over and again in the *Phenomenology*. Hegel fuses the macroscopic field of historical knowledge with a microscopic enlargement of the turmoil within each mind as it confronts the reality of other minds and tries to be equally—or more—real.

An older mode of representation, such as medieval allegory, depicted these clashes as a battle that takes place in the mind or soul. For Hegel, the warring allegorical figures of that mode capture the truth only in the form of archaic and shadowy tokens that the dynamism of history eventually fleshes out. The symbol, as distinguished from allegory, and considered by Hegel an advanced mode of representation, overcomes abstractness by fused concrete universals from which the idea shines forth with sensuous radiance. Reality is not given but achieved: The very fugitiveness of the real, the split or noncoincidence of person and world, of subjective and objective being, obliges a labor that redeems imagination from the twilight zone of abstraction as well as the terror of unreality.

To excerpt Hegel is tricky. His prose is like Penelope's web, in that it manages to reconstitute itself and defer interminably the final stage—here the end of history and closure of the dialectic. Somewhat arbitrarily, then, I will take my illustration from the final pages of the *Phenomenology*'s section entitled "Spirit in the Condition of Being Certain of Itself: Morality."

❑   ❑   ❑

In humanity's collective advance toward "Absolute Knowledge," Hegel posits a transition that leads, after the Enlightenment, from moral certainty to a purely spiritual religion consistent with full self-consciousness. God now appears as an intuition of *progressive* thought that has achieved self-certainty but is not trapped into a rigid, enclosed, unforgiving selfhood. The duel of ego with ego, inevitable when confronting others, cannot be resolved unless it is lifted to a level where opposites are reconciled without ceasing to be a duality. Hegel calls this stage "Self-Consciousness at home with itself"—not unhappy, that is, not seeing itself as alienated. This advanced stage is attained once a potentially deadly recognition of the otherness of persons or groups becomes acknowledgment by shedding its antagonistic edge and yielding to the inner, motivating power of "pure knowledge"—a concept that recalls Spinoza's "intellectual love" of God, although in Hegel it is joined to understanding history rather than nature. "The reconciling affirmation," he writes, "the 'yes' with which both egos desist from their . . . opposition, is the existence of the ego expanded into a duality, an ego which remains . . . [by that act] one and identical with itself, and possesses the certainty of itself in the complete relinquishment of itself and its opposite: it is God appearing in the midst of those who know themselves in the form of pure knowledge."[1]

The reader may feel, as I do, that God pops up here like the god out of the machine in ancient Greek drama, when the action has reached impasse and a superior force must intervene. Yet even this philosophically engineered deity testifies to Hegel's own striving to locate, in addition to the whole that is the truth, each new manifestation of spirit, its precise logical and historical, agonistic and concrete, moment.

I have quoted Hegel not only to show the tenacious grip of the concept of spirit as it merges with the reach and self-emancipation of the human mind but also to recall the mental strength, rather than the endless verbal dexterity, of such a thinker. Hegel's peculiar strength includes a rejection of that simplified historical and material determinism later revised into him. He is not satisfied with historical explanation. History is indeed the scene of actualization, the play- or battleground of spirit. But what goes on there, the actualizing passage from abstract to concrete, has an internal intellectual momentum that is described in extraordinary detail by the dialectic.

Despite all the talk, however, about actualization and reconciliation on the one hand and opposition, self-alienation, and the labor of the negative on the other, the vastness of Hegel's totalizing perspective does not succeed in envisioning history as a necessary and justified scene in which the agency of spirit leaves no scars. The scar, the traumatic or ecstatic memory trace, is never entirely erased and so becomes, whether we like it or not, the foundation of our sense of reality.

◻ ◻ ◻

I suspect that Hegel's internal perspective in the *Phenomenology*, a very large book that rarely identifies by name the historical outcomes it alludes to, is still indebted to a spiritualizing Christianity going back to

Saint Paul's transcendental if exploitative lifting ("Aufhebung") of the Hebrew Scriptures. (See chapter 7, "The Letter as Revenant.") Instead of rejecting the "Old" Testament as a limited or distorted reception of a divinely revealed truth, Paul applied a powerful, polemical mode of interpretation that preserved it as a prefiguration. Mary, for example, becomes a new and greater Eve. A divine yet historical agent, she supersedes the woman who anticipates her in this extended salvation history. Antebellum and residually Puritan America is still conversant with that same Christian typology, through which it saw itself as the new Israel. It redeems itself by that larger identification. "Escaped from the house of bondage, Israel of old did not follow after the Egyptians; to her were given new things under the sun. And we Americans are the peculiar, chosen people—the Israel of our time; we bear the ark of the liberties of the world . . ."[2] (Melville, *White Jacket*).

Paul's interpretive move invokes the living spirit of the savior, a presence surviving not only through his teachings but also after his death as Holy Spirit and Comforter, in order to revoke the (supposedly dead) letter of the Judaic mentality, its constricted view of sin, law, and tradition. Hegel, like Paul, extends salvation history, but by a vision of the human intellect. The latter progressively subsumes enmity and contrariety and moves forward through mental fight and endurance from empty universals to the concreteness of historical actualization. Rarely if ever have intellectual and spiritual worked together so closely rather than frustrating each other.

Today, though, Hegel's importance does not reside primarily in the details and intricacies of the historical dialectic he traces. That dialectic, in fact, exacerbates a sense of the difficulty of narrative intellectual history. Contemporary debates on the origins of totalitarianism (they involve Hegel's own theory of the state and often attack the "Enlightenment project") present an overdetermined and even emotional genealogy. Do we have the conceptual instruments to discern how cultural causation works?

What mainly remains alive and valuable is Hegel's respect for each successive, superseded stage. Past cultures, or their spirit, are not treated as errors and obstacles but as necessary antecedents not to be disregarded. Their trace must be internalized if the mind is not to fall back into a fatal solipsism. Hegel talks of the "prodigious labor of world history" and of the length of a journey that has to be endured, in which every moment is necessary. One can object to what has since been vulgarized as the March of Time; but that march, in Hegel, is more like the sequence of pictures in a gallery, made gravid by extraordinary passages of pathos that endow the portrait of each era with its own authenticity, and so found modern historicism.

❑ ❑ ❑

The generations that grew up in the aftermath of World War I often link their anxieties to a *regressive* phenomenon characterized by T. S. Eliot as a dissociation of thought from feeling. Eliot feared that a free-floating intellect, joining with the revolutionary's contempt for the past, would corrode what was left of traditional ceremonies and local customs and so undermine a historically cumulative national identity. Yeats's "A Prayer for My Daughter" shares that concern and evokes what already seems like a lost innocence. By definition, a wasteland cannot bind genius to locality or incorporate thought as feeling.

Eliot constructs a dubious historical narrative—in form like a Hegelian genealogy yet backward rather than forward looking—that locates the crisis of dissociation in early modernity and the Protestant schism in Christendom. (Other contemporary trends posit the gradual destruction of an organic rural community where labor blossomed and the intellect remained integrated with the arts of daily life.) Poets like John Donne, Eliot claims, caught up in the religious and political turmoil of the Reformation, live at the edge of a dissolution yet maintain a unified vision of the departing unity. Even Shakespeare, compared to Dante, cannot unify experience and fails at times to create adequate symbols, or "objective correlatives," for what he seeks to express. Modern poetry, it is suggested, should draw inspiration from that exemplary, complex, moment. This meant, in effect, downgrading a second great literary Renaissance, that of the Romantics.

"Who Needs Goethe?" (chapter 10) has as its subtext "Who Needs Wordsworth?" and tries to undo Eliot's simplified historical scheme. Not only to set the record straight (Eliot, in fact, had a nuanced appreciation of Wordsworth and Goethe) but to honor the struggle against inauthenticity—in history as a whole, or in modernity—waged by

Hegel, the Romantics, and many post-Romantics. Any close reading of Hegel, and Goethe and Wordsworth, will show that, although troubled by a sense that history has taken a decisive turn, they do not locate this turn in the past or claim it ushered in a decadent, irreversible structure of feeling. Their focus is on radical alterations occurring in their time, and they maintain a hope inspired by the French Revolution.

◻   ◻   ◻

The revolutionary years from 1776 to the end of the Napoleonic wars are the temporal site of enormous intellectual, economic, and industrial turmoil as well as of heightened democratic and national feelings. Acute questions are raised about whether traditional ways of life can survive. Wordsworth in *The Prelude* describes how, between 1793 and 1795, "Sick, wearied out with contrarieties/[He] Yielded up moral questions in despair."[3] He could neither accept nor dismiss a rejectionist attitude toward the past. Social and political history was being unmasked as the story of slavery, not liberty. Whether we turn to Rousseau's notorious "Man was born free, yet everywhere he is in chains,"[4] or Kant's essay on the Enlightenment as an emancipation ("dare to know"), or Schiller's *Letters on Aesthetic Education* (dare to play . . .), or Wordsworth's *Prelude*, or the poetry of Blake, Byron, and Shelley, what is taking shape is an intellectual and spiritual manumission.

The "mind-forged manacles," of course, dismantled by Blake's ambitious poems, were also tangible chains that fettered slaves and degraded "the human form divine."[5] The aspiration to transform a narrative about near-universal bondage into a story of gradually achieved freedom meant that the past and its literary classics had to be either disowned or radically reinterpreted. Blake recognized the sinister and repetitious reality of the past but chose to face it down by the sheer force of a poetic and often subversive Bible of his own, an anticlerical, energy-liberating "Bible of Hell."

His type of enthusiasm, therefore, remains close to what contributed to Wordsworth's moral perplexity: ideologies that divided the "man to come . . . as by a gulph"[6] from him who had been. In some, including Blake, that break was understood as a divestment: a return to Adam Kadmon (First or Primal Man) and the unfallen human condition. Matthew Arnold's *Culture and Anarchy* would lump all such ideologies under the name of Jacobinism: "violent indignation with the past, abstract systems of renovation applied wholesale, a new doctrine drawn up in black and white for elaborating down to the very smallest details a rational society for the future."[7]

Included in this "new" doctrine are both pietistic and secular philosophies of inner light extensively described by Goethe and Hegel. In addition to religion-based enthusiasms exalting a private revelation, and originating in a variety of radical Protestant sects, there was a situationist trust in what *The Prelude* described as "the light of circumstances, flashed/Upon an independent intellect,"[8] and further—although not in Blake—the ruthless application of analytic reasoning to human affairs.

Wordsworth, having overcome his own crisis, tries to correct his generation's despondency, after what is widely perceived to be the French Revolution's failure. His autobiographical account of the restoration of imaginative hope and power—as a poem, *The Prelude* enacts its own claim—is the first to evoke in vivid if episodic detail an individual mind's developmental history. Wordsworth concentrates on a youngster's iffy socialization together with the growing awareness of his calling—crucial factors in the formation of personal identity. The poet's recovery begins in the midst of moral perplexity, when early and intensely localized memories revive his sense of "Nature" as an animistic, sometimes frightening, yet ultimately benevolent, tutorial agency. Once he combines the call to be a poet with the progressive if troubled path to self-identity, once he decides to give voice to his childhood as well as to "English" nature, Utopia no longer demands that the past—personal or national—be excised by radical political surgery.

❑   ❑   ❑

A final reflection, by way of this triad of opening chapters. Recent writings, a flood of them, take up the legitimacy of moral philosophy. They revisit a question formulated with the advance of secularism in the eighteenth century: Can rationally cogent grounds be found for ethical pronouncements? The possibility of devising a political morality, however speculative, and avoiding disastrous positivisms or political religions is also the latest cottage industry of the law schools. Wittgenstein concluded that there were matters philosophy should not attempt to justify by its procedures, and many feel the same about validating on propositional or logical grounds specific interpretations of art. My concern with "authenticity" and "spirit" is a way of linking ethical talk to art once more, while taking into account the contextual historical pressures art articulates in its own way.[9]

The aesthetic response, seen by some as an avoidance or escape, may be as much foreknowledge as response. Like philosophies of history inspired by Hegel, but less discursively, art raises the issue of human freedom: of the self-determination of the individual and often of the collective with which the individual identifies. The persuasiveness of art needs the supplement, however, of an interpretive practice that includes art itself rather than being applied from the outside. How does imagination become a reality principle? How does the unreality of art lessen the sense of unreality that so often invades us?

Ideology, however grand, is not adequate as a reality system. The Christian conflation of spirit and freedom, for example, and the humanistic pairing of truth and freedom—two great ideologies that merge in Hegel—reduce to empty clichés if we neglect the historical controversies that led Cardinal Newman in his *Apologia* to adopt an "antagonist unity" as his persona. Newman is not only aware, before the letter, of the principle of positionality; he also knows that some role-playing is inevitable, even in a nonfictive autobiography.

The unreal real tends to prevail unless two conditions are satisfied. First, the writer's work must be honored for the imaginative force in it that makes received opinion or a fixed reality principle appear to be a false bottom, as in a magical deception; then the writer's situation is honored, which cannot happen if the adversarial embrace between an emerging self and historical circumstances does not take place. This embrace, however, does lead to the danger of a mimetic identification with force majeure, so that ideology critique is always necessary.

Let me illustrate these assertions briefly by citing slave narratives as a generic example. Hegel's "History" is the story of human liberty achieved by respecting the precarious face-off between self and self, self and other. His analysis of liege lord (master) and bondsman (slave) in the feudal age became famous and influenced both political and psychological treatments of the often mortal struggle to recognize, and so emancipate, an oppressed class. Actual slave narratives eventually enter that epic legend of the centuries called history. They seek to "tell a free story," that is, to free the narrator from inner as well as outer bondage. For despite the legal emancipation of the victims, their testimony may still be distorted by a sense of sin or inferiority, by the tainted self-image they live with or which they assume remains in the mind of others.[10] Yet having acquired literacy (this is often a crucial part of their chronicles), the ex-slaves, whose exemplary act has only recently seeped into the cultural consciousness, realize themselves along the same lines that canonized modernist artists.[11]

Not only does what they say have documentary importance, but the act of writing itself, the will and courage to communicate, takes on performative value. Hence a strange light falls on our admiration for the modernists. What is the *Néant*, the Nothing, against which Mallarmé contends as if in crisis? Why do artists like him claim that style is everything and subject matter indifferent? What beyond a conviction about the vanity of human affairs, which any moral or religious person can share, incites their obsession with unreality—hopeless virginity, meaninglessness, phantomization, or sheer, unrealized potentiality— which is then countered by an astonishing faith in pure artifice, even in a religion of art?

Flaubert writes in a famous letter of 1852: "What seems beautiful to me, what I should most like to do, would be a book about nothing, a book without any exterior tie, but sustained by the internal force of style."[12] And in a later correspondence he mentions his pleasure on seeing a bare wall of the Acropolis. "I wonder if a book, independently of what it says, might produce the same effect?" It is impossible to imagine such sentiments in slave narratives or other victim accounts.

Perhaps the rise of realism, the very thing that made it possible to find an audience for narratives of social suffering, leads to a passion for purity in art that is not an evasion of reality so much as a troubled kind of tribute to reality. Artists survive in that way the other side of realism: the tide of print, *fait divers*, and copy. Mind empties itself of older forms of containment in order to grapple better with realities but therefore confronts its own sterile essence, or the truth of the trivial, or a dulling repetition of the miseries of the world. Its ascetic or aesthetic labor must then avoid producing a mere duplication of the unreal real (Flaubert) or the real unreal (Mallarmé).

Flaubert's ingenious doublet, Bouvard and Pécuchet, is a demotic analogue to Mallarmé's Hérodiade and her mirror image: We feel the simulacrum encroaching. "They think I am in love with the real," Flaubert remarked about readers of *Mme Bovary*, "but I execrate it; it is out of my hate for realism that I undertook this novel."[13] Thus the irritant that produced the pearl continues to be creative; so does, despite the modernist's desire for a pure or else absolute kind of art, the will to communicate:

> The extreme austerity of an almost empty mind
> Colliding with the lush, Rousseau-like foliage
> of its desire to communicate . . . [14]

That communication-compulsion, linked today with an urge to be accountable, if only to oneself—even, possibly, with the urge to preempt judgment by becoming "Jean-Jacques, judge of Jean-Jacques"— remains constant.

❏   ❏   ❏

Will all art, then, end as a portrait of the author or a species of life-writing? That is a question raised in the next chapter. Artifice, however, is not inevitably on the side of transparency, or the will to expose hidden feelings and thoughts. Publication includes intellectual cunning, as we learn from philosopher and scholar of Greek culture Leo Strauss. Societal pressure and outright censorship generate intricate and devious modes of writing. What seems straightforward often conceals an esoteric meaning. Psychoanalysis has suggested, moreover, that the mind is deeply formed by a lasting deposit of what was suffered by humankind collectively as well as by what is experienced early in life, so that an internalized form of censorship, together with an equivocal style, seems inevitable.

The power of plain speech, however, the moral force of testimony in particular, does not lose its appeal. It promises to liberate representation from both an externally imposed censorship and that ingenious, self-generated obliquity. *We fantasize a public mode of expression whose truth will make us free.*

Alas, what we actually see around us is quite different. Artistic freedom, in the contemporary climate, means tolerating deviations from the accepted norm and at times making deviation the norm (to the point of advertising a movie as "A Motion Picture Deviation"). An unusual degree of license tends to rouse a sentiment of powerlessness in the artist. Creativity, finally unimpeded, seems to persecute the creator who cannot live up to it. The impasse between an ideal of public discourse aiming at transparency or normative understanding and more devious, artistic kinds of speech has not been resolved.

The fusion, moreover, of a society of communication with a society of the spectacle has already led to a myopic celebration of photogenic factors and an unthinking ethic of exposure and disclosure. One effect of this is the wasting of minds by semifiltered masses of information whose impact is caught by the popular proverb "garbage in, garbage out." The continued presence, and recrudescence, of religious politics aims at a state of ultimate transparency, and stops at nothing, paradoxically not even at dissemblance, to unveil a Manichean world, an anatomy of reality as stark and judgmental as the Apocalypse. Even moderate attempts to redeem what is regarded as the wasteland of modernity, by merging once more the forces of the state and of religion (by what Kenneth Burke in the 1930s named a "sinister unification"), result in conflict resolution becoming almost impossible: Negotiation involves compromise, and compromise is not possible when political strife touches religious and especially messianic convictions.

Cultural prophesy, when imbued with such apocalyptic fervor, is based on an idea of authenticity or spiritual fulfillment that is absolute and brooks neither ambiguity nor critique. Pleasure, as Lionel Trilling pointed out in a prescient essay of 1963, "The Fate of Pleasure,"[15] is no match for a militant spirituality that devalues human and secular fulfillment as a specious good. To abide the negative (in Hegel's sense) is as hard as to nourish faith by the evidence of things not seen. There is a temptation to allow a coercive and purely ideological transparency to compensate for that lack of visibility. The tardiness of the messiah— the unreal presence, or simply the unreality of the spirit, its inadequate human and social embodiment—prompts cycles of rage and frustration that lead to renewed catastrophe. From that perspective, history turns out to be not the story of human liberation but one wounding after another, a narrative of scars left in the wake of spiritual violence.

❏   ❏   ❏

While my treatment of the intersection of moral, political, technological, and literary/linguistic issues is essayistic rather than systematic, I wish it to respect historical as well as personal associations whose density make art, and even the art of criticism, the source of a lasting if difficult pleasure. That density is related to the rich darkness or non-transparence characterizing literary language and artistic expression generally. My last group of essays, then, is a scrutiny of the conditions under which, presently, we study art. "Who Needs Goethe?" "The Virtue of Attentiveness," "Democracy's Museum," and "Aestheticide" envision a renewal of aesthetics by valuing the art in art. I try to transmit an awareness of how art's peculiar stylization, its divergence from narrow concepts of imitation, induces a marked, near-physiological response: a memory not confined to strictly bodily events but encompassing in a viable form both greater and smaller trauma.

PART II

CHAPTER 4

REALISM, AUTHENTICITY, AND THE NEW BIOGRAPHICAL CULTURE

I t is Friday, March 31, 2000. I am thinking about my essay. It hardly matters what date it is, but the concreteness of that marker is strangely comforting.

Two "signs of the times" in the *New York Times* catch my attention. One is a full-page ad for a Sotheby auction featuring master photographers. It reproduces an Edward Weston photo, "Hands against Kimono," valued at between $100,000 and $150,000. The blurb describing it reads in part: "This bravura print of Tina Modotti's hands is one of Edward Weston's most sensitive studies of his lover."

Why would the photo's value be less, I wonder, if its attribution were uncertain? And how much do the biographical details, the specificity of the woman's name and role in Weston's life, add to its value?

The second item is a review by Michiko Kakutani of *Blonde*, Joyce Carol Oates's fictionalized biography of Marilyn Monroe. The review is unusually harsh, accusing the author of "shamelessly . . . using the life of Marilyn Monroe as a substitute for inventing an original story" and so to cash in on the star's legend. Oates freely changes the real names either into other or allegorizing nicknames: "the Ex-Athlete"(Joe DiMaggio), "the Prince" (President Kennedy), "the Playwright" (Arthur Miller), "the Blonde Actress" or "Miss Golden Dreams" (Marilyn herself).

What Oates has done, I surmise from the review, is not all that different from a recent tendency to move historical fiction into the present, to rehearse or re-create lives and events within the direct memory of many contemporaries. A genre has emerged that hovers between fiction and reportage and even mixes historical actors with invented observers.

The elder novelists, however, unless their purpose is topical satire, avoid a roman à clef that needs no key. They elide the source of what initially inspired them—the "germ" of the whole, as Henry James called it. At the same time, they may find a way of novelizing it as a structural trace that conveys the feel of contemporary fact. I glimpse such a trace in the striking and mysterious newspaper advertisement that is the pivot of Heinrich von Kleist's *Marquise of O.* Also in the quite ordinary request for information about a missing person found in the *Paris-Soir* of December 31, 1941, a notice that, in December 1988, forty-seven years after its insertion, catches the attention of Patrick Modiano's narrator in *Dora Bruder.*[1] It initiates a quest that takes up Modiano's entire novel.

The impact of the *fait divers* of newspaper (and now TV) signals a new phase in the relation of fiction to contemporaneity. In both Kleist and Modiano it is an ad, conspicuous in the one case, deceptively inconspicuous in the other, that yields a clue to the story of a life. Everything else about the two narratives is different. That a marquise, during the turmoil of the Napoleonic wars, resorts to a public medium in order to find her rescuer-rapist implies a daring solecism, a desperate if courageous act on the part of a nobly born woman. In Modiano, however, the ordinariness of the medium emphasizes the deceptive ordinariness of the event. The missing girl for whom the novel (but is it a novel?) is named had no power of self-determination except for the "fugue," or escapade that may have doomed her. She disappears twice: as a runaway in the winter of 1941 and again in June of 1942 when she was probably seized in one of the roundups of Jews in Paris.

Is Modiano's narrative history or fiction? *Dora Bruder* offers, at first glance, nothing to sustain fictional suspense except the removal of a mystification. The "Vichy syndrome," as the historian Henri Rousso has named it, covered up till the 1980s the part played by the French police in the deportation of Jews. The first-person narrator of *Dora Bruder,* eventually identified as Modiano, retrieves by his research a single, unknown girl's life—and death—from obscurity: He makes her name live, or, rather, reveals through it a collective fate.[2]

But there is a mystery because we are left to conjecture why he should engage in precisely this quest, motivated by an announcement seen by chance. He has no personal or family relation to Dora, except in the sense in which her last name implies universal kinship. He says only that he is familiar with the *quartier* where Dora lived and experienced an adolescent rebellion at the same age. His family, being Jewish, found itself in a comparably dangerous situation in wartime Paris. He also betrays regret for losing the city he knew while growing up, which is being altered by postwar changes.

❑   ❑   ❑

It is impossible to decide from internal evidence whether the gradually recovered details of Dora Bruder's fate are fictive or present an actual slice of history. At once detective and archival researcher, the self-burdened narrator meets the discipline of history on its own ground, producing a persuasive facsimile.

Yet *Dora Bruder* cannot be called "faction." The author respects his remoteness from the events, and the narrative "I," although distinctive enough, tied to certain memories and caught up in the search, has only a spotty autobiographical density. Sparse details about the author's life[3] contrast with the increasing weight of facts about Dora's fugitive passage across the landscape of a disastrous epoch.

Without being impersonal, then, Modiano's "history" achieves a representational quality similar to neoclassical *récits* that report terrible events rather than depicting them on stage. Its narrator, however, is not an eyewitness, as in those *récits*. He is a belated observer, drawn as if accidentally—through no more than a printed trace—to an act of necromancy that rescues Dora from the anonymous mass of Holocaust victims.

❑   ❑   ❑

Two questions are correlative to any discussion of realism in its contemporary phase, when autobiography, biography, testimony, and confessional memoir invade both fictional and nonfictional space. One is the liaison between the "I" and historical events, as in *Dora Bruder* or in W. C. Sebald's *The Emigrants*. The second is the status of the "I," which is (1) a character in the story, (2) seemingly coincident with its narrative double, and (3) a peculiar linguistic entity.

Let me deal first—and briefly—with the triple status of the "I." As a character it is entirely variable: reticent in *Dora Bruder* and *The Emigrants*, flamboyant in confessional literature or self-exposé, a style shifter in E. L. Doctorow's novel, *City of God*.[4] This chameleon quality is partly enabled by a linguistic feature. While "I" has the semantic consistency of a name, being a pronoun backed by a noun (the name of autobiographer, biographer, or novelist), it is, at the same time, what linguists call a shifter, and allows the identity of the "I" to vary with the (imagined) context of narration. Call it semantically opaque—like most proper names—but syntactically transparent.

The "I," despite or because of that variability, continues to serve as the premise for a promise to reveal something factually true. This expectation proves to be deceptive, or very intricate. Together with certain related words ("now," "here"), the "I" is either an empty universal or part of an imaginary, if credible, biography—more precisely, thanatography (death- rather than life-writing). Reading *Dora Bruder* in the context of Modiano's other novels, an obsessive pattern emerges, one that suggests a deep-seated identity puzzle.

The pattern I refer to includes tracing the passage of a missing person, who may turn out to be the narrator himself, as in *Rue des Boutiques Obscures* (1978). "I am nothing. Nothing but a clear silhouette," is how that novel begins. It goes on to situate the "nothing" in a prosaic way, disclosing that the speaker is referring to his amnesia.[5] In *Voyage de Noces* (1990),[6] however, the literalizing device of amnesia is dropped. Everything slips into a sentiment of unreality, a permanent *fugue*, and the narrator has to grasp at various identity-scraps: addresses, places previously visited, phone numbers, and, as in *Dora Bruder*, a classified ad for a missing person ("On recherche une jeune fille . . ." etc.).[7]

Modiano has confessed to blending "reality and fiction. . . . a procedure producing a certain uneasiness that would not arise if readers were sure of finding themselves either inside a totally imaginary situation or else in historical reality."[8] This uneasy *clair-obscur* is his specialty, and it conveys his revolt against a deadly bureaucratic world, whether French or fascistic, and where only persons with identity cards have the right to exist—at the risk of being summoned or rounded up.

Yet Modiano's fascination with vanishings remains intriguing. A sustained contrast governs his novels. Particular places as well as persons—places fitfully illuminated by the people who pass through them—come to the fore and endow his pages with a ghostliness reminiscent of old photographs and homemade movies. Moreover, he elides, as I have mentioned, much of his own biography to allow Dora's absence to be the focus, heightened by a contrast between "the extreme precision of certain details" and "the night, the unknown, the forgetfulness, the nothingness all around them."[9]

To adapt one of Freud's observations: The dead girl's imaginative impact is stronger than the living might have been. The fullness of the empty center called Dora suggests an incarnation arising from an "absent memory" that afflicts a postwar generation of Jewish writers. (In Klarsfield's *Mémorial*, while Dora Bruder is listed as deported with Convoy 34 on September 18, 1942, place and date of birth are blank.) Not having directly experienced the Holocaust era, members of that generation are compelled to research, rather than recall, what happened in and to their families. The descendants' imagination is haunted by absent presences.[10] *or present absences*

The engagement, then, that retrieves in the form of a personal quest the memory of an unwitnessed reality lifts the element of romance in this kind of fiction to a new level of seriousness. It is a form of belated witness complementary to the memory that returns in the testimony of eyewitnesses. By now the popular appeal of these testimonies may have increased memory envy in two respects. First, the testimonies are by people akin to Dora Bruder, rather than exclusively by those who played important roles in or after the Holocaust. Second, they reinforce the wish, always latent in us, for strong, identity-shaping memories.

❑   ❑   ❑

We reach, here, our other concern: the relation of the invented or reconstructed "I" to the historical as a form of realism. Does historical fact always further the realistic mode? In fiction, the specificity of the famous name, of "Marilyn Monroe" for instance, may not have much effect, once the surprise wears off. Only when the name is unknown ("Martin Guerre," "Dora Bruder") or unrevealed (the bearer of a secret identity) or made evocative by a literature of its own (as in Joyce's use of Homer's Ulysses) does it become an intriguing index. Otherwise its reality claim is no greater than that of the pro-name "I," which always both reveals and conceals its meaning. Name recognition, then, is only initially an advantage, somewhat like having an inside position on the racetrack.[11]

The fact is that fictional narratives must generate an interest independent of a coincident reality. There is an ironic reversal of the priority of real to fictive. The "Anne Frank," the "Philip Roth" of a Philip Roth novel, or the "Paul Auster" in a Paul Auster story ("City of Glass" in *New York Trilogy*) have their own confusing and disconcerting lives. That is demanded by the self-fashioning, self-inventive element associated with modern originality, a rebellious, break-away quality that competes with the narrative patience and extensively described settings found in most great novelists. Not only do the characters in this "double game" of fact and fiction try to get away from the author and reclaim their power of agency, but authors may become characters themselves and seek a public, real-life installation of fictive alter egos.[12]

Here we glimpse once more the originality of *Dora Bruder*. That work is not only a careful piece of research, or a simulacrum blending reality and fiction. Rather, its noncoincidental relation to the real-life Dora Bruder reveals the truth of fiction's reality-claim. The post-Holocaust memory, haunted by historical fact, becomes a freely, even lovingly bestowed form of imagination. *Dora Bruder* illuminates the imagination's power to identify with the very puzzle of identity by going out of one person and re-creating another person. That the circumstances are tragic, that this life of Dora Bruder is also a death, only intensifies the affinity between memory and imagination in a time of endless mourning. The ordinary, deeply lodged feeling of nothingness in oneself makes something of the absent other. Call it—this creation out of nothing—an ultimate defense against nihilism; also a defense of literature against the doubt that arises when a simple listing of names, of deadly statistics, and an occasional photo account for those lives with a refusal of pathos that seems absolute.[13]

❏   ❏   ❏

What we savor in realistic fiction is not only the vitality of the characters. It is also, as Ortega y Gasset once remarked, the novel's power to turn us into provincials of its world, of a setting so carefully observed that it becomes a milieu, life-giving or life-impeding. That milieu has disintegrated in Modiano, although the houses and streets bear mocking vestiges of it, pieced together by his meticulous re-creations. In Sebald, however, a specious miracle is described: The displaced persons build for themselves a new milieu with a solidity that camouflages past suffering and deceives for a time even the narrator. Indeed, Sebald introduces photos into his stories that claim to represent realia in the life of the emigrants, photos that function as attestations of his characters' near-zoological camouflage, of their seeming stillness and integration rather than alienation.

If authors, moreover, borrow historical figures, especially well-documented ones, the risk grows that the issue of authenticity will surface. We cannot suspend disbelief when known circumstances are denied or tinkered with. There is an existential, irreversible quality to those facts that renders clearly fictive insertions unconvincing.[14]

In certain cases, of course, a penumbra of doubt continues to unsettle received history: Oliver Stone exploits this in his film on the Kennedy assassination. Counterfactual theorizing, moreover, and science fiction's alternate realities abound. But we sense in these instances—as in detective stories generally—a skeptical or even gnostic element that deprives appearances (the familiar world, received history) of their apparent truth. An anxiety develops, expressed rather than alleviated by fictional suspense, that nothing is what it appears to be, that everything, eventually, will turn out to be deceptive, manipulated, counterfeit.

It should not come as a surprise that received historical fact is felt to be as fallible as any other. Historians themselves have as their principal task to affirm or disconfirm it. But while the stylistic demeanor of history-writing remains, on the whole, impersonal, today it often merges with a writing in the first person no longer shy about itself.[15] Every truth claim in this area is shadowed by the awareness that it may be history fiction despite itself.[16] What does surprise, however, is that fiction as a sustained mode distinct from historical representation should be threatened—as memoir, journal, testimony, and faction usurp all other realisms.

With the expansiveness of first-person writing the defense of gossip often comes at the expense of fiction. There are other challenges too. Reality TV, in which it is impossible to tell spontaneous from faked or rehearsed, competes with a realism long outflanked by the hydra-headed genre of romance—the latter presently spawning new techno-wars in heaven as on earth. If the subject in question remains the "I," its integrity is harder to spot when surrounded by special effects. Could the "I" too be such an effect? Who, where, is the center of all this decentered magic? Who is real, the main character of the sci-fi movie *The Thirteenth Floor* asks at one point: How do I know I am not an optical illusion, a bundle of computer-driven electrical charges?

❑   ❑   ❑

E. L. Doctorow's *City of God* struggles to regain something of realistic fiction's threatened integrity. It mixes veristic vignettes of contemporary life with fantastic riffs. There are no fewer than four first-person narrators, including a novelist. Among the fantastic parts are cerebral digressions on "cosmosity," antianthropocentric speculations that spook the urban comedy striving to transform its chaos into a City of God yet failing to displace the human as the measure of all things. Cosmic space cannot become place and certainly not a redemptive milieu. At the novel's end, despite the city's drift toward apocalyptic havoc, a man and a woman are left, a kind of Adam and Eve working to rebuild society through the Noah's Ark of a modest Upper West Side synagogue.

Doctorow's prose gravitates only slowly toward a personal form of containment, a clearly delineated "I." Yet the story line, while devious and interrupted, is not complex. Everett, the novel's novelist, recounts the spiritual picaresque of Timothy, a lapsed priest, who will eventually marry a woman rabbi. The narrator glimpses a form of redemptive heroism in the priest's adventures, in his own brother's harrowing task flying a bomber in the second World War, and in stories from the Kovno ghetto during the darkest days of the Holocaust.

The Kovno episodes, in particular, approach faction. They recall John Hersey's *The Wall* (1949), a novel that re-created the Warsaw ghetto uprising. Hersey's *Hiroshima* (1946) was justly famous as a narrative equivalent of photojournalism, but for his novel Hersey had to rely on eyewitness accounts in the YIVO Institute for Jewish Research. From these he "invents a memory," that is, a character contemporary with the events he recounts for posterity.[17] Hersey would later become wary of such powerful metajournalistic re-creations.

Doctorow, too, invents a contemporary to chronicle the liquidation of Kovno's Jews, but adds a twist: The lapsed priest is the one who hunts down and retrieves a lost Kovno archive. In addition, the novel's novelist, who calls himself a "faux Pop" (mocking the priestly honorific of "Father"), insinuates himself into the life of all his characters—some of whom are still in process, still being invented.

The very ease with which writers or cineasts deceive us, moving like Doctorow between gritty simulacra of daily life, archival quests, and dream-like or imaginative fugues, betrays the doubt that has penetrated our sense of reality, radicalizing the eternal question about the truth of appearances. As an explicit symptom of this, Doctorow's novelist describes an affair with a woman whom he persuades—if only as a plot he conceives for a movie—to lure her husband into a situation where the latter's identity is nullified, because the lover's perfect counterfeit has successfully taken his place.

Moreover, that the narrator calls himself a "faux Pop" links *City of God* to the search for a true father or authority figure, a search that is a constant in Anglo-American history from early religious revivals to contemporary confidence hucksters. Does the "faux Pop" also link up with our new biographical culture, its claim of realism?

❑   ❑   ❑

To answer—and conclude—I will look at one of the more interesting of a recent spate of academic autobiographies. Jane Tompkins's *A Life in School* is the conversion narrative of a teacher who reviews her quite ordinary life, starting with "the dark corridors" of P.S. 98, through college, graduate training, and many years as a professor in various universities.[18] The book tells of a late awakening to the fact that schooling has left out what school is for: life and community building.

Nowhere does the author find a holistic education. Her diagnosis, at once political and spiritual, is that the system substitutes authority for an alive teaching, and she recounts her not-always-successful efforts to relinquish authority in the classroom. Even when the classroom, by the instructor removing herself as authority figure, is made free and safe for the students, it becomes unsafe for the teacher, who used to be shielded by the mask of authority but is now open to the quirky as well as just criticism of her students.

I single out this memoir because it seeks to exorcise one type of "faux pop"—that is, false authority—without falling prey to another "faux pop," false populism or facile notions of community. It illustrates the search for authenticity motivating most autobiographies. Here is someone who was always an aspiring student and became a successful scholar-teacher. Yet her book, unsparing in its depiction of her schooling, is marked by an equally unsparing self-portrait.

The "I" that reveals itself is neither apologetic nor vaunting. Nor does it have quick remedies for personal loneliness or the incapacity of our schools to draw students toward a vital sense of kinship, cooperation, and community. Instead it returns continually to a dissatisfaction with the very self that describes a delayed awakening. It achieves, albeit at the cost of being relentlessly unfunny, the accumulative force of a bildungsroman.

Tompkins's awakening was prompted by a duo of repeated dreams exposing her fear of authority and investing it with two separate meanings. There is the fear of personal failure, related to the power a teacher has over you, and which was instilled from the very beginning of the author's life in school. But later there is also the fear of becoming an authority figure yourself—a fraudulent one. Tompkins writes that the dream of being exposed as a fraud is experienced in one form or another by thousands of teachers at the beginning of each school year.

Once upon a time, awakenings of this kind were followed by revivalist movements. But in this book the spirituality is ecumenical and dressed down. It is not unthinkable, then, that the autobiographical wave we are experiencing is a contemporary version of a perennial anxiety whose classic examples are Augustine and Rousseau.

I draw two lessons from the above. Autobiography, at its best, is neither ego trip nor history fiction but rather, as in Tompkins, a clear-sighted analysis together with a refusal to impose pedagogical or social solutions that could provoke further tyranny and iatrogenic suffering. Whether the hypocrisy of half-baked ideologies is punctured by the earnest realism of memoir-writer and novelist, or—since "the worst returns to laughter"—by picaresque forms of hilarity is less important than that the relation between description and prescription be as complex as in a work of art.[19] Let there be a greening of the pedagogical element. So that, to quote Wallace Stevens, "The green falls on you as you look . . . /That elemental parent, the green night,/ Teaching a fusky alphabet."[20]

The drive, moreover, to be totally embodied and yet transparent, a drive fostered by today's biographical and self-biographical culture, by all those candid constructions or reconstructions, cannot expunge a lingering fear of personal inauthenticity.[21] This fear need not be as explicit as the torments of self-examination undergone by seventeenth-century seekers for evidences of grace or the integrity of their conversion. But it is often the unmistakable subplot. Even should authenticity be, according to Henry Louis Gates, Jr., "among the founding lies of the modern age,"[22] how far back does that other untruthful term "modern" extend? I prefer, adopting a phrase from Shelley, to think of authenticity as an "illustrious superstition."

CHAPTER 5

TELE-SUFFERING AND TESTIMONY

Why was the sight
To such a tender ball as the eye confined?

—*John Milton*, Samson Agonistes

Television is a mechanism bringing us images from far away while making itself as invisible as possible. To be effective, it cannot relinquish this magical realism, this counterfeit transparency. Arguably, TV shares that characteristic with print or other media: To cite a common definition of imagination, they render what is absent, present. Yet TV's difference from a verbal or literary medium is quite clear. Novels, or histories in book form, respect the absence of those absent things more: Their distance is factored in, not only by deliberate devices that expose a (relatively) invisible author's rhetorical manipulations but also by the difference between the mental activities of viewing and reading. TV, to generalize, conveys the illusion not of making absent things present but present things more present (than they are or can be). Even when devoted to information rather than fiction, TV emits a hyperbolic form of visuality.

Of course, like literature, TV can become self-conscious and blow the cover of its magic by showing within its pictures a camera taking pictures or a monitor reflecting them. But it does so, usually, only to increase its authority as an objective mediation, or rather to make us think of it as a medium rather than a mediation. Showing the camera is showing what you shoot with: It is no longer a concealed instrument.

Those opposed to the modern world's iconomania can shun the cameras but would find it futile to smash them. Cameras are not icons but productive of them, and the network by which they send images is redundant rather than place-bound, so that any damage would be merely symbolic. In fact, although a religious rhetoric denouncing the lust of the eyes is still heard, many faiths have succumbed to the medium and adopted it for profitable evangelical propaganda.

I do not want to give the impression that TV is purely a mechanism. It is, indeed, the most powerful means we presently have for the production of images (if we consider the downloading of images on the Internet simply a further extension of TV's potency). Yet behind the mechanism there are its directors or agents, removed by the magic—the automatism—of photography. The interaction of TV's image production and those who coordinate or manipulate it is a lively and self-complicating topic. Not without reason has journalism (now dominated by TV's influence on the general public) been called the Fourth Estate. Sociologists and others have begun a full-scale critique of the managers who set the conditions of reporting and viewing for the medium: They suspect a "structural corruption" that makes it ineffective to try to modify by discursive means (such as this essay) what goes on.

There exist, no doubt, genial filmmakers who attempt to criticize the image through the image; and I will soon describe the Yale Video Archive's further attempt to do just that. But it is hard not to agree with French sociologist Pierre Bourdieu that anyone who goes on television will suffer a loss of autonomy and that the self-analysis occasionally nurtured by TV journalists only feeds their "narcissistic complaisance."

□   □   □

Now and then a murderous incident like the 1999 Columbine School massacre by two Colorado teenagers incites a flurry of speculation about the influence of the imagery video brings into the home. The television set or a computer with video games has become, as it were, a new hearth. But is it a controlled, domesticated fire we have brought into the castle of our privacy?

As parents, my generation tried to limit the viewing of TV, primarily to prevent neglect of homework or a sidelining of intellectual and socializing influences. Increasingly, though, the problem does not involve only the proper allotment of leisure time. What is viewed comes into question, and the very modality of watching. For not only are violent films available on a 24-hour basis, but newscasting itself, on the same continuous basis, transmits daily pictures of violence, suffering, and destruction. One of the simplest axioms of psychoanalysis holds that hyper-arousal leads to trauma or inappropriate psychic defenses: It seems clear enough that, while human responses are not uniform, and our psyches are quite resilient, this intensification has its impact. We live in an artificially enhanced visual culture, but it is premature to claim that we have visual culture.

The issue of TV's responsibility for social violence is a complicated one. The medium does not present a seamless web of images. Its hypnotism is far from unalloyed. The medium is more talky, in fact, than most cinematic composition: It adds layers of words to juxtaposed visual excerpts. In addition to the words and snatches of music that come with the relayed images, we have the anchorperson's or moderator's commentary. News, talk shows, music montages (MTV), and documentaries, therefore, may be the ultimate TV, rather than retailed Hollywood-type films. Moreover, while films usually hide the fact that they are episodic and present themselves as wholly new and startling (although playing on continuities bestowed by famous actors or character types), TV not only likes to serialize programs but allows arbitrary breaks for advertising that disturb our concentration without quite dehypnotizing it.

We take our eyes away from a book in order to think or else to rest them, letting what has been read go deeper. In contrast, TV offers (also because of the ease of channel surfing) not real breaks or reflective pauses but one audiovisual representation after the other. Its "flow," in short, at once isolates certain sequences and distracts us from them. The reality effect of its imagery, therefore, is heightened and diminished at the same time. This is one reason why it is hard to generalize about the contagious effect of TV violence: It all depends on whether your inner reception is tuned to what tries to invade you and won't let go or, alternatively, to the interruptions—visual and verbal—that dissipate it.

❏   ❏   ❏

One clear danger, however, should not be overlooked. Increasingly, as on-the-spot news reporting and other live broadcasts, especially the wilder kind of talk show ("My sister has two lovers") gain TV share, the reality effect of what is viewed verges on an unreality effect. The reason may be stated as follows. When reading fiction or seeing it in cinematic form, we adopt what S. T. Coleridge called a "suspension of disbelief." We know those multiple gory deaths in action movies are faked and that a considerable supply of ketchup is used. But what can keep addicted viewers, especially young ones, from a more fatal "suspension," which consists in looking at everything live as if it were a reality that could be manipulated? The unreality effect that turns what we actually see into electric phantoms is a new and insidious psychic defense.

Good fiction quietly posts many signs that imply "No Way Through to Action." It constructs reflective detours that convert reading into a many-leveled interpretive act and remind us we are dealing with simulacra. The problem with TV, however, is that, only a click away, and an intimate part of home, it becomes a treacherous servomechanism conspiring with a residual, delusory omnipotence of thoughts. While for most of us TV simply hard-copies the eye, making the "tender ball" less vulnerable, for some it may produce a mental atmosphere that makes it appear as if the very place we live in also came from that box. "Televised reality," Norman Manea has written, "becomes a self-devouring 'proto-reality' without which the real world is not confirmed and therefore does not exist."[2] The world is then no more and no less incredible than what confronts us in the news or ever-more horrific movies.

It is not that there must be a direct link between violent scenes depicted on TV or film and the brutal acts of teenagers; we surely know how confusing, precarious, and potentially catastrophic the passage from adolescence to maturity is, independent of a supposedly malignant TV effect. But there probably is a *derealization* of ordinary life that causes some youngsters to act out—like a game or drama whose roles they assume—their pain, disillusion, or mania. Animated gadgets rather than people inhabit a world of that kind, and it is easy to fall into the Manichean mind-set of "them and us" or "the good and the bad guys," fostered also by increasingly formulaic and ferocious movies. Youthful idealization of certain role models often goes together with an underestimation or even scapegoating of a despised group.

❑ ❑ ❑

Concerning this derealization, it is astonishing to reflect that only forty years ago, one of the most significant books about the cinema, Siegfried Kracauer's *Theory of Film*, bore the subtitle *The Redemption of Physical Reality*. It argued with great cogency that "Film renders visible what we did not, or perhaps even could not, see before its advent. [Film] effectively assists us in discovering the material world with its psycho-physical correspondences. We literally redeem this world from its dormant state, its state of virtual nonexistence."[3] Kracauer dealt with film as the fulfillment of the realistic effect of black-and-white photography. The cinema, he claimed, was animated by "a desire to picture transient material life, life at its most ephemeral," whether "street crowds, involuntary gestures" or "the ripple of the leaves stirred by the wind."[3]

Compared to this view of the medium, what we see in movie houses today should be called *photoys*. They are ghostings of reality, not its redemption. What, for example, is being rendered—made visible—by *The Matrix?* There are, no doubt, some strong "psycho-physical" sensations produced by this film's mastery of special effects: the way, for example, it carries the tendency of a body-piercing generation to an extreme by undermining the integrity of personal flesh. So, in addition to the doubling and out-of-body experiences intrinsic to its story line, near the beginning of the film there is a brilliant visual pun when the movie's reluctant hero is "bugged" by a disgustingly alive mechanical insect inserted via the navel into his innards. This inverted parturition recalls Nietzsche's insight that all preconceptions arise in the entrails. It is as if we had to return there to see the world without prejudice.

Yet ordinary sense data enter this film only in the form of incongruous scenes: of a here-and-now that can no longer be securely confined to a single location. As Christian painters often surrounded earthly events with heavenly figures, doubling the locus of the action, so every significant adventure of the hero, however external or apparently objective, has its echo in an invasive internal change dramatized as physical agony or the labor pains of rebirth. Moreover, a devious topology leads to defamiliarized interiors that remain absurdly familiar. The contraption to which people are strapped before they undergo their psycho-physical journey is a conflated image of a dentist's chair, an electric chair, and how astronauts are buckled up before the launch. Similarly, although we traverse seedy if potentially mysterious passageways to get to the Oracle, when we meet her she is in an ordinary kitchen baking cookies. And, despite the importance to the film of mobile communication, at a crucial final moment the hero steps into the interior of an old-fashioned phone booth, a retro effect that recalls (affectionately enough, but hardly realistic) Superman's transfiguration. In a sense we never get outside—outside of the movie studio producing all these effects.

What kind of reality, then, are we shown? Interestingly enough, we are not as far from Kracauer's "redemption" as might first appear. It is precisely a redemption of physical reality that is being aimed at—radically, comically, ingeniously, despairingly—by movies like these. The motif of redemption, in fact, governs *The Matrix*'s plot: to find "the One" who has the guts to free us from a world of appearances that limits or controls human perception and presumably keeps us from experiencing the *real* real world.

Yet in truth the movie offers only an engineered reality—an assemblage of phantasms, of illusionistic contraptions that seek to get under our skin yet rarely do so. In fact, in order to remain in the human, it relies on a few sentimental or fairy-tale episodes, such as a life-giving kiss. When Kracauer, then, writes that the cinema is uniquely equipped to "redeem this world from its dormant state, its state of virtual non-existence," he lays bare the ghostliness of existence revealed by cinematic photography's own countergnostic, technological quest romance. I continue to prefer poetry's economy of means, as in these (admittedly imploding) stanzas of Emily Dickinson:

> I heard, as if I had no Ear
> Until a Vital Word
> Came all the way from Life to me
> And then I knew I heard—
>
> I saw, as if my Eyes were on
> Another, till a Thing
> And now I know 'twas Light, because
> It fitted them, came in.
>
> I dwelt, as if Myself were out,
> My Body, but within
> Until a Might detected me
> And set my kernel in.[4]

❏ ❏ ❏

It may have been my own reality hunger, as well as the duty of memory, that made me take part in a project to film Holocaust survivors. Founded in 1979 by a New Haven grassroots organization, the project was adopted by Yale, which created in 1981 the earliest Video Archive for Holocaust Testimonies. Working with the archive, I became more aware of the power and the limits of film and video.

Our aim to record on video the stories of survivors and other witnesses proved more complex than we had assumed. The idea was to put people with direct knowledge of those grim events before the camera and let them speak with the least possible intervention. A series of authentic autobiographical accounts would emerge and contribute to the collective memory of a time passing away together with the eyewitness generation. That time would soon be available only through history books.

The project was instinctively right in seeking to extend the oral tradition by means of video testimony and in allowing the voices of witnesses to be heard directly in an embodied, audiovisual form. But

we only gradually understood the communal implications of the en-
terprise and its potential impact on memory and the communicative
environment.

Let me illustrate what we learned by discussing a number of practical issues that arose. How does a venture like this balance the seduc-

tive magic of photorealism—expressive of the wish to make the
survivors and their experience more evidential—with an anxiety about
intrusion and voyeurism? Should we not hold such an archive to be a
sacred deposit and shield it, for a time at least, from the merely curious or prying? We turned to a law school professor who wrote an
opinion quoting Justice Brandeis's "Sunlight is the best disinfectant."
We obtained informed consent from each of the interviewed and
made sure they understood that their testimony would be a public act
of witness open to all who came to consult it in the university library.
Moreover, visitors to the Yale Archive were asked to read a statement
that laid out the reasons for the testimony project.

When I look back at the first two years of filming, I realize what
made the issue of privacy more sensitive. The survivors who came to
be interviewed were totally supportive; but others—a few historians as
well as some survivors not yet interviewed—felt uncomfortable watching the tapes. What disturbed them was partly the emotional, intimate
texture of these oral histories, but chiefly their video-visual aspect.

Indeed, among the almost two hundred testimonies initially
recorded, I now see inspired but also, at times, irritating camera work.
Wishing to project the act as well as narrative of witness, we often
sought what one of the project's founders, adopting a legal term, called
"demeanor evidence." The result was excessive camera movement.
The supposedly "imperturbable" camera (Kracauer's word) zoomed in
and out, creating Bergmanesque close-ups. Eventually we advised that
the camera should give up this expressive potential and remain fixed,
except for enough motion to satisfy more naturally the viewers' eye.

Another decision also involved the visual sense. Should witnesses be
recorded in a studio or at home? Our choice was at first forced on us
rather than thought out, yet proved to be fortunate. There was so little
funding that space provided free on the unoccupied floor of a building
became a makeshift studio and more feasible than transporting equipment and interviewers from one home to the other. The makeshift stu-

dio was sparsely furnished: chairs as necessary, a backdrop curtain, and sometimes a plant. What we sacrificed was the kind of colorful, personal setting we would have found in the survivor's home, and which helps when videography has a film in mind; what we gained (this realization came later, and we stuck with our ascetic decision) was not only simplicity or starkness but a psychological advantage. The interviewees, in a sparse setting, entered their memories with less distraction, or, to put it differently, they could not divert their attention to this or that familiar object. There were also fewer disruptions—such as a child crying, a dog barking, a telephone ringing—to disconnect the flow of thought.

Another decision was for the camera to focus exclusively on the witness and not show the interviewers. In retrospect, I think we might have included at least an initial verification shot of the interviewers; but we were determined to keep the survivor at the center, visually as well as verbally. Despite TV's disdain for "talking heads," that is exactly what we aimed for. The survivor as talking head and embodied voice—a more sophisticated technique would merely distract viewers. We were not filmmakers, even potentially, but facilitators and preservers of archival documents in audiovisual form. In short, our technique, or lack of it, was homeopathic: It used television to cure television, to turn the medium against itself, limiting even while exploiting its visualizing power.

I suppose we did sacrifice by this effacement of the interviewers— heard and not seen, and trained to ask only enough questions to make the witnesses comfortable, to keep them remembering, and sometimes to clarify a statement—a certain amount of transparency. For interviewers have a special importance in this kind of oral history. They are positioned quite differently from investigative journalists. Yes, they do seek to elicit information, often of historical value. Yet basically their purpose is to release memories of what happened "in the deep backward and abysm of time": not yesterday or a short time ago, but as far back as forty years when the project started in 1979, and sixty by today.

This act of recall cannot be accomplished without respecting the Holocaust's continuing impact on the life of the witnesses. Afterthoughts and associations often arise in the very moment of giving testimony; the past is not confined to the past. The best interviews result from a *testimonial alliance* between interviewer and interviewee; a trust relation forms, in which the search for facts does not displace everything else. Such an alliance, however, is a framing event that lies beyond the scope of the camera. It cannot be made transparent (in the sense of visually readable) but needs the sort of mediation author and psychiatrist Dori Laub and others who know the Yale project have given it. When I talk of the project's communal frame, a return of trust, a wounded trust, is involved. The interviewers—indeed, all persons associated with the project—form a provisional community and become representative of a larger community, one that does not turn away from but recognizes the historical catastrophe and the personal trauma undergone.

◻   ◻   ◻

Memory, we have learned from Maurice Halbwachs, and again from Pierre Nora, always has a milieu. How do you photograph a memory, then, how do you give it visibility, when that milieu has been destroyed by Holocaust violence as well as the passage of time? But experiences do remain imprinted on the mind, set off by the very absence of what inhabited the original space. Our foreknowledge of mortality may even enhance what has vanished. The quiescent or subdued memory image endows photos with a physical aura. The effect is that of a still-life (even when the camera is in motion): A ghostly presence emerges, an unquiet spectral demand for reintegration that lends credence to Kracauer's film theory.

Holocaust videography, of course, to achieve a return of memory through photographed testimonial speech, can place the victims back in what is left of their milieu of suffering, as Claude Lanzmann often does in his film *Shoah*. It pictures, for example, a field or grove of trees, now quite innocent, and which defeats the camera-eye as in Michelangelo Antonioni's *Blow-Up*. Lanzmann even arranges a remarkable mise-en-scène by placing a barber, whose duty in the camps was removing the prisoners' hair, into an ordinary barber shop. However effective this device may be, we sense its artifice. It is best to resuscitate memories by simply raising the internal pressure with the assistance of non-aggressive interviewers.

Ideally, these interviewers become more than questioners: They comprise, as Halbwachs said, a new "affective community" that substitutes, however inadequately, for the original and tragically decimated milieu. But here an unresolved contradiction casts its shadow over the video testimony project in the dot-com era. Will the work of memory retrieval and its communitarian aspect withstand the "imperturbable" camera, its cold, objectifying focus, and now, in addition, the impersonal market forces of electronic recall and dissemination?

I have suggested that survivor videography does build in some resistance by counteracting the glossy or ghostly unreality of seemingly realistic yet increasingly surrealistic TV programs. In part this is because the testimonial words do not fade out, replaced by a cinematic simulacrum of the events being described. Although the testimonies range over time and space, the camera's mobility, as well as its visual field, remains restricted to a person speaking in a particular place, at a particular time. While presenting testimonies in audiovisual format may add an expressive dimension, even that is not an essential feature—for the speaker's bearing and gestures could also distract from the story being told. What *is* essential is the mental space such minimal visuality ("I see a voice!") allows. Witnesses can "see" better into, or listen more effectively to, themselves; and viewers too respond to that intimacy.

All our efforts at Yale were directed, then, to capturing the personal story; and to maximize the witnesses' autonomy during the taping process, we did not limit the time of the interview or impose any conditions whatsoever. Yet our decision in this regard was based less on sophisticated thinking about TV than on the fact that victims of the Shoah had been brutally deprived of precisely their personal autonomy. The camera, also, because it focused on the face and gestures of the witnesses, was anything but cold: In fact, it "reembodied" those who had been denied their free and human body image in the camps.

I am less sure, however, about the success we will have in taming postproduction procedures. As distance learning becomes standard and machine-readable cataloging takes over, archives of conscience like ours may not be able to resist being turned into megabytes of information, electronic warehouses of knowledge that marginalize the other values I have mentioned. This greed for more and more information, for positivities, which has already accumulated an extraordinary and melancholy record on the Holocaust, has not yielded appreciable ethical lessons. The heaping up of factual detail may even be an excuse to evade the issue of what can be learned. Yet it is not enough to say "nothing" can be learned; that no lesson can stand up to the enormity of what happened. If only because such a position neglects the testimonial act as such, and the gulf that appears, in the aftermath of Auschwitz, between the possibility of testimony—which extends to visual and verbal representation generally—and Sarah Kofman's axiom: "Speak one must, without having the power."[5]

❑　　❑　　❑

Having described the communal frame of memory retrieval and the potential impact of survivor videography on the medium, I am tempted to make a final and very broad generalization. It shifts the focus from the survivors to those who look at their testimony and ultimately to the quality of our gaze. "What others suffer, we behold," Terrence des Pres (a brilliant, literary-trained cultural observer) once wrote of the modern condition—with reference, in particular, to the increased technical power of optical transmission.[6] We become, through the media, impotent involuntary spectators; it was so with the events in Bosnia, and then in Kosovo. It is no longer possible not to know. But the effects of this traumatic knowledge, this tele-suffering—Luc Boltanski, a French sociologist, has named it *souffrance à distance*—are beginning to be felt.

One difficult effect is that of secondary traumatization, through a guilt, perhaps a shame, implanted by becoming aware of evil or simply of such suffering. We know more about identification with the aggressor than identification with the victim; a bond sometimes grows between persecuted and persecutor, between the kidnapping victim, for instance, and the abductor. Sympathetic identification with the victim, however, is taken for granted, so that strong side-effects have drawn less attention. In the humanities, where the subject of trauma has only begun to be recognized, we spend more energy criticizing psychoanalysis than dealing with what is fruitful in trauma theory.

That we learn through our own suffering is a cliché that targets abstract or book knowledge: The real issue, however, is whether we can learn from the suffering of others without overidentifying. To overidentify with the victim may have consequences as grave as to identify with the aggressor. Indeed, I suspect there may be some convertibility in the form of a movement toward coldness or cruelty when it becomes too hard to take in something that so intensely wants to be forgotten or mastered. We fear not just the image of suffering itself but also the sense of powerlessness that accompanies it—the obsessive thoughts and a drift toward desensitization. Without empathy no art, especially no fiction; yet the management of empathy is not easily taught.

The Holocaust testimony project, an active if belated response, relays terrible stories, yet in a bearable way, most of the time. It, too, creates a bond, as I have already said. In the telling, the psychologist Judith Herman has remarked, the trauma story becomes a testimony; and in the hearing of it the listener, who as interviewer enables the telling, is a partner in an act of *remembering forward* that obliges us to receive rather than repress inhuman events.

So the worst returns to haunt later generations. But it also gives them a chance to work it through. That is still a crude way of putting it, however. We know from Primo Levi's *The Drowned and the Saved* that the "ocean of pain" for the survivors rose instead of ebbed from year to year and that many among them were afflicted with a shame that could not be cleansed.[7] In fact, as these stories circulate, in the form of video testimonies, and generally as written memoirs or fictionalized accounts—as they gradually, and not always in a conscious manner, reach the public, we see the beginning of a rather astonishing phenomenon.

❏   ❏   ❏

I call it memory envy. An extreme case may be that of Binjamin Wilkomirski, whose *Fragments* was hailed as the most authentic depiction so far of a child survivor of the Holocaust.[8] Yet the chances are that Wilkomirski was brought up in Switzerland and never saw the inside of a concentration camp.[9] His identification, nevertheless, with survivor experiences is quite convincing. The author internalizes what he has heard and read, and it emerges as his own experience. Here the creative and the pathogenic are hard to tell apart. Some deep envy is at work, particularly in those who have no strong memories themselves—"strong" also in the sense that the memories bestow social recognition. The pressure to own a distinctive identity, however painful, plays into this: better to recover false memories than none, or only weak ones.

An equally interesting though very different case is Harold Pinter's play *Ashes to Ashes* (1996). It depicts a woman, Rebecca, who is being interrogated by her husband about the sadistic practices of a former lover. Rebecca seems to have tolerated or been hypnotized by them. Perhaps she is still under their spell. The Holocaust is never mentioned, but her mind, like Sylvia Plath's, lives in its penumbra—in a memory, perhaps a fantasy, dominated by male violence, the loss of babies and of the innocence they evoke. Her husband is unable to bring her back; his very questioning becomes another kind of violence. As in the setting for survivor testimony, the stage is bare of props and the only action is a (tormented) interview. It comes as a shock to hear Rebecca repeat, at the end and climax of the play, the words of a woman who had her baby taken away (I quote verbatim here but leave out the "Echo," which, in the play, repeats the last words of each phrase):

> They took us to the trains
> They were taking the babies away
> I took my baby and wrapped it in my shawl
> And I made it into a bundle
> And I held it under my left arm
> And I went through with my baby
> But the baby cried out
> And the man called me back
> And he said what do you have there
> He stretched out his hand for the bundle
> And I gave him the bundle
> And that's the last time I held the bundle
> And we arrived at this place
> And I met a woman I knew
> And she said what happened to your baby
> Where is your baby
> And I said what baby
> I don't have a baby
> I don't know of any baby[10]

The words were a shock because they reproduce with omissions and slight changes those of a survivor in a Yale testimony.[11] I read them first in a *New Yorker* review of Pinter's play after it was staged in America two years later. We glimpse here how diffusion occurs: how Holocaust memory influences *affectively* a wider public. For it is improbable that Pinter could have seen the Yale testimony in question. It is far more likely that he saw those words in a book by Lawrence Langer, who was the first to study the Yale archive in *Holocaust Testimonies: The Ruins of Memory* (1991). That book did not quote these particular words, but a later book by Langer, *Admitting the Holocaust* (1995), does—in a chapter, interestingly enough, on Cynthia Ozick's "The Shawl."

In Pinter the original memory-milieu of the survivor's words is elided. No one could guess that "Echo" is, in a sense, a real person, namely Pinter, whose mind has played back, almost verbatim, a description of the trauma of deportation. We pick up clues about the Holocaust context earlier in the play, but this final monologue clinches the matter. Yet what is remarkable here is less context than resonance: The Holocaust has invaded Rebecca's (and the dramatist's) consciousness to such an extent that no further historical specificity is needed—indeed, to be more explicit might limit the power and pathos of this short play.

We have no technical term I know of to describe the playwright's symbolic method, although Aharon Appelfeld too, in some novels, and Norman Manea in short stories, allows the setting of the action to be at once recognizable and unspecific. (The kind of denial depicted in Albert Camus's *The Plague*, whose context certainly includes the wartime persecution of the Jews in France, is conventionally, but effectively, allegorical.) However unique the contextualizing event, Pinter wishes to make the woman's narrative express a general aspect of the human condition. One is left wondering how often this occurs in literature—how often we fail to identify the elided circumstance. Perhaps this is what Aristotle meant, when he said that poetry is more philosophical than history. In Greek tragedy, moreover, with its moments of highly condensed dialogue, the framing legend is so well known that it does not have to be emphasized. A powerful abstraction, or simplification, takes over. In this sense, and this sense only, the Holocaust is on the way to becoming a legendary event.

In Pinter's case we can trace how the historical referent almost elides itself. The very resonance of the event both broadens it and makes it vanish—a pattern like waves from a pebble thrown into water. Key phrases have migrated from a videotaped testimony to a scholarly book, to a popular play, to an influential magazine's review of the play. *Ashes to Ashes*, however, is an unusually conscious case of memory envy. Holocaust imagery has been adapted rather than appropriated, and Rebecca's passion narrative suggests a sympathetic rather than total identification. Her repetition of the survivor's account is a self-redeeming, if nonconsoling, reenactment.

❐   ❐   ❐

Two concerns remain. At what point does diffusion become commodification and banalize, rather than universalize, a new representational genre (the video testimony), or Holocaust memory itself? Will everything end up, not even in a scholarly book, or as the climax to an enigmatic and moving play, but as a series of conventionalized iconic episodes variously packaged? A second concern, more distinctly ethical, is Pinter's use of this incident. Imagery from the historical Holocaust is made to fuse with a very private and precarious mental condition. Some might characterize this as exploitation. Yet it may be, I have suggested, an inevitable and even appropriate development. The pathos of the testimony moment loses its specific context precisely because it arouses a widespread anxiety—here concerning the loss of a child and the traumatic repression of that memory. What others suffer, we should suffer.

Try to suffer, that is. The entire problematic of how we can feel for others—and continue to feel for them—surfaces here. The pressure to respond with empathy (not an unlimited resource) is enormous, and it produces what has been called compassion fatigue and even boredom. But it could also incite anger and hate: first, perhaps, turned inward as a form of self-disgust (and leading to depression should we deem ourselves insufficiently responsive), then turned outward as a sadistic or callous action, and completing in this manner a vicious cycle. This cycle is inevitable if we overidentify, in the very name of morality, with the victims, or do not respect the difference between their suffering and our own. As Primo Levi and Charlotte Delbo, a French poet and survivor, have observed, even the words that seem to describe that suffering become false tokens when it comes to the Shoah. "Hunger" and "tomorrow" do not mean in everyday language what they meant in the camps.

At this point, art and especially literature disclose their truest reason. Art expands the sympathetic imagination while teaching the limits of sympathy. Such teaching hopes to bring the cognitive and the emotional into alignment. There is no formula, however, for aesthetic education of this kind: It must start early and continue beyond the university, perhaps for a lifetime. It is rarely prescriptive, and, although it may schematize itself as a set of rules (as a poetics or a hermeneutics), the type of thinking involved seems to import a structural moment of indeterminacy that escapes the brain's binary or digital wiring. A sort of unframed perception becomes possible, a disorientation that is not to be confused with skepticism or nihilism. Even the painter who titles his picture "Six Unintelligible Figures" holds it together and creates a focus for thought.

Because to think suffering is different from thinking about suffering, it is not the absence of meaning that disturbs Maurice Blanchot, for example, but its presence: More precisely, what disturbs him is the temptation to foreclose "the writing of disaster" by assigning meaning too quickly. "Danger that the disaster take on meaning rather than body." "Keep watch over absent meaning." "Try to think with grief."[12] Visual literacy is even further behind in recognizing this challenge than literary study. While Kracauer's axiom that the cinema "aims at transforming the agitated witness into a conscious observer"[13] recognizes how important a human resource film can be, it understates the moral problematic: the guilt or shame accompanying sight and the vicissitudes of empathy.

Today the dominance of the video-visual has become a fact of life as clear as other global influences. It has a bearing on both morality and mentality. However difficult it is to disenchant the medium of TV, we must approach it as more than a source for entertainment or information. Above all, "useless violence" (a phrase coined by Primo Levi to describe Nazi brutality), when routinely transmitted by TV in fantasy form or real-time reportage, should

lead to intense self-reflection. The hyperreality of the image in contemporary modes of cultural production not only makes critical
thinking more difficult but at once incites and nullifies a healthy illusion: that reality could be an object of desire rather than an aversion to overcome.

CHAPTER 6

TESTIMONY AND AUTHENTICITY

The dead cannot praise, nor all those who go down into the silence.

—Psalms

Victor Klemperer writes on May 27, 1942, fearing discovery of his journal and risk of deportation and death if that happens: "I shall go on writing. That is my heroism. I will bear witness, precise witness!"[1] The precision of this forcibly retired professor of Romance languages is invaluable: He documents daily life in Nazi Germany, including the corruption of its language, and makes vivid the threats, humiliations, house searches, and other harassments Dresden's few remaining Jews had to undergo. Klemperer reports everything, day in, day out; his "precise witness" is part of the authenticity of these diaries and enhances the fact that a personal document of such scope, contemporaneous with the events, has survived.

The quality of authenticity I have mentioned is easier to recognize than to define. Our sense of historical veracity enters into it, a sense created by the author himself, who chronicles a plethora of telling details that convey the nightmare. Yet such precision cannot be a criterion for authenticity in all witness accounts, because the conditions in which witness is borne are not always the same.

Klemperer's clarity and scope are those of a privileged observer, in the sense that while his movements are restricted, he is not imprisoned and further has the means and the leisure to write. In the camps, as Primo Levi observed in *The Drowned and the Saved*, almost none of the inmates had an extensive view of what was happening. Their experience of the concentration camps during the time of victimage was generally limited to barracks, job, or squad.[2] Only a few privileged prisoners, or a political deportee like David Rousset, who was part of the communist cadre of his camp, might gain a more total view of *l'univers concentrationnaire*. Rousset gathered enough knowledge that he could publish soon after liberation *The Other Kingdom*, a coherent account of the infra-structure of that "universe."[3]

The ideologically determined fate of Jews in the hierarchy of the camp system led to a paradox noted by Levi. Those who survived, he felt, were inadequate witnesses because of their restricted angle of vision, but also because the few who managed to see more had inhabited a "gray zone" of compelled yet morally ambiguous choices. Their later reportage, therefore, might be evasive or self-exculpating. Levi describes the fact without passing judgment. His stern conclusion, however, is that the truest witnesses were those who could no longer witness: the submerged, the dead.

Levi's paradox makes us, in our post-Holocaust awareness, uncomfortable. We do not wish to question survivor testimony. It is its own justification. Yet Levi's self-scrutiny, coming from a person with his experience, cannot be overlooked. And it leads into a larger issue raised on almost every page of his memoir *Survival in Auschwitz*. What lesson are we to draw from the behavior of human beings subjected to the most humiliating and systematically dehumanizing conditions? His paradox concerning the possibility of authentic testimony is a challenge to the generations to come, like his cautionary poem, "Consider If This Is a Man."

I want to review some responses to Levi's challenge. Not necessarily dependent on him, they raise the question of what defines authentic testimony. Jean-François Lyotard in France and Giorgio Agamben in Italy develop their positions in a sustained philosophic manner, while Dori Laub, a psychiatrist and himself a child survivor, writes from within the context of actual survivor testimony.

❑   ❑   ❑

I begin with a brief notice of Lyotard. He intervenes against the negationists, especially those who deny that the gas chambers were instruments of mass murder in the overall plan of the "Final Solution." To prove the industrial fabrication of corpses—to prove it by the criteria of the negationists—the dead themselves, gassed and cremated, would have to speak. The negationists, therefore, sin not only against historical fact but also against the victimized community, which is doubly a victim, being slandered by the charge that this fabrication is of its own making. "The plaintiff becomes a victim," Lyotard writes in *The Differend*, "when no presentation is possible of the wrong he or she claims to have suffered."[4]

If the denial of the possibility of testimony about the role of the gas chambers in the extermination is at the center of Lyotard's inquiry, Agamben bases the very possibility of authentic witness on the dead, or living dead: in camp slang, the "muselman" ("Muslim"). This phenomenon from the camps and ghettos was well known: The name designated "the irreversibly exhausted, worn out prisoner close to death" who had fallen into a profound, totally passive depression.[5] Unlike Bruno Bettelheim (a camp inmate for a relatively short time, and later a famous psychoanalyst), who sees in such surrender a negation of the human, of a defining, inalienable margin of free will, Agamben refuses to deny human status to the muselman. If our civilized concept of dignity cannot cover that kind of destitution, then ethical thinking is faulty and has to be changed.

Agamben therefore answers in the affirmative Levi's "Consider If This Is a Man" (also the original title of *Survival in Auschwitz*), which asks what defines moral behavior in light of the death camp's systematic degradation of its victims. The muselman's muteness is like an injunction to rethink the human: "to deny his humanity would be to confirm the verdict of the SS, to repeat their conduct. . . . But, if there is a region of the human where these concepts have no meaning, then we are no longer dealing with ethical concepts, for no ethics can permit itself to exclude from its province a part of the human, however ungrateful it may be, however painful to consider."[6]

Dr. Laub, for his part, confirms Levi's paradox by a paradox of his own. He views witnessing as an "impossible" act, at least in theory— not because the death camps defy description but because the Nazi machine, when it did not murder the victims, tried to make sure the survivors' view of themselves would be so severely injured, their self-image so darkened, that they would be unable to testify. Or, should they speak, no one would believe them; and this additional injury would seal the silence. In short, even in their afterlife, once out of the camps, they would not escape the fate of the muselman.

Laub's insight might seem related to Agamben's, that muselmän-ner are the "integral" witnesses (the word is from Levi), not only because they challenge our ethical concepts of what is human but also because they are "the radical refutation of every principle of obligatory communication."[7] Yet Laub, cofounder of the first project to systematically videotape survivors, wishes to restore a damaged or deeply buried ability to speak and so to testify. He does not compel witnesses, even should it seem necessary (Claude Lanzmann, in the film *Shoah*, does pressure them) but seeks to unblock a channel of communication by a process that removes disabling distortions from the survivors' self-image.[8]

Laub's position is close to my own. Testimony and trauma struggle with, against, each other. In this struggle the defeat of undistorted witnessing should not be taken for granted. Survivor testimony, although it may remain devious in some respects, or self-deceiving, or elliptical and occasionally erroneous with regard to historical fact, is eminently interpretable. It is partly a flashback, an obsessive monologue like that of Coleridge's Ancient Mariner in the poem of that name. But it is also a narrative in search of itself that depends on a voluntary rather than a hypnotized listener, on a caring and careful ear. Witness is made possible when representatives of an "affective community"[9] create a testimonial alliance between survivor and interviewer.

Agamben might agree, but we cannot be sure because his book is all about the theoretical location of authentic or "integral" testimony. Wishing to join an ethics of testimony after Auschwitz to a philosophy of speech formulated independently of Auschwitz, he runs a certain risk. Is he not exploiting the Holocaust as an extreme occurrence in order to exemplify a well-known thesis? It holds that the intimate sense of a personal unity of consciousness, of being present to oneself and the world, depends on very fragile support: on speech acts (*l'événement de parole*) that are themselves dependent on a special category of words like "I" and "now." These flexible linguistic signifiers named "shifters" include personal pronouns, deictics (like "these" and "those"), and adverbs of time or place. Their meaning as referents depends entirely on the context of the utterances in which they occur. In that way they create a powerful illusion of direct address, immediacy of inscription, and self-presence.

Agamben does not argue explicitly that the language of testimony breaks down only because of a disabling of "I" and "now" as shifters. But if I understand him correctly, he does link the breakdown of speech to the catastrophic silence of the muselman who turns into an "integral witness"[10] because of what cannot be spoken about in terms of focusing on "this" place, "this" ("now") time, or the injured, even destroyed, self-presence (the "I") of the victim. The disturbance of the shifters is related to what Agamben calls language's "constitutive 'lacuna,'" and it reinforces the nonspeech (le "sans-langue") of the mute witness.

Now, what we learn about speech after the experience of the camps is a legitimate topic. And testimonies in this regard, both by what they say and the fact that they are able to say it, are important actualities. For a time after the war, and perhaps even today, speech testifies to speech itself as an act of which the inmates of the camps were deprived, and it strives to enter once more into free, normal human occasions.[11] Agamben's linguistic theory of testimony, however, makes the very vulnerability of speech in both ordinary and extraordinary circumstances the defining mark of the human.

❑   ❑   ❑

What is really at stake, then, is post-Holocaust discourse. Indeed, Agamben delegates himself, like Levi, to be a proxy for the muselman. Mute and nameless, the muselman seems to be more present to Agamben than he was to himself and comes to represent a new riddle of the sphinx. He is said to be an *antiprosopon*, one who has seen what cannot be seen without dying, and who himself becomes unseeable, "faceless." (The *antiprosopon* was associated in ancient Greece with the myth of the Gorgon.) Agamben provides the *antiprosopon* with a face, in philosopher Emmanuel Levinas's sense of that concept. His abject, medusa-struck condition is a call and challenge that the human in us cannot evade. It is this power of address, even when mute, Agamben identifies with the truth of testimony.

Who has not felt that inarticulate yet powerful solicitation in more ordinary circumstances? The Philomela project of giving or restoring a voice to the voiceless, of overcoming trauma or a passivity too deep for words, emanates, for example, from Saint Paul's picture of the nonhuman creation groaning to be redeemed (Romans 8:19 ff), from orphic visions, from Wordsworth's empathy for "mute, insensate things," from the genre of the riddle, and even from moments of unavailing eloquence, as when an insomniac poem of Levi's enjoins the swarming ghosts of the submerged, the "sommersi," to leave him be.

Yet I find Agamben's formulation disconcerting. In his desire not to exclude the muselman and, by extension, the wretched of the earth who have been forced to live without dignity or decency, his position neglects, when it comes specifically to the Holocaust, thousands of survivor testimonies that actually exist. By substituting an eloquent generalization for close, empirical study, Agamben preempts consideration of what Lawrence Langer has called, in his pioneering book of 1991, the "ruins of memory" in survivor testimony. On the subject of dignity, however, Langer and Agamben are in broad agreement. What is salvaged from the experience of the camps is, precisely, *not* human dignity. "The muselman ... keeps watch over the threshold of an ethics and a form of life that begin where dignity ends."[12]

In this way a limit experience is used to connect ethical and (non)verbal in all speech. The form of life that begins where dignity ends is also inherent in silence or inarticulacy. The human being is now defined not primarily as the animal who speaks but as one whose silences may speak.[13]

Agamben goes very far in developing his paradoxical theme. His *tour d'horizon* of the major topics of philosophy covers the nature of internal time consciousness, the phenomenology of the emotion of shame, a modern concept of biopolitics and sovereignty, the discovery of shifters in linguistics, and the metaphysical or religious issue of "what remains."[14] Principally, though, theory's function here is helping the ethical observer to face something faceless. It is our reaction to the figure of the muselman, what we deduce from his extreme example, that matters. Agamben puts forward a theory of how utterance is not genuine without a passivity raised to the second power. It is a passivity, a strength of reception (akin, perhaps, to Keats's famous "negative capability"), an empathic going-out of oneself and subsequent depersonalization that points not just to an absence of the human—or to the shame of being human that silences the will to speak—but also to the presence of something non-human. "Humans are humans insofar as they testify to the nonhuman," Agamben writes.[15] We approach here, if implicitly, a theological concept: that of Christ's self-emptying, or *kenosis*. But surely that concept identifies the divine rather than the human as what is emptied out in order for an act of sacrificial witness to be consummated.

Agamben's closeness to religious thought and sensibility is not my main concern. Rather, that the muselman becomes, in effect, an unmoved mover. By focusing not on a suffering felt by the sufferer (for the muselman is by definition the bearer of an unfelt or unconscious passion) but on what *we* should feel, how *we* should respond, the ethical thinker as secondary witness is made to enter a symbolic sphere that challenges or even lies beyond the ethical. The relation between that symbolic sphere (in which a zombie is ensouled) and historical reflection of the ordinary kind remains unclear.[16] In a recent novel based on his personal experiences in Buchenwald and of the muselman, Jorge Semprun remarks, not without sarcasm:

> The best witness, the only true witness in reality, according to the specialists, is one who has not survived, who has gone to the end of the experience and is dead. But neither the historians nor the sociologists have so far resolved this contradiction: how to invite these true witnesses, the dead, to their conferences? How can they be made to speak? That is a question, in any case, which the passage of time will settle: soon there won't be any more embarrassing witnesses to encumber memory.[17]

Let me summarize, very briefly, my discussion so far. To talk about the authenticity of moral life in the camps or similar conditions is problematic—always excepting some remarkable episodes. Moreover, to found authentic testimony on the silence of the dead, or of the impassive muselman, evades the entire question concerning the authenticity of the witness accounts that do exist. *What is true is that all such witnessing, when the threat of immediate death has been removed and the witness testifies in freedom after the event, remains under the shadow of that death experience.*

❏   ❏   ❏

Levi's paradox did not seek to invalidate the witness accounts of those who survived. The ascription of a special status to victims who went under, functions, in *The Drowned and the Saved*, more as moral admonition than as metaethical challenge. Nazi soul murder, in any case, did not succeed in silencing the survivors; instead, we have an outpouring of testimonies in roughly three waves: immediately after liberation, then after the Eichmann trial, and, gathered in more systematic fashion, the oral documentation of the last three decades.

The issue of authenticity, of course, does not go away because of that unexpected and massive result but widens its orbit and touches each of us. The burden of how to be a witness to the witness—how to attend, interpret, and value the testimonies—clearly falls on all for whom Nazism's "culture of death" is a frightening riddle. There is a duty of reception. Professional historians often avoid it, claiming that only contemporary testimony, like Klemperer's or that of the Lodz ghetto documents, have sufficient authenticity.

What does authenticity mean to historians? Three criteria, ideally, should be satisfied: the witnesses' attested, immediate presence to the events; their testimony recorded even as the events occurred; and factual precision. The more time that elapses between the event and the witnessing of it, the less reliable historians believe testimony to be[18]—where reliability means that witnessing should furnish, despite small, contingent variations, one and only one version of what was experienced. A hypothetical original version is privileged. This move is not unlike what we find in Agamben, except that he invests only the muselman with the potentiality of truthful disclosure. Yet in oral testimony taken many years later, different witnesses often see things differently or even see different things. This may also happen with a single witness, whose memory is not static but evolves.

While presence, reliability, and precision (these qualities being established not only by a testimony's intrinsic force of style but by the convergent agreement of several sources) are important factors in corroborating the competence of witnesses, they do not exhaust the issue of authenticity. Indeed, it is unclear whether "authentic," with its moral overtones, can be used by historians. "Authentification," perhaps, as when the source of a document is evaluated. Even applied to imaginative literature, the word tends to be discordant. Do we ask whether a certain poem, novel or film is an "authentic fiction"? The word—although Agamben, following Levi, uses "integral" rather than "authentic"—is at home only in moral philosophy. Even there, unless we bring to bear an entire system of thought, like that of Kierkegaard or Heidegger, it strikes one as being the "je ne sais quoi" of ethical thought.[19]

Still, Agamben's search for integral testimony, while not underestimating the importance of historical facts, does contest their adequacy to *understanding* the Holocaust. The impasse, he writes, "is essentially that of historical knowledge: the noncoincidence of facts and truth, of constatation and comprehension." It is to be regretted that he acknowledges that noncoincidence by a discourse that fails to come to any but abstract terms with most actual testimonies.[20]

◻   ◻   ◻

Testimony, today, has become a major nonfiction genre beyond the specific instance of the Holocaust. It may have reinforced parallel forms in other cultures, such as the Latin American *testimonio*. Vernacular, especially when orally transmitted, and with the semiarticulate eloquence of unrehearsed speech, the witness accounts coming out of the Shoah have raised public consciousness toward other genocidal acts, both earlier and later. They may even have encouraged the explosion of confessional and autobiographical narratives generally.

It makes a difference, I think, whether we approach the topic of testimony and authenticity from the side of authenticity or from the side of testimony. In Agamben, at his most cogent, the two are a biunity. But usually he places the issue of authenticity foremost. This leads to the bracketing of actual testimonies. He does not ask, for instance, what perception of time we find in witness accounts, or how that contributes to their status as truthful and valuable report.

Such questions cannot be answered without studying the witnesses' time-consciousness through the unusually spontaneous narratives they often provide. Kant, Husserl, Heidegger, Foucault, Binswanger, Levinas, and Benveniste (all discussed by Agamben) may or may not be relevant, but the priority belongs to a new corpus of utterances.

Concerning the testimonies' relation to historical time, even historians might concede that they gain as well as lose something when gathered belatedly. It is not only that the catastrophe itself has continued to live on in the survivors, but also that since both written and oral utterances take place in a specific memory milieu, that milieu, as well as the survivors' later and accruing experience, influences the moment of recollection.

Oral testimony is especially susceptible to this temporal and cultural imprint. Even if, in a well-conducted interview, considerable initiative is left to the survivor, the interview partners usually come from a different generation. One sociologist has already tried to compare American and French interviewing procedure.[21] The language in which testimony is given can also make a difference: Those who returned to their own country or language have a different relation to it than émigré or displaced person. These aspects cannot be bypassed if we wish to understand, and perhaps foster, a new art of memory.

Arts of memory, moreover, are subject to technological change. The modern archive is not a passive repository: It encourages, even helps to generate, new materials. The video testimony is such a proactive medium. As an extension of an older oral tradition, although existing alongside print culture, the electronically recorded interview has its own situated reality and needs careful description.

◻   ◻   ◻

Let me briefly suggest what should be considered. Whether collected in the form of audio or video, we expect the witness accounts of survivors to be verifiable, even when we do not value them only for the information they contain. Governed by a realistic mode of narration, and claiming the authenticity of autobiography—indeed, enabled by a testimonial compact between interviewer and interviewee—these narratives are performative as well as informative. They bring into the present a cry that must continue to be heard—a cry not so much of juridical accusation as of a human suffering too often silenced because society is afraid to acknowledge its voice or because the individual fears the return of trauma. Extreme incidents, it has often been noted, fall out of experience and must find some other mode of coming-to-knowledge. I believe that literature and art have always served to create forms of representation that open a blocked channel of transmission and the retrieval of a truthful recollection.

It is not surprising that memory lapses occur in this literature of testimony, given the pressured situation. Some lapses may be as eloquent as the moments of silence that also punctuate witnessing; but they are not inevitably taken to be valuable. Oral testimony, moreover, does not try for chronology, narrative suspense, or even a story line. It can attempt them, of course, especially when repeated and revised in print. But as oral performance, it holds us in a different way. The action we follow is less a plot that goes from climax to climax, from salient point to salient point, than a self-evolving sequence, more supple and associative, one that often displaces the accent or punctuates unpredictably the recounted action, disclosing the stress of individual mind as it retrieves in the very moment of narration what has been suffered. This observation brings me to my special interest: video as a medium for the testimonial act.

Concerning the video testimony, I want to limit myself to four observations. First, Pierre Nora connects the appeal of oral, and particularly audiovisual, history to the sense of directness we have become accustomed to through the media. Our taste for the everyday life of the past, and the biographies of ordinary people, displays, he says, "the will to make the history we are reconstructing equal to the history we have lived."[22] But it remains unclear whether this intense desire for a direct, (tele)visual experience compensates for the indirectness of the past (increasing, because history, in an era of transformations, recedes from memory faster than ever) or for the poverty of the present—a rich poverty, related to media that trap us in the false present of simulacra.

My second point is that the shaming of the victims in the Shoah was linked to an oppressive gaze intending to implant a permanent feeling of nakedness and vulnerability. That gaze, in fact, took away their right to a sense of shame: A vicious *Schadenfreude* acted out an anti-Semitic rhetoric that denounced the Jew as dangerously without shame. Videotaping the survivors can have, therefore, a very basic, compensatory function. They are seen and listened to, as fully human, even when recalling their former nakedness.

My third observation stresses a pedagogical concern. What will have the best chance of getting through to young people in the future? We have entered an audiovisual age. The classroom, like the museum, is changing. I am devoted to books; I believe print literacy is essential. But it will have to be reinforced (rather than displaced) by TV, Internet, and film. Everyone knows how important docudramas are in conveying to a large audience something of the terror and pathos of the event.

Finally, the video testimonies are a new communicative genre whose features we are still discovering. They reject a realism based on illusion and do not fade into archival footage or a reconstruction of the scenes evoked. There is no attempt to gloss over the fact that these are interviews, and of the kind the industry has labeled "talking heads": The technical means of transmission are not elided by an art that hides art. The mechanics simply facilitate the interviewees' ability to recall and record. In short, the mechanics of videography hardly interest. The deliberate creation of an archive—"the materiality of the trace, the immediacy of the recording, the visibility of the image"[23]— is important, but not for a progressive technique of representation.

What *is* essential, because conveyed with unusual directness, is the survivors' defining struggle with trauma or loss. We glimpse the flux and reflux of consciousness, as witnesses grapple with what has escaped or overwhelmed memory. Memory itself is remembered.

❏   ❏   ❏

I have looked at the topic of testimony and authenticity mainly from the side of testimony. I will close by focusing on it from the side of authenticity. This difficult concept, which I can no longer evade discussing directly, presupposes not only a methodical wariness all scholars should practice but the existence of two kinds of simulacra: forgeries, always possible once a formal mode of expression is well established, and imitations that are more than opportunistic—also, probably, more dangerous, for they can deceive their own author, who becomes a confidence man to himself. It is likely that Binjamin Wilkomirski's *Fragments* presents such a case.[24]

While historical research is not powerless to unmask such authentic fakes (the fabricated memoir about the suffering of a victimized group also turns up in other areas), their presence, like that of all fictions, explains something about Holocaust deniers who cry fraud all the time. What motivates the deniers, if we look to their rhetoric, is a vicious *modern* anti-Judaism. From the time of Richard Wagner, anti-Semitic propaganda has depicted the Jew as a "plastic demon" (Wagner's phrase), that is, a demonic shape-shifter in his ability to assimilate. Wagner was updating a linkage between two despised social groups, Jews and actors or pseudo-artists, perhaps on the basis of the former's "alleged cosmopolitanism, ready adaptability, and linguistic virtuosity."[25] "What good actor today is *not* a Jew?" Nietzsche asks in *The Gay Science*, giving the whole issue an ironic twist. "The Jew as a born man of letters," Nietzsche continues, "as the true master of the European press, also exercises his power by virtue of his histrionic gifts."[26]

Wagner turns a normal suspicion of tricky resemblance into an obsession focusing on the phantasm of the alien who can counterfeit national character in order to subvert it, who is radically inauthentic, rootless ("semitic"), and emotionally frigid—except when it comes to money, which, in its materialistic immateriality, its abstract and international form, becomes his weapon to liquidate local, racial, and cultural identities. Upon emancipation, a considerable number of Jews (as Nietzsche observed) became writers and journalists, especially as the professoriat was not open to them for a long time. Later many were associated with Hollywood. The Holocaust, then, the deniers ask us to believe, is just another exploitative Jewish forgery, a propaganda trick to make money and undermine national honor. For the deniers it does not matter how much contrary evidence is brought forward, since that evidence merely demonstrates the cunning of the shape-shifting demon.

This picture plays on one of our deepest fears: that there may exist a realm of the inauthentic so close to the authentic, so dissembling/resembling, that, basically, the distinction between the two cannot be decided except by an intuitive and assertive act of faith. Or by the argumentative act of the scholar who, like Agamben, introduces a caesura into this realm, establishing by a reasoned distinction the exact status of what is deemed to be authentic.

Thus in an era of simulacra, of increasing saturation by the media and new, vast sources of information or disinformation, the critical faculty, always at risk, can turn desperate and feel adrift in a demimonde of tendentious, superficial, or manipulative images. Our natural suspicion of appearances is inflamed to the point where a new gnosticism is born, now in the area of ideology rather than religion. The tentacles of this gnosticism, in the form of political theories that destroy common sense and claim to demystify appearances, inspired many adherents of totalitarian regimes with paranoid fervor (Milosz's *The Captive Mind* confirms that) but also, in Western democracies, entangles extreme racist and anti-government groups. Freedoms of thought and speech are not a sure-fire defense against the schizoid feeling that the world we live in is not the real world.

The fallout from the fact that so much of what we know depends on the mass media has been explored by the German sociologist Niklas Luhmann.[27] A striking example of what he calls "manipulation wariness" is the claim of Goran Matic, a minister in Slobodan Milosevic's government, who announced during the Kosovo conflict "that what the world had assumed were refugees—driven from their homes by Serbian police and paramilitary units—were in fact 3,000 or so ethnic Albanian 'actors,' paid $5.50 each . . . by the CIA to take part in a NATO 'screenplay.'"[28]

Holocaust deniers, obsessed by inauthenticity, could claim, despite thousands of survivor witnesses, that here too the evidence is faked, that we are shown a propaganda parade of testimonies. The slander that the Jews control the media and perhaps all sources of information would only play into that Manichean picture. I do not know a remedy for anti-Semitism or similar kinds of xenophobia, which are a sickness deeply and perversely rooted in something idealistic: an obsession with certainty, clarity, and authentic being. I do know, however, that what Tony Judt has called "a sustained preference for a priori reasoning over human testimony"[29] continues to undermine both reason and testimony.

PART III

CHAPTER 7

THE LETTER AS REVENANT

The noise surrounding recent literary criticism suggests not only a busy urban street but the repair jobs blocking it. Denunciations of that criticism's "antihumanistic" bent are part of the din. To some extent, of course, these are brought on by the polemical stance of influential thinkers like Michel Foucault, for whom "humanism" is not humanistic enough—in the sense that it still covers up, by its sentimental and spiritualizing vocabulary, a power struggle that demands a materialistic perspective.

Curiously, though, this materialism often assumes characteristics previously attributed to the party of spirituality. "Can we find an analogue of matter in the order of thought itself," Jean-François Lyotard asks in *The Inhuman*. "Perhaps words themselves," he continues, "in the most secret place of thought, are its matter." He means that words cannot disappear into the thought that thinks them. "They are innumerable like the nuances of a color- or sound-continuum. They are always older than thought." One cannot get rid of them any more than of "the Thing." Yet matter, he also insists, is something "which is not *addressed*, which does not *address* itself to the mind (what in no way enters into a pragmatics of communicational and teleological destination)."[1]

Almost against my will, I too take pleasure in such expressions as "social reality," "realism," "productive," "matter," "material culture," "cultural materialism," "the materiality of the signifier," because they have become terms with pathos and weight, and act as shorthand to say that critics or artists are now truly demystified. Reality, we think, could we find its socioeconomic determinants, might yield its secrets and become more real—less opaque, that is, less of a limit to human understanding, perhaps even an imaginative fact that cooperates with rather than blocks creativity.

Take Michel Leiris's short treatise on the painter Francis Bacon. He titles it *The Brutality of Fact*, but his vocabulary remains within the orbit of terms that derive from the sphere of spirit. He insists on the immediacy and self-sufficiency of Bacon's painting in the following words.

> As if it had its own life and constituted a new reality instead of being a simulation . . . a canvas by Francis Bacon, whatever the elements worked into it . . . is what is apprehended at once and imposes itself without the least detour, independently of all judgment for or against. Though alien to whatever, near or far, might recall a theology, it is the very type of real presence achieved by the figures that animate such works. . . . [T]he viewer without preconceived ideas makes contact with an order of flesh and blood reality.[2]

Leiris wants us to feel that Bacon's paintings are realities, not simulacra; realities, moreover, bringing us closer to a life present for and to us. His description evokes a material construct that, once created, seems to have an independent existence. This is a spiritual position because it puts us in an unmediated relationship to the work of art, while materialism insists on the mediations rather than on what is unmediated and therefore runs the risk of becoming formalistic in trying to match what is "worked" into the canvas with the real-life conditions of acts of production, transmission, and reception.

Leiris does nuance his perspective by remarking on the tension between Bacon's "realism" and an intensity that is surrealistic and so may scorch and repel rather than attract the viewer. "Real presence" is brutally real, and it is Bacon's virtue to reveal that fact in his depiction of ordinary as well as quasi-mythic portraits. Yet one could substitute the words "unreal presence" and get almost the same effect; and I suspect that "unreal real presence" is what should have been said.

My purpose is not to second-guess a brilliant and conscientious writer, but to suggest, in the words of the nineteenth-century materialist Proudhon, that, do what we may, our language is "plena Jovis," by which he meant paratheological, full of god terms. Like planet Earth itself, a mythic or animistic language seems to have cooled and fixed itself at some point as a terrain; its spiritualism, therefore, however secularized and whited out, bleeds through; even extreme attempts to modify it remain a negotiation.

❑   ❑   ❑

Words wear out, of course, new coinages do occur; and by now literature comprises a heterocosm, an expanding universe whose precarious unity is threatened by cyberspace. Yet there is no reason to suppose that certain basic laws governing the old economy of literary space will change. When Jacques Derrida invents the word "paleonymy" (rewriting or overwriting), he refers to the material conditions of verbal production, but these conditions effect a change that must be described as metamaterial, if not spiritual. By "paleonymy" the writer installs himself in the received language, especially its hot-button expressions, such as "culture," "realism," "liberty," "equality," "spirit."[3] (For William Blake, to change the venue, they were "devil" and "angel," "nature," "mystery," "religion," "pity," and so on.) These words have accrued a fan of meanings; they undergo, as an older stylistics used to say, a *Bedeutungswandel*, or changes of signification. We can't throw out or totally elide them; even to trash them by devices such as irony and parody keeps them alive.

The modern literary imperative to estrange language or make it new respects that dynamic. Derrida allows for a play of meaning; he shows how words, as part of concept systems, have been historically complex; he "deconstructs" the militant, false, or shimmering oppositions they generate. Deploying an exegetical rather than transformative method, his capacious analytical mind *inscribes* itself into the received and elaborated texts, creating further layers of signification.

Basically, then, as Plato said, words written down become orphans; we cannot descend to the dead authors for a clarification of their intent, and so they depend on our interpretive wit or charity. Reading is necessary after all. Even if, as Paul de Man liked to say, it usually tries to get rid of reading. He meant that most professional readers seek to ignore the difference between sense perception and cognition. These seem to merge in oral modes of communication but remain divergent in written media, despite an infusion of aesthetic charm. In fact, the perceptibility of formal elements, intrinsic to the pleasure of literary texts—whether these forms are residues of sensation or epistemic constructs—resists cognition as well as helps it. If there is a mystery in letters, it is as commonplace and surprising as the inscribed letters themselves in their unexpected combinations: Reading, materially dependent on the ground and figures of inscription, cannot free message from medium in order to intuit the former directly.[4]

Spirit is usually associated with immediacy or the transparence of the medium, its elision through the vehicular force of the message. The letter is usually associated with what the German-Jewish philosopher Ernst Cassirer called the curse of mediacy. Derrida mourns the inadequacy of words as much as anyone does, but he also views it as a challenge and stages a sort of saturnine celebration: Writing disseminates what cannot be returned to its source (the parent/author of the words), allows new graftings, and so makes possible an intellectual harvest freed from shibboleths of a classical or narrowly conceived finality.

Another way of putting this is to say that the letter as vehicle, or the prior, once-authoritative text, can never be erased: It is, by the sheer fact of alphabetic existence, as well as its inertial meanings, the ghostliest of creations, at once opaque and transparent, persistent and barely noticed. If the text's letter substratum were noticed more, if it had that virtue of continuous self-evidence without bringing the act of reading to a stuttering halt, critics and interpreters would be out of a job. The ghostly life of the letter—which also founds intertextuality— is what is being reinserted into the history of interpretation by present-day literary theory in order to refute both an arrogant philosophy and an overconfident, charismatic evangelism.

Recent literary theory, then, has two aims: to modify the hegemony of materialistic explanation *and* to fight a long-standing imperious spiritualism. The field named aesthetics had resisted these extremes. But today aesthetics faces charges that it is covertly ideological or spiritual, even somehow to blame for an "aestheticizing of politics" that made fascism attractive. The task of maintaining, like Kant, that there is an aesthetic judgment, irreducible to either materialism or a spiritual finality, has become harder.

❑   ❑   ❑

I will focus on exploring whether spirituality still can be associated with art, however troubling the word "spirit" has become to those who know the history of religious triumphalism as well as the ravages of fascism's so-called spiritual revolution. Fascist jargon, rowdy, slogan-infested, arrogant, is the precise opposite of Emmanuel Levinas's "One comes not into the world but into question." Maurice Blanchot also seeks to avoid a heroic or will-to-power phraseology: He characterizes the (willful) unwillfulness, the barely spoken character of that inner and unworldly resistance, by alluding to Herman Melville's Bartleby, the scrivener, who obstinately repeats "I prefer not to." A nonconsent of this kind, Blanchot writes, "belongs to the infiniteness of patience; no dialectical intervention can take hold of such passivity. We have fallen out of being, an outside where, immobile, proceeding with a slow and even step, destroyed men come and go."[5]

This evocative statement does many things at once. It points to what Theodor Adorno called a "negative dialectics," one that purges Hegelian versions of progressivity or transcendence. It appropriates, at the same time, a distinctly moral vocabulary independent of Foucault's type of activism. Finally, it evokes the haunting, contemporary disaster that gradually moved to the center of Blanchot's thought. The image of those "destroyed men," their repetitive as if eternal motion, does not come from Dante's *Inferno* but from the death camps. It echoes Primo Levi's description of the *musulmänner* in *The Drowned and the Saved*. (See chapter 6, "Testimony and Authenticity.")

Blanchot's strong, if allusive rather than specific, historical reference scandalizes because it suggests a passivity that cannot be spiritualized (interpreted as martyrdom, for example) yet honors sheer endurance. A modern materialist protest it certainly is not. Indeed, the problem is how to renew an image of spiritual action without employing for that purpose tainted words. Insofar as the fate of the Jews (principally, not exclusively) is involved, the question of Christian culpability enters. In its own historical development Christianity failed to recognize a spiritual quality in Judaism—the way Judaism abides patiently, although not without apocalyptic stirrings, the delay of the messiah. The Church also failed to recognize the spirit in which Judaism dealt with ceremonial and legislative detail, especially after the destruction of the second Temple. Judaism as we know it today was created in good part by transforming Temple worship into the *shulchan aruch*, the prepared table, that is, importing the sacred altar and its rites into home and synagogue. Torah shrine and family table become converging foyers. Instead of valuing this loyal project, one that produced feats of interpretation often as astonishing as those of Saint Paul and other Fathers of the Church, Christianity viewed it as mere obstinacy and materialistic blindness.

It is painful to raise the issue, but how much was contributed to the Holocaust by an anti-Semitism ideologically transmitted and ingrained through the opposition of "spirit" and "letter"? This polemical religious dichotomy charged Judaism with respecting the letter rather than spirit of Scripture. Too often in the past the dichotomy turned "spirit" into a pawn of the most violent urges. In particular, it justified persecution by characterizing the Jews as sunk in a textual and carnal materialism that fostered invincible ignorance or even diabolical blindness.

To clarify contemporary criticism is also, then, to recall certain historical givens connected with anti-Judaism. All the more so because a powerful combination of Christianity and the pagan classics engendered during the Renaissance a literature of Christian humanism. The greatness of that literature—say, from Dante, through Ariosto, Tasso, and Calderon, to Spenser, Donne, and Milton—is not affected by what I will say, but lingering critical assumptions based on it are. Because of that literature's prestige, there had to be both a dehellenizing and dechristianizing of criticism in order to gain an alternate vision of the interpretive act. A redemptive notion of literalism—even of materialism—became necessary. In this respect, an acquaintance with *midrash*, the main vehicle of the Jewish exegetical tradition, has recently helped to remove the ignorant side of the prejudice against the letter. Levinas, for example, describes how the Hebrew Bible exceeds what it originally said under the pressure of an interpretive method that does not have to posit a spiritual or transfigurative level of meaning:

> What [Scripture] is capable of saying goes beyond what it wants to say. . . . it contains more than it contains . . . an inexhaustible surplus of meaning remains locked in the syntactic structure of the sentence, in its word-groups, its actual words, phonemes and letters, in all the materiality of the saying which is potentially signifying all the time. Exegesis would come to free, in these signs, a bewitched significance that smoulders beneath the characters. or coils up in all this literature of letters.[6]

❏   ❏   ❏

One does not have to be religious to recognize the historical link between interpretation and faith-based assumptions about the relation of letter and spirit. Let me review what is well known. Guided by the apostle Paul's transfiguration of the Septuagint, Christian evangelism sought to displace rather than actually replace the text of the Bible. Paul founded a hermeneutics together with a new religion; the two are inseparable. With Pauline Christianity the text of the older dispensation is not abolished; instead, through systematic reinterpretation a hierarchy is established that still influences our concept of spirituality today, although it has almost no resonance in Judaism. "Jewish law," Blanchot remarks, distinguishing it from the Christian position, is "the inscribed word with which one does not fool, and which is spirit because it is the burden and the weariness of the letter."[7] Yet Paul's "fooling" saved the Hebrew Bible for Christianity by suggesting that its historical actors could be read as prefigurations of a new revelation. He claimed to speak for a "spiritual Israel" hidden in the text.

Book 3 of Augustine's *On Christian Teaching* is a classic restatement of Paul's "Christian freedom" compared to "Jewish slavery." Christian freedom is freedom from the literalism of Jewish ritual law and, generally, from a literal interpretation of what has come to be known as the Old (superseded) Testament. Freedom and spirituality are contrasted with Jewish slavery, that is, with the carnal or literal interpretation of Old Testament commandments, rituals, and narratives. So, for instance, Ezekiel 36:23–29, a passage ending "And I will cleanse you from all your uncleanliness," becomes a prophecy about the New Testament, and the "you" addressed is made to refer not only to a chosen remnant (Paul's "spiritual Israel," designating the Jewish Christians of his time), but potentially to all other peoples through "a promise of the baptism of regeneration."

Augustine develops Paul's notorious axiom in 2 Corinthians 3:2–3 and 3:6 that "the letter kills but the spirit gives life." He goes further, however, and associates this universalizing dictum with a rule that allows a leap from species (the particular people to whom Ezekiel refers) to genus (the category that transcends the species—for example, all who become Christians). But this type of transcendent leap is not consistently made. So, when Ezekiel complains (36:17–18), "The house of Israel lived in the land and they profaned it by their ways and their idols and sins; their conduct before my face was the uncleanliness of a menstruating woman," then, claims the saint, "It is easy . . . to understand this of the house of Israel, about which Paul says 'see Israel according to the flesh' [1 Corinthians 10:18], because the people of Israel did or experienced all these things in the flesh."[8]

Augustine moves, as the spirit lists, progressively from species to genus, or sticks, as in this case, to the species, trapping Ezekiel in his own prophetic hyperbole, in a trope of uncleanliness that is not allowed to be a trope. Suddenly Augustine, in order to inculpate the fleshly Israel, is himself the literalist; he has no wish to appreciate the candid realism of the Hebrew Bible, which acknowledges a people's creatureliness and imperfection. For the Hebrew prophets see no way to improvement except through graphic and powerful denunciations demonstrating that the gap between Israel and God has become so wide that it threatens the covenant. Ezekiel himself does not claim to speak in the name of a man purer than the people he addresses; and it could be argued that the very fleshliness of the prophet whom Victor Hugo called—admiringly—the "dung-prophet" ("le porc-prophète") emphasizes the fact that Israel as a nation must redeem itself before it becomes a redeemer nation. It must be redeemed in the flesh, moreover; the flesh is not separated off from the spirit. Using menstruation as a trope of uncleanliness is problematic, but such fleshly matters are dealt with, not avoided, by ritual regulation; this nonseparation of the flesh is one reason it is so difficult for Judaism to engage with Christian spirituality.

The Christian Fathers emphasize the older rites of purification but not for the same purpose as the prophets. The rites are made characteristic of carnal Israel and its primitive stage of spiritual development. They are mocked for their legalistic detail or transformed into Christianity's divinely efficacious sacraments. The Christian reformer does not honor the biblical writers for their searing self-assessment but holds all the self-recorded sins of the Jews against them, as if these flaws were predestined and could not be purged without faith in the new revelation. Eventually the greatest sin becomes that of continuing in sin, of not accepting the new revelation.

The divergence and then schism between Judaism and Christianity is legitimated by different concepts of what is authoritative in the text of Scripture. Pauline Christianity sees everything in the Old Testament—poetry, legends, commandments, histories—as a revelation accommodated to the limited insight of the Jews. A New Testament, a supersessionist illumination, frees the text from legalism and literalism. From the perspective of a *Jewish* "spirituality" of the letter, however, the biblical record shows insight, not blindness. Progress comes not through a simplification or abolition of ritual behavior, although Israel's prophets warn again and again that moral qualities must accompany ritual observance for the nation's purification to occur. The advance made by the founding rabbis in the tragic time following the destruction of the Second Temple is expressed in a famous Talmudic saying: The Jews may have forsaken God, but never the Torah. Faith here is faithfulness to the text, more specifically to a double Teaching, one transmitted in writing, the other "by mouth." Through an extreme elaboration of what the Sages call the Oral Law, its defense and often transvaluation of even the smallest mitzvah, Jewish ritual and its basis in the Torah engrave the heart, mind, and flesh of a people faced by powerlessness and dispersion.

These regulations, derived by the rabbis from a written and unchangeable Bible, although denounced in the New Testament as pharisaic, include instructions concerning every aspect of bodily and spiritual cleanliness. Holiness is ideally conceived as a seamless garment of scriptural thoughts and Scripture-inspired acts, from dawn to dusk; that is why, after vigilance is involuntarily suspended during sleep, the traditional *modeh ani* (Thanksgiving) prayer on awakening praises God for keeping the soul pure in sleep—which hints at a sinister and polluting force, active in the darkness, although never named. Whether it makes sense to say that Judaism has its own kind of spirituality or not, the latter is very different from what develops in Christianity.

❑   ❑   ❑

My concern is with the extreme, and still influential, Pauline reduction of the non-Christian Jews to a "fleshly" people blind to its own spiritual potential. I have no quarrel with the interpretive yield of the spirit/letter dichotomy, its imaginative daring; nor is it my aim to reverse values in this binary opposition for the simple benefit of the letter. It is the early ideological fallout and later the nearly total neglect of Jewish exegetical traditions (with the signal exception of Renaissance Christian Hebraists), that is sad and often pernicious. Already in Augustine we see quite clearly both his hermeneutic slight-of-hand and self-arrogation of grace—the attempt to restrict the importance, in providential history, of the Jews, while opening the covenant to all "the nations." Christianity wished to distinguish itself, says Augustine in *On Christian Teaching*, "by the novelty of grace, not nobility of race, and by mentality, not nationality." Except for what is implied by "grace," a word too confidently used from a Jewish point of view, yet which basically derives from the doctrine of chosenness, this Augustinian declaration is as clear as a bell and the true, universalistic core of Christianity.

We cannot but note again how closely allied faith and hermeneutics are. Listen once more to Paul talking about the Old Testament: "You are our letter, written not with ink but with the spirit of the living God, not on tablets of stone but on the fleshly tablets of the heart" (2 Corinthians 3:2–3), which derives, as Augustine notes, from Ezekiel's "I will give you a new heart and a new spirit, and I will take away from your flesh the heart of stone and give you a heart of flesh" (Ezekiel 36:26). Stone, flesh, spirit; the progression is clear. Or listen to Augustine himself when he writes of the Jews in Christ's time, this time in a nonsimplifying way:

> Because they were very close to being spiritual—for although they did
> not know how to interpret them spiritually, the vows and signs con-

cerned with the world and the flesh had at least taught them to worship the one eternal God. . . . So Christian freedom has liberated those whom it found enslaved to useful signs—they were, so to speak, not that far away—and by interpreting the signs to which they were subjected has raised them to the level of the things of which those were signs. These people formed the churches of the holy Israelites."[9]

To sum up: An impasse is created when the text-bound character that joins Christianity to Judaism is also what comes to divide them. Paul, in his emphasis on faith—a virtue that fosters belief in things not yet, or fully, visible—invents an interpretive method that makes a new text appear from within the old, a text that foretells or confirms the story of Christian redemption. Paul is shameless in purging from the Hebrew Bible everything but a self-fulfilling prophecy of the passion (*humilis*) and triumph (*gloriosa*) of Christ. He calls this perspective on the Hebrew Bible spiritual, accusing Jews who do not accept it of being blinded by carnal interpretation and so lacking the faith necessary to accept Christ as redeemer. (For Jews, that "faith" would mean faithlessness, an abandonment of *emunah*, the trust that assigns redemption and resurrection directly to God and God alone. But that is another story.) And it is perfectly true that Judaism, in its formative period, which coincides with rabbinical teachings that make up the Talmud (teachings derived from the Bible by the powerful exegetical instrument of *midrash*), does not include a formalized "spiritual sense" among the levels of meaning it develops—although the possibility of *sod*, an esoteric level of significance, is always present. There is *pshat*,[10] the simple or literal meaning, and there is *drash*, the inquiry into that meaning, which uses a large variety of methods insofar as the Bible is not only the proof text for law-finding, for *halakha*, but also for *aggada*, bible stories retold or explicated as wisdom literature in the most diverse and ingenious ways.

❐ ❐ ❐

The evolution of rabbinic exegesis is a complicated story: We are dealing with centuries of intensive scriptural interpretation.[11] One thing is clear, however: The letter/spirit dichotomy is totally inadequate, considering how Judaism envisaged the reception and transmission of revelation. The *Mekilta* of Rabbi Ishmael, an early *midrash* collection, says that what was heard at Sinai and "seen" through the mountain's thunder and lightning (Exodus 20:15)—that is, by way of an ear that became a visionary organ—had as many facets as there were Israelites present. This multivocality, moreover, did not diminish immediacy of understanding. "As soon as the utterance came forth [from God's mouth], they [the Israelites at Sinai] interpreted it."[12] *Midrash* itself still strives to hear and see that way; it senses the proximity of an aural Torah, its fluidity and malleability, and whether the mediating text is transmitted by oral or written means. Moses as human intermediary, articulating and transliterating God's voice, provides a conduit that respects the limits of each recipient. The rabbinic axiom that the Bible speaks in the language of man takes that direction: It recalls the distance (as well as Scripture's alleviation of it) between God and humankind, between His voice and our capacity to hear and understand.

Midrash plays with the idea that already the first Hebrew letter, the *aleph*, which is also the proto-letter of the first word of the Ten Commandments, the aspirate of "I," *anochi*, in "I am the Lord thy God," might have been overpowering. Yet when the *Mekilta* claims that at Sinai everyone understood according to their capacity, it suggests a concept of inspiration joined to one of accommodation rather than of withholding. The emphasis falls on generosity, not economy. The power of God's charged, fully vested utterance includes that flexibility of address and is, if anything, heightened by the divisibility of the divine word and later, the exegetical parsing of the text.

This principle of accommodation was turned in Pauline Christianity against the Jews: Their revelation is said to have been limited by divine foresight, because they were not worthy to receive full measure. The Synagogue had a veil over its eyes and chose to continue in ignorance even when that veil, with the advent of the Messiah, could have been removed. The Church claimed to have received a spiritual and transfigurative way of unfolding the text. As late as Thoreau this ecstatic concept of "translation" remains, although the Scriptures for him include the sacred classics of all nations. There is a written form of expression "too significant to be heard by the ear, which we must be born again to speak."[13]

Jewish exegesis, then, did not feel a necessity to add a spiritual sense, nor did its language refine itself into a decorous classical idiom. Although not lacking stylistic features of its own, it remains sermonic, linguistically multilayered, and unashamedly vernacular in diction, as well as explicitly text-dependent in its references to the Bible. It is the literature of Judaism before the modern, "Enlightenment" period, and blocks rather than fosters a distinctive, quasi-autonomous mode of imaginative writing. But there is often an interesting contamination when it is difficult to tell whether the sacred text has entered the commentary or commentary the sacred text.

A daring antiliteralism is not absent, moreover. Even without the Kabbala, we find what scholars have named "allegoresis," perhaps introduced via the Hellenic heritage of Philo. Through allegoresis Rabbi Akiba saved a sensuous chant, the Song of Songs, for the canon, declaring that it described the holiest of mysteries, the love between God and Israel. Akiba's redemptive skill probably had a very practical as well as mystical aim: counterbalancing the passionate emphasis on divine love in Pauline Christianity.

❑ ❑ ❑

It is time to return to the contemporary scene. My remarks will remain brief and risk overgeneralization. Jacques Lacan, seeking to define the action of the unconscious, disputes the Christian commonplace that the letter kills while the spirit gives life. He would like to know "how the spirit could live without the letter." Even so, he adds, "the pretensions of the spirit would remain unassailable if the letter had not shown us that it produces all the effects of truth in man without involving the spirit at all."[14]

Judaism enters writers like Lacan and Blanchot because it has endured that long disaster called its history by rarely succumbing to the worst aspects of messianic expectation. Having rejected Christianity, Jews acquire a historical patience based on the continuance of secular time: on the absence, or deferred advent, of the redeemer, an attitude Christian persecutors portray as a self-imposed limitation and curse. In historical Christianity, Jews are caricatured as the unassimilable other and associated with what has already been mentioned: crass literalism or a blind resistance of letter and legalism to spirit. Blanchot revalues that resistance as being close to what Lacan called "insistence," rather than self-blinding, unspiritual, uncreative.

Even Freud, according to Lacan, did not fully realize what he had uncovered when he laid bare the duplicity of words. In structuring the Unconscious, they also block insight into their own, repressed impact. The inscriptional force of the verbal, even when fragmented or atomized into letters, is now recognized as more than an archaic superstition or magical belief. This recognition, of course, did not have to wait for a literary rediscovery of *midrash*. Nor for such late, fictional re-creations of letter-mysticism as Borges's *Aleph* (in *Ficciones*). It is manifest in every literary text, even when that does not claim to be primarily literary: John Donne's sermons, for example, hardly inhibit the poet in the preacher, and display an extraordinary verbal density as well as doctrinal dexterity. Their message is that the spirit that gives life is also given life by the letter.

To complicate matters, those lettered words, even when they compete with other expressive instruments, are relatively ascetic. They are strangely abstract signifiers rather than pictorial icons or hieroglyphs, and as such seem to break with phenomenality—although they are invested, in some theories, with a quasi-magical, mimetic, or even "performative," effect.[15]

From an ascetic point of view, then, literalism—better, lettrism or literality[16]—restrains a spiritualizing and triumphalist verve that would overwrite the text of Scripture by a transcendent type of interpretation. In Judaism, Scripture is closer to God than any mediating figure—even if Jewish writing continues to imagine, carefully and ironically (think of Kafka's or Walter Benjamin's evocation of the messianic moment), an opening toward finality and unmediated vision.

In short, we are asked to view the Word that leads to wisdom not as the *logos* of the gospel of Saint John: not as a redemptive illumination, blessing those who acknowledge it, cursing those who do not, and eclipsing or abolishing a previous word. It is, rather, a dangerous medicament. Within Judaism, particularly, lettrism may always have been a homeopathic remedy to manic and murderous forms of spirituality.[17]

❏   ❏   ❏

Where does all this leave the literary? What is the relation between literary and literal? Literariness "illuminates" rather than writes over or evangelizes the letter. It touches back to the verbatim like Anteus to Mother Earth. It is not, to borrow a figure from Donne, "the spider love that transubstantiates all."[18] However exalted the content of a literary work may be, the text is preserved by resisting the readings it incites. A textuality appears that is as stubborn as Jews are in Christian eyes. A letter-bound remnant impossible to dissolve maintains a kind of self-presence, refuses to collapse under ideological suasions or the sheer multiplicity of the commentary. In that sense it continues to "abide the negative" and traumatic historical change. Trauma, because it is at once unrepresentable *and* affective, gives the impression of what Kristeva has called a "symbolic collapse." But that collapse is averted when Judaism refuses to go into exile from the word. As Scripture, revelation even seems immune to its own archaic and disruptive energy, to the very traumatism it has so often provoked. In Gershom Scholem's oft-quoted formulation (see his letter on Kafka to Walter Benjamin, September 20, 1934), even when the text of revelation has lost its meaningfulness, it still asserts itself. Like trauma, what revelation means is at once unintelligible and deeply felt. "It has *validity* but *no significance*."[19]

This constant return of the letter produces a complex fidelity. I would like to describe it as *a cure of meanings by the text*. Blanchot, too, though faithful to the expressive or symbolic potentialities of language, glimpses a thereness, an *il y a*, that wounds arrogance and undermines stability of meaning. There is a night, according to his lyrical story, *Thomas the Obscure*, that issues from "a wound of thought which no longer thought itself."[20] According to Blanchot, the literary—related to Philomela traumatisms that threaten to disable speech yet find their way to a new kind of signifying—survives when the correspondence between words and "guardian thought" is menaced by spiritualistic deception and gross propaganda, or by the substitution of violence for *entente*.

"The one who encounters the other-in-his-otherness [*l'Autrui*]," Blanchot declares, "can only relate to him by deadly violence, or by the welcoming gift of the word."[21] We cannot, then, give up speech without giving up what is characteristically human; speech is the only place where we meet in understanding and potential amity, despite the otherness of the other and the pull toward speechless violence. "Speech invites man to no longer identify with his power."[22]

❏   ❏   ❏

The stumbling block for every deterministic social theory of literary expression is the formalism of literature. Literary forms outlive catastrophic events, as they do their original intent. Such formalism, paradoxically, while approaching what Scholem calls a zero point of meaning, allies itself to a sense of materiality, to basic and solid inscription. For if, as Blanchot believes, "the glory of a 'narrative voice'" prevails, whatever the content of our speech, and if it is in the nature of artistic words to aspire to permanence, to be showy, seductive, stubborn, then language and thought will remain after a disaster, as they were before, "exterior" to each other.[23]

Here "exterior" denotes a measure of conflict between language and thought, an imperfect harmony or productive dissonance. But if materialistic interpretations suffer a defeat, so do spiritualistic ones. Spiritualizing interpretations cannot spirit away the letter. The letter is "that which remains" and so resists any messianic/catastrophic foreclosure of time. Derrida opens his most original work, *Glas*, with "Quoi du reste . . . ?," signaling up front that neither philosophic nor literary endeavors can achieve their ideal without a remainder. Something is always left over. "Let us divvy up eternity to make it transitory," Blanchot suggests ironically at the end of *The Writing of the Disaster*. He also quotes Levinas: "To admit the effect of literature on humanity—that is perhaps the ultimate wisdom of the West in which the People of the Bible recognizes itself."[24]

CHAPTER 8

TEXT AND SPIRIT

The face-to-face with the text has replaced the face-to-face with God.

—*Edmond Jabès*, Le parcours

E ven a casual observer of the worldly scene or of news that besieges ears and eyes and becomes increasingly a confusing talk show with endlessly extemporized sense and nonsense, even you and I, who are that casual observer, cannot fail to notice how often the supernatural turns up as a topic. Let me excerpt a moment close to Christmas 1997. "In Books, It's Boom Time for Spirits," runs a headline of "The Arts" section of *The New York Times* (Tuesday, November 11, 1997). The very next week, this same section, devoted to Robert Gobert's installation piece in the Los Angeles Museum of Contemporary Art, features a Madonna standing on a drainage grate with a cruciform pipe through her belly, which elicits the curious headline "Religion That's in the Details" (not only entrails) and adds "A Madonna and Drain Pipe Radiate an Earthy Spirituality." The number of best-sellers on near-death or out-of-body experiences is well known; spirit raptors proliferate; and the recovered memory syndrome has insinuated not only devastating suspicions about family values but also made stars of obscure people who claim to have lived previous lives as saints, warrior-heroes, and Amazonian queens.

Serious scholars, too, turned from their literary preoccupations to write, as Harold Bloom has done, on *The American Religion* and, with the approach of the millennium, on omens, angels, avatars, and such. Bloom's survey of Christian and heterodox movements since 1800 envisions the year 2000 as the triumph of an unacknowledged, specifically American religion, in which the "soul stands apart, and something deeper than the soul, the real Me or self or spark, thus is made free to be utterly alone with . . . a free God or God of Freedom" who loves every American with a personal love. Bloom would like to stand aloof, but finds he too is part of this scene—as American as Emerson or Whitman. "Religious criticism," he says, "even if it seeks to banish all nostalgia for belief, still falls into the experience of the spiritual, even as literary criticism cannot avoid the danger of falling into the text."[1] Although there is nothing new in the antics of hucksters and televangelists, or meeting the Lord in the air (in a spaceship, no less, according to Louis Farrakhan), or weeping statues, or miracles on Broadway (Tony Kushner, *Angels in America*), or the amazing ease with which both preachers and skinheads claim to have heard the call of God, it is time to reflect on this bullishness in the spiritual market.

Did the mere approach of the year 2000 act as a magnet? My initial thought is that there is enough craziness in traditional religion itself, I mean imaginative, poetic craziness, so that this sort of human circus is unnecessary. At the same time I agree with William Blake that imagination is religion's birth mother, always trying to free its offspring, the poets, from strictures of doctrine. But then one remembers a different aspect of the spiritual impulse, that it is never entirely disinterested: It often breaks through as the compulsive side of those whose disgust with the human condition—with themselves or others or politics—becomes intolerable and who tend to advocate purgative schemes of reform.

To write adequately about spiritual experience—or what is called such—would need the tolerance and comprehensiveness of a William

James.[2] Indeed, the task of distinguishing between spirituality and spiritism seems endless. The question of where spirituality is today is also complicated by the increasing predominance of visual texts, particularly movies. How "spiritual" is a film like *Seven* (1995), written by Andrew Walker? It is one of many staging the city as an evil place that requires purification through a punisher or avenger. Based on the Christian typology of the Seven Deadly Sins, it tracks a murderer's grisly serial killings in pursuit of a spiritual quest. The killer himself imposes the scheme of the Seven Deadly Sins on randomly chosen victims, and the surprise is that, while outwitting the police, he allows himself to be killed at the end as a sacrifice to his own scheme—because he embodies one of those sins. There is no spiritism here of the supernatural kind; but there is a borderline sense of the uncanny, as in so many detective stories, where a fiendish force seems to outmaneuver human reason. The rational wins only because the murderer (or author) wants it to, in order to save the concept of motivation. *Seven* cannot be dismissed as the gothic exploitation of religious mania; it is a ghastly hyperbole demonstrating how sinister that mania becomes when the spiritual life runs amuck, when its claim to mark and fight evil is seized by a despairing intensity that leads to flamboyant acts of proclamation.

In general, the detective-story format of looking for clues that do not yield easily to looking, and mock in their cunning character the noisy, clumsy pursuit of the police, points to the need for a different kind of *attention*. In such films, there is a glut—gluttony—of sight that cuts across all attempts to render these moral fables spiritual. Perhaps the spiritual can only be caught at the margin, glimpsed, not focused on; it evades being incorporated, or fixed as a purely visual event. In *Seven*, there is a short moment in a police station where, quite implausibly, strains of classical music are heard—an allusion, perhaps, to a more striking scene in another film, *The Shawshank Redemption* (1994), in which music of that kind transports the prisoners in the yard to a world they have not known and may never know again. Brushed by the wings of that music, they stand still, in their inner space, attentive; then the miraculous notes evaporate into the grim round of their daily existence.

My aim is to cover only one aspect of spiritual experience, that which involves "listening" to texts. This aspect of spirituality is linked to my previous examples through the quality of attention that texts, canonical or noncanonical, foster. In what follows I begin with literature, and the reason is personal, coming both from my training and the fact that Jews are still a text-centered community.

◻   ◻   ◻

Many have claimed that something read, even as fragmented as a single sentence come upon by chance, has made a radical difference and set them on a new course with spiritual implications. This happened most famously to Augustine; the *tolle lege* ("take up and read") episode from his *Confessions* recalls the magical practice of the *sortes Virgilianae* or *sortes Bibliorum*, in which you opened Virgil or the Bible and decided on a course of action by taking the first verse that met your eye as an oracle. The practice survived into Methodism and was known to George Eliot, whose Dinah Morris in *Adam Bede* seeks divine guidance "by opening the Bible at hazard."[3] Saul Lieberman, a distinguished scholar of the Talmud, speculated that this sort of divination was also behind the curious notion of *bat kol*, "daughter [or echo] of the voice [of God]," heard in an era when He was no longer audible, or, as the Bible puts it, when open vision had ceased—the era of postprophetic teachers who between the second century B.C.E. and the fifth C.E. were the founding fathers of orthodox Judaism.[4]

The perplexed soul would go out of the house of study into the street, and words accidentally heard (often Scripture verses) were to be a deliverance, indicating the path to be followed. (To "follow a *bat kol*," an expression based on Isaiah 30:21, is mentioned several times in both the Jerusalem and the Babylonian Talmud.) Some of these sounds must have penetrated the scholar's house; but perhaps his devoted attention, his *kavanah*, kept them out. The celestial *bat kol* could also appear in dreams or daydreams. This audism has something desperate about it; it is clear, from such incidents, that "the spirit blows where it lists," or that, to cite Bob Dylan, the answer is blowing in the wind.

In order to respect secular experience, to see in it a potential hiding place of the spirit—not unlike the way art after Marcel Duchamp values trashy occasions—we eavesdrop everywhere. Chance disrupts or challenges, as so often in novelistic plots, a potential ethics. The surrealists say that such encounters reveal an *hasard objectif*. Today we don't necessarily consult Virgil or the Bible and turn them into a lottery; but the world, the very world from which we seek refuge, still opens to divulge accidental epiphanies. Modern Age spiritism of this kind may have begun with Baudelaire's *Fusées* (Fireworks): They describe a type of trance that parallels a depth experience also yielded by hashish but extends it like a magical varnish over anything and everything, including "la première phrase venue, si vos yeux tombent sur un livre" (the first-come phrase, if you happen to look into a book).[5] Poetry itself, Baudelaire suggests, is the product of an intelligence lit up by an intoxication of this kind.

Often today, our learned psychedelic adventurers, instead of consulting the *bouche d'ombre* of a sacred volume, mix yoga-like meditational practices with conventional forms of ecstatic prayer and chanting. The act of emerging from a period of concentration, of isolated study or brooding, into the promiscuous clamor of the street or the sad variety of books one admires and cannot make one's own, seems to hide a sensuous need, the wish for a *coup de foudre*, a choice as absolute as Emily Dickinson's

> The soul selects her own society
> Then—shuts the Door—
> To her divine Majority—
> Present no more—[6]

Grace, akin to love, amazes, because it occurs involuntarily among the impossible diversity of human beings with whom one wishes to be intimate. Indeed, as we have also seen with the Branch Davidians or the Jonestown suicides, the need to love or to cleave to a strong, ordering voice, whether that of a guru or the text he claims to embody, is essential to this kind of communal spirituality. Many are deceived when the promise of life, of rebirth, produces its own *rigor mortis:* in Dickinson's words, a closing of the valves of attention "Like Stone."[7]

❏   ❏   ❏

Myself, I have never graduated beyond Fortune Cookies; and even those lost their charm when I opened one and received the all-too-probable message: "What you have eaten isn't chicken." But I admit that as a student of literature, and as one who reads a lot, in the canon as well as miscellaneously, there are times when a passage has taken my breath away: when I have been tempted to call the impact of such a text spiritual, and supposed that others would also call it such. The first case I will take up is perhaps too good, in that the subject matter is already in the religious realm.

I read Cardinal Newman's *Gerontius* again, a play structured as a viaticum, or ultimate rite of passage. It describes the individual soul passing from the instant of death to the judgment seat. It was not so much Newman's daring conception that held me, as he shows the dying man moving like a somnambulist along that fatal path, accompanied by the voices of the funeral mass and the intercession of orders of angels. What held me was an early moment in this process, when Gerontius expresses his terror: terror of dying, *timor mortis*, but also of God's judgment closing in. Newman places heroism at life's end, as it is overwhelmed by pangs related to the physical agony of death, pangs that contain an intuition of damnation:

> I can no more; for now it comes again
> That sense of ruin, which is worse than pain,
> That masterful negation and collapse
> Of all that makes me man. . . .

In this prayerful monologue Gerontius does not address himself to God, Christ, Mary, or other intercessors—until seized once more by a spasm of fear. The comfort of address, of being called or being able to call upon, is removed, as he begins a free fall, dying alone, without steadying hand or voice:

> as though I bent
> Over the dizzy brink
> Of some sheer infinite descent;
> Or worse, as though
> Down, down for ever I was falling through
> The solid framework of created things. . . . [8]

Like Gerontius, at that moment, we realize how ordinary life bears us up; so that if the term "spiritual" can enter appropriately here, it also refers to the gratitude one owes created or material things for their support. The earth generally does not give way; and we trust our body, for a time. There are intimations, however, that this confidence cannot last: At the end of our life, or at the end of days, or indeed at any time in the course of individual existence, we are deserted, a trapdoor opens, the pit yawns. It is then that spirits enter or reenter and the immediate frontier becomes death.

In considering the colorful aspects of a free-floating spirituality as well as one closely linked to religion, I will try to avoid cornering myself into a decisive definition of the phenomenon itself. Like Nathaniel Hawthorne in "The Celestial Railroad," I am anxious not to become a Mr. Smooth-it-away. I suggest, then, that we often seize on one event, whether disturbing or exhilarating or both, that cuts across a relatively careless, wasteful, ignorant life. We focus on what was revealed—on what turned us around, not necessarily from bad to good but toward a sense of purpose and identity. The quality of attention so aroused is not necessarily the outcome of a religious exercise: It can involve the act of attention as, in Malebranche's phrase, "the natural prayer of the soul." Or there is Keats's wonderful analogy: "I go among the Fields and catch a glimpse of a stoat or a fieldmouse peeping out of the withered grass—the creature hath a purpose and its eyes are bright with it."[9]

Readers, poetically inclined, yet also distracted by passages that seem to stand out, must find a way to go where these lead. Such readerly absorption is, I think, becoming rarer, not just because books have multiplied and the World Wide Web is there to be manipulated, but also because film has become a major art form; and film is panoramic, requiring a more diffused as well as exigent attention, one that hypnotizes through a variable zooming and focusing. The tyranny of the eye, the simple pleasure of filmic omnipotence, combines distraction with a faux-semblant of concentration.

Of course, some intensity of the visual has always existed; the use of religious icons or the meditative "exercises" of Ignatius tell us how important images, inner or outer, have been. Or, as in D. H. Lawrence's "Bavarian Gentians," written a few months before his death, the coming darkness renders the visible more visible, counterpart of a kindly light purely and intensely nature's own. The poet calls the dark blue flowers black lamps from Dis, the god of the Underworld. Their burning darkness contrasts with Demeter's pale lamps and acts as the poet's spirit guide or *psychopompos* to the region of the dead.[10]

Yet unless the discipline of reading has first come about, without being routinized by print culture, it is doubtful we can even approach an analysis of spiritual value, at least in our civilization. In many conversion experiences, as William James has shown, terror and turmoil are allayed (or incited and allayed) when a voice is heard uttering Scripture words.[11] Poetry's dense phrases have a parallel effect: They often induce a contemplative mood, asking to be carried longer in the womb of the mind, and do not bring a premature and disenchanting clarity to birth.

❏   ❏   ❏

Is spirituality, then, linked to the sense of the individual as such being found, or found out? That those affected feel directly called or addressed is probably more important than recognizing whose voice it is or the exact content of the call. A sudden, mysterious utterance outflanks the resistance to being identified or known too well. Is not the oldest—and youngest—game that of hide-and-seek? Shock, surprise, self-consciousness, unanticipated arousals of guilt or joy, even a negative correlative of these, "Blank misgivings of a Creature/Moving about in worlds not realized"[12]—such radical moments, not always verbal, although demanding a verbal response or a temporal, sustained act of consciousness, may not constitute the spiritual as such or bind it to the ordinary life we lead. Yet they furnish a disruption from which we date a conscious birth.

The individual is always singled out, is always one of three stopped by an Ancient Mariner, transported by a musical phrase, "looked at" by a work of art, as when the archaic torso of Apollo admonishes the poet Rilke: "You must change your life."[13] There is a heightened sense of place or virtual embodiment. The spiritual in those moments approaches ecstasy yet does not leave the body except to enter, at the same time, a specific visionary space. So Jacob at Beth-el: "How full of awe this place!" (Genesis 28:17). Compare the flashbacks of trauma: "I think I would have no trouble even now locating the spot on the median strip of Commonwealth Avenue [in Boston] where they [the repressed experiences of many years ago] emerged out of that darkness. . . ."[14] Krzystof Kieslowski's film *The Double Life of Veronica* (1991) intimates how strong and sensuous the pull is toward union with a second self that is always somewhere else, and whose absent presence is felt as a loss, even a disembodiment. This ghostly, complementary other is as endlessly mourned as its reintegration is desired. Aesthetics classifies such ecstasies as sublime; religion, generally as full of awe. They exalt, terrify, and humble at the same time.

Individuation of this sort seems to be essential even when the newly minted person flees from it into the arms of a brotherhood, sisterhood, or God. It is notoriously difficult, as we all know, to distinguish the sense of election from mania. Then how do we get from such instances of spiritual experience to a communal bond without betraying or falsifying them? To hear voices is a form of madness; random textual surprises are borderline cases that interpolate the reader and can be amplified as inner quotations, cryptomania, or internalized commands. Yet once we have redeemed that madness by turning to methodical exegesis, are we still in the precarious domain of being singled out, or do we simply confirm what we already know through doctrine? Have astonishment and awe turned into dogmatic faith?

We should not underestimate the importance, negative or positive, of hermeneutics in religion: an activity that flexes the meaning of a canonical text. The methodical character of hermeneutics tries to minimize eccentric responses by establishing a true, authoritative, original meaning. Yet everyone who has ventured into the field of interpretation, even when it represents itself as a discipline or a science, knows the polyphony if not cacophony of exegesis and how endlessly interesting it is to try to meet the challenge of texts. Although we take for granted that the voice of God is no longer heard in the way the boy Samuel heard it, or which would make the interpreter reply "Here I am," a part of us returns to certain texts as to vestiges in which strength of spirit condenses itself and could achieve what Robert Frost memorably called "counter-love, original response."[15]

❏   ❏   ❏

I have given my essay the title "Text and Spirit" because it has always puzzled me how dependent spirituality is, not only on books—necessary for cultural transmission, once there is dispersion, or as the oral tradition becomes too complex—but on textual issues. The rivalry of religion with religion could not continue without systems of interpretation that activate in specific ways the faith community's Scripture, which may be a book shared by several religions.

It must already be clear, in any case, that there is a link between text and spirit when textual incidents, in the form of fragments, are like a voice falling into us, taking hold of us. Although elaborated and restored to their first or another context, such audita remain snatches from a ghostly conversation or a more absolute book. I have represented this receptivity to spiritualized sound as a psychic and existential fact. Moreover, I have stressed its contingency, as religion itself often does when it depicts a divine intervention: A prophet is unexpectedly called, a commanding voice is heard, a rebus or inscription appears.

But I have also said that the orthodox hermeneutics we have inherited, while respecting life-changing responses to source texts with canonical status, seeks to limit these.[16] Although some passages are more astonishing than others, and through as yet unknown mediations even ordinary biblical pericopes can have a startling effect, both religious and literary theories of exegesis take much pride in the doctrine of context—a predetermined context, shielding the reader from subjectivity and speculative excess. Similarly, in evangelical or charismatic movements, where startling conversions—even convulsions—are expected, what takes place is, as it were, programmed in and becomes a sacred or, at worst, sacrilegious mimicry.

The force of the fragment, then, surprises, because it comes from outside, even when that outside is within us. It does not matter how we analyze the psychic fact; what is important is that a metonymic textual condensation, this appearance of word as vision, *leads back* to a source text, or is the germ, as in creative writing, of a *leading forward*, a transformative moment that creates its own narrative support.

❐   ❐   ❐

In talking of spirit, we have an obligation to go first to where the word *ruach* appears in the Hebrew Bible. After "In the beginning God created the heaven and the earth," Genesis discloses that "the earth was unformed and void, and darkness was upon the face of the deep." The *ruach elohim*, which "hovered over the face of the waters," is close to that darkness on the face of the deep. But this might suggest that chaos, the *tohuvabohu* of unformed earth and water, may have preexisted; in which case the creation would not be *ex nihilo*, out of nothing, but only a form-giving event. The Bible's opening phrasing defeats that thought; and the "spirit of God," with the formless darkness mere backdrop, manifests itself as a commanding voice instantly originating light. Yet even here, in this place of power, as the poet John Hollander has remarked, "Light is called, not torn forth."[17]

In the second chapter of Genesis, there is a subtle parallel to the spirit hovering over the face of the waters: "there went up a mist from the earth, and watered the whole face of the ground" (2:6). This is a transitional sentence that could be joined either to the previous verse describing the barren, soon-to-be-fertile, earth or to the next, which retells the creation of humankind: "Then the Lord God formed man of the dust of the ground, and breathed into his nostrils the breath of life; and man became a living soul." The words for breath and soul are not *ruach* but respectively *neshamah* and *nefesh*. As a picture of the creative act, there is something gentler here and more intimate: a proximity of divine to human that is not felt in the first creation-of-man account (Genesis 1:26–29) despite the theme of *zelem elohim*, of being created in God's image.

In fact, where we might expect the *ruach* to reappear, as in Genesis 3:8, we find instead a voice, "the voice of the Lord God walking in the garden." The earlier depiction showed the spirit of God as a hovering force in the formless darkness; in the later picture, however, the mist rising from the ground and watering the face of the earth is an image taken directly from nature, and the creation that follows is distinctly anthropomorphic, in that its subject is literally the shaping of a man, while the very art of description is friendly and naturalistic. Genesis 3:8, moreover, augments the idea of a relation between *ruach elohim* and voice, the voice that generates light. Without, to be sure, a definite body, that *ruach* voice now addresses and interpellates the lapsed human being, an act that can be said to call it to consciousness or conscience.

If my analysis is correct, *ruach* is not anthropomorphic (it is, if anything, closer to theriomorphic); yet as a speaking and intelligible voice it moves toward a pathos at once human and sublime. *Ruach* never forfeits its quality as a numinous, awe-inspiring source. This is borne out when we enter the later, more historical era of Judges, where the voice of God, while still manifest, often escapes those who search for it. The episodes that focus on the relation among Samuel, Saul and God are particularly disturbing: indeed, here the verb *lidrosh*, the root of *midrash*, meaning to seek out the voice, first appears.[18]

The episodes are disturbing because while God's relation to Samuel remains familiar, allowing responsive words or obedience, the pressure on Saul is terrifying. Saul is an *am ha'aretz* (a simple, earth-bound fellow) going to the seer for a mundane, bumpkin-like purpose, "Can you give me guidance where my asses are?" and being confronted by a fearful demand, a question that is not a question at all but an astonishing, exalting imposition: "And on whom is all the desire of Israel? Is it not on thee, and on all thy father's house?" (Samuel 1:9:20). Samuel then predicts Saul's journey home, which culminates in his joining a band of prophets: "And the spirit of the Lord will come mightily upon thee, and thou shalt prophesy and be turned into another man" (Samuel 1:10:1–7), where "come mightily upon" translates *zalachat*, "seize" thee or "fall upon" thee (cf. Samuel 1:11:6 and 1:16:13). A power of transformation is evoked, akin to that of the *ruach* in the first lines of Genesis.

Clearly, the open vision and voice are passing from Israel. The presence of God returns in the prophets, but with more violence, ambivalence, chanciness, and—in Abraham Heschel's formulation—pathos: so the *devar-adonai* is like a burning fire consuming Jeremiah's heart and bones (Jeremiah 20:9). God's *ruach* reverts to something of its aboriginal manifestation: We are made to feel its incumbent mystery and transformative violence more than its intimacy.

❐   ❐   ❐

It is well known that the sealing of the canon of Hebrew Scripture is linked to the recession, if not disappearance, of prophetic voice and vision. With the destruction of the First Temple, then decisively with the destruction of the Second and Bar Kochba's defeat, inquiry of God must go through *midrash*. The Sages may still be looking for asses, but these include the Messiah's donkey. Those rabbis are not shy; they assert on the basis of Deuteronomy 30:11–15 that the Law is not in heaven but among them in the earthly tribunal; indeed, they abjure the authority of the *bat kol* and seek to shut down the prophetic impulse, even as Saul banished the witches whom he was nevertheless forced to consult. This means, in effect, that spirit has become textualized; inquiry of the Lord, in the postprophetic and postpriestly era, is mediated by the recitation, reading, and contemplative study of Talmud Torah.

This multilayered commentary continues to call itself an oral tradition, however, and claims descent from Sinai; the image of direct transmission, through the voice of God or "daughter" of that voice, is never entirely given up. To read in the Talmud, or to extend its inquiry, becomes a religious experience itself.[19] Priest and prophet are replaced by the figure of the rabbi of exemplary learning who walks with the Law (*halakhah*, the path), even as the righteous of old had walked and conversed with God.

The rabbinic revolution, as it has been called, seals the canon and draws the consequences of that closure. In the Sages' own hyperbole, God is made to say of an errant Israel, "Would that they abandon me but keep my Torah!"[20] This expresses, of course, a fear that *God* has forsaken the community; in captivity and dispersion, only the Torah remains. But whatever dryness of spirit ensues, whatever constriction and narrowness of purpose, the act of reading strengthens and takes on a quality of prayerful recitation—of a crying to God in words of the canonized text as well as a listening for His response.

One might think that how *midrash* usually atomizes Scripture would diminish the latter's eloquence. Such divisions certainly sin against plot or story, the very features that entice us to look at the Bible as literature. What matters in *midrash* is the verse, or part of the verse, even a single word or letter. Meaning is achieved by the montage of biblical patches. Gershom Scholem once called this "mosaic style" of the great halakhists "poetic prose in which linguistic scraps of sacred texts are whirled around kaleidoscope like."[21]

What I have tried to do is sketch a minimalist theory of spirituality, influenced mainly by the Jewish commentary tradition. Some will be disappointed by this modest approach. Spirituality is a word with great resonance, yet I have not extracted large, exalted structures of sensibility or discourse. Were I to do so, I would have to respect an entire midrashic sequence or collection and show how words dim the eyes as well as refresh them, insofar as visuality and idolatry may be linked. I would also have to deal with the issue of anthropo/gyno/morphism, or divine pathos: a fertile, if always disputed, well spring of religious energy. I would have to stay longer with the way *ruach* breaks into voice, becomes voice-feeling; and, close to the heart of the throat, threatens to turn the human response into a stammer. I would also have to recognize that, in Judaism, with a Messiah who tarries, "hope" must be a central theme, wherever and however it manifests itself. The very word "spirituality," moreover, still seems somewhat foreign to traditional Jewish thinking and observance: It got preempted by Pauline Christianity. Only to Levinas might it be applied: His theology evokes a vigilance, even an insomnia, that keeps human finitude, traumatized by the infinite, from enclosing itself in "the hegemonic and atheistic self" for which life reduces to equanimity.

◻   ◻   ◻

There is one further generalization I want to venture. It returns to something almost as equivocal as dreams, namely the gift of speech and what Dante and also the German-Jewish religious thinker Franz Rosenzweig call its "grammar:" voiced thinking that becomes writing and seeks a coincidence of spirit and letter. That coincidence is rare and demands a price—an engagement that takes time, perhaps a lifetime. For there is no guarantee that poetic words, ancient or modern, will make sense, or the same sense, to different readers throughout history. In fact, the more earnest our attention to language, the more the conventional links dissipate, and a nakedness appears in the words as words, one that both arouses and threatens the process of intellection.

We often feel, then, that biblical words say too much to be received: their anagogical force, while breaking what Rosenzweig calls the shell of the mystery, can make us feel as poor as Edward Taylor, the Puritan poet:

In my befogg'd dark Phancy, Clouded minde,
Thy Bits of Glory, packt in Shreds of Praise
My Messenger [his poetry] doth lose, losing his Wayes.[22]

We cannot presume to win spiritual coherence lightly, when the spirit itself is so often figured as a preternatural, disruptive intervention. The not-foundering of communication under that pressure is unusual, for speech could turn into nothing more than a contiguous mass of alien sounds. Perhaps, then, shards, *klipot*, Edward Taylor's "Bits of Glory . . . Shreds of Praise," must suffice.

Let me end by recounting what happened to Martin Buber. His path to the great Buber-Rosenzweig translation of the Bible was very complex, but one episode stands out.[23] Well-acquainted in early youth with the Hebrew original and then with several translations, including Luther's, he noticed shortly after his Bar Mitzvah that he read the Bible with literary enjoyment—a fact that upset him so much that for years he did not touch any translation but tried to return to the *Urtext*, the original Hebrew. By then, however, the words had lost their familiar aspect and seemed harsh, alien, confrontational: "sie sprangen mir ins Gesicht" (they dared me to my face).

Thirteen years later—one thinks, therefore, of a second Bar Mitzvah—he attended the funeral of the founder of modern Zionism, Theodor Herzl, and came home feeling oppressed. Reaching for one book after another, everything seemed voiceless and meaningless (*stumm*). Then, as if by chance, and without expecting much, Buber opened the Bible—and happened upon the story of how King Jehoiakim had Jeremiah's scroll read and consigned piece by piece to a brazier's fire (Jeremiah 36:21ff.); this went to Buber's heart, and he began to face the Hebrew once more, conquering each word anew, as if it had never been translated. "I read [the Hebrew] aloud, and by reading it this way I got free of the whole Scripture, which now was purely *miqra'* [vocal reading]." A few years later, while again rereading a biblical chapter out loud, the feeling came over him that it was being spoken for the first time and had not yet been written down, and did not have to be written down. "The book lay before me, but the book melted into voice."[24]

Buber has not left us a reflection on why the "found" passage from Jeremiah affected him so powerfully, and he does not refer explicitly to the *bat kol*. But his stated wish to "get free of" Scripture by first converting it into an aural experience is remarkably candid. The Hebrew root *qara'* in *miqra'* may have helped as a first step toward a retranslation of the Bible that challenges Luther's strongly vernacular version. *Qara'*, as in *qryat sh'ma*, denotes the action of calling, of a crying out or reciting, as well as naming: The content of this prayer is, after all, a naming of God. *Qara'* as "reading" never loses its residual meaning of "calling out." Moreover, in the episode from Jeremiah, the verb *qara* (when spelled with ayin rather than aleph) is a near homonym of "tearing"—a sacrilegious act on the part of the King and which recalls two distantly related events. First, the destroyed scroll is rewritten by Jeremiah's scribe Baruch, a doubling that could recall that of Sinai's tablets as well as raise the issue of the relation of written to oral Torah. Both Buber and Rosenzweig try to express the link between text and spirit in a radical way, one that goes through the restitution of its oral or aural resonance, but otherwise do not seek to transform the Bible by any type of spiritualizing interpretation. "*Schrift ist Gift* [Script is poison]," Buber quotes Rosenzweig, from a letter shortly before their work of translation began, "holy *Schrift* included. Only when it is translated back into orality can I stomach it."[25]

The episode from Jeremiah, moreover, leads intertextually to II Kings 22, in which Hilkiah the High Priest discovers a Book of the Law (*sefer hatorah*) in the temple and Shaphan the scribe reads it to King Josiah; but there the King tears his clothes,[26] not the scroll, and has it read aloud to the assembled people. II Kings near its inception had recounted the story of Elijah and Elisha: how Elijah ascends in a whirlwind and perhaps leaves to his disciple a "double portion of . . . *ruach*." Here, too, we go once more from prophecy as open vision to the discovery of a scroll that must provide vision by inquiry, by a midrashic process linked to recitation and research. The fiery chariot and horses carrying Elijah away, become, when Elisha is lamented (II Kings 13:14–15), no more than a figurative allusion, an exclamation ("My father, my father, the chariots of Israel and the horsemen thereof!") expressing a fear that the *ruach* will depart from Israel with Elisha's passing. Despite the sporadic persistence of prophecy, the spirit will now have to reside mainly within the temple of a text.

I leave the last word to Levinas, who suggests that talmudic and midrashic literature shows that "prophecy may be the essence of the human, the traumatism that wakes it to its freedom." Thought itself is an elaboration of such a moment. "It probably begins through traumatisms to which one does not even know how to give a verbal form: a separation, a violent scene, a sudden consciousness of the monotony of time. It is from the reading of books—not necessarily books of philosophy—that these initial shocks become questions and problems, giving one to think."[27] The prophetic consciousness, reading, and the ethical converge, wherever self-identity, challenged by otherness, instructed and roused by it, becomes "la spiritualité de l'esprit."

CHAPTER 9

TRANSPARENCY RECONSIDERED

ON POSTMODERNISM, FUNDAMENTALISM, AND OTHER DARK MATTERS

La transparence est trop belle pour être vraie.

—*Jean Baudrillard*, La transparence du mal

T he issue of messianic politics remains very much alive. When we look at the contemporary world, at significant factions in the Middle East, messianic politics cannot be put down as a species of Y2K nuisance. Religious expectation turns too often into a provocation for time to end or to reveal its innermost direction. Secular systems too—those of Saint-Simon, Spengler, Yeats—incite a species of cultural prophecy that foresees a necessary cycle of life-renewing catastrophes.

"Postmodern" as a temporal marker invalidates that kind of cultural prophecy. It suggests a disenchantment that is final, or self-perpetuating. The period concept of modernity as breakthrough and decisive renewal seems to have lured us once too often. Although cultural prophecy, as Yeats pursued it in *A Vision*, still tries to draw a principle of hope out of disenchantment, the sense of a merely destructive end draws nearer. "The best lack all conviction, while the worst/Are full of passionate intensity." The modernist who wrote this was already a postmodernist.

In this charged atmosphere, there is a surprising revival of hermeneutics, not as the ancient art of explicating sacred texts, or searching for an interpretive key to disclose the exact date of the Messiah's or the Beast's advent, but as an intrinsic and permanent mode of questioning. Reading now goes together with appreciating the friction of words, the *temporality* of a rhetoric that serves to restrain precipitous ideologies of progress or a flight into the future, like that of Walter Benjamin's Angel of History. Head reverted, facing a ruinous past, the angel is driven forward by a "wind blowing from Paradise." It was also Benjamin who said he wanted to take literary criticism more seriously than anyone before him—as if its task were to enter that angelic force field and extract hope from a vista of destruction despite the messianic politics causing the destruction.[1]

My subject, then, is the function of literary criticism at a time when postmodern and fundamentalist perspectives clash without hope of accommodation. As a term, "postmodern" implies that we have entered a new epoch and, more significantly, that "modern" is no longer an adequate concept. (In that particular respect the fundamentalist mentality fosters a premodern kind of postmodernity.) I begin with Gianni Vattimo, a fluent analyst of the postmodern, who defines it as exhibiting two salient characteristics.

□   □   □

The first of these acknowledges the historical odds against drawing meaning out of the disenchantment of meaning. The disenchantment at issue derives as much from the abandonment of liberal hopes in mankind's progressive emancipation as from the frustration of New Order or fanatical end-time thought characterizing the political religions. "The ironic-nostalgic inventory of the talismans of progress," Vattimo writes, "is perhaps the only 'utopia' still possible," and he asks what kind of "indispensable discursive apparatus" or "rhetorical accessory" might be capable of "keeping strict faith with disenchantment."[2] Given the disastrous course of utopian thinking, its murderous application by Nazism and Communism, and the revival of religious politics, especially in the Middle East, the inability of progressive thought to replace utopia by a permanent mode of critical thinking forebodes a world in which ideological warfare spills out at any point into actual war.

Critique, as a wary and interminable discourse, should have, Vattimo therefore insists, a more-than-subversive thrust. He understands how hard it is to remain without the support of convictions. In the pursuit of science and learning, passionate intensity can accompany methodical doubt—there too, as Descartes and Pascal demonstrate, an "end" beyond middle and muddle is grasped at. The postmodern form of critique finds its positive dimension through hermeneutics. A religious watching-in-patience that in the past acknowledged yet also tempered apocalyptic expectation is replaced by a broadened concept of *reading* as the scrutiny of nonsacred as well as sacred texts. Reading becomes a distinctively temporal, even temporizing, activity, requiring something more than the count-down of numerology or its variants. It makes time rather than seeks to speed it up. Whereas numerology wishes to anticipate the end, or a definitive, fulfilled present (*parousia*), reading practices associated with a historical hermeneutics have made room in—extended—a time pressured by apocalyptic expectation and political impatience. They create a livable secular space within a "time without end."

In what sense, however, is Martin Heidegger's version of hermeneutics, for example, a reading? Does it not call for a liberation of hermeneutics from its dependency on texts—except those of a few great poets? It is Being itself, according to Heidegger, not the text, that "calls" to us in those poets. Heidegger uses his Husserlian base (the phenomenological "return to things") as an existential prop to convert into something positive as well as critical (*fragwürdig*) a sustained dismantling of both metaphysical and humanistic assumptions. Reading is made to coincide with a speculative archeology, an etymological deconstruction of received Greek or German texts. Thus Vattimo simply honors a text-centeredness Heidegger cannot really escape, however far out his interpretive ventures go.

What associates Heidegger and Vattimo closely is an awareness of "the counterfinality of reason." In human relations, meanings attained by reason are also dissolved by it, perpetually constructed and deconstructed, rather than disclosing an underlying, objective design that can be made transparent. A plurality of worldviews, which is the result of that dynamic, of that movement of counter-finality, both founds and unsettles secular thought.

Hermeneutics, then, retains its importance for any *horizon* of truth because of its age-long experience with the necessity of (re)interpretation. It exposes the deceiving simplicity of the media we use for communication while engaging the never entirely transparent meanings accumulated and sedimented by tradition. These meanings can be simplified, but the ethical risk of so doing is greater than that of remaining aware of their plural nature. Once language, symbolism, and tradition are seen to be the depositories of a "generous error" (this is how Shelley, the English poet, puts it), not completely separable from truth by future enlightenments, then a double hermeneutic is necessary: of restoration as well as of suspicion, to employ the useful terms introduced by the French philosopher Paul Ricoeur.

❑ ❑ ❑

The importance of the residue or remainder we call tradition, to an age that substitutes plural and relativizing worldviews for a fabled universal discourse, is described as follows by Vattimo. He writes in the last chapter of *The Transparent Society* ("Ethics of Communication or Ethics of Interpretation") that hermeneutics has sought

> to affirm historicality as *belonging:* the experience of truth does not occur in the reflection of an object by a subject committed to self-transparence, but rather as the articulation—or interpretation—of a tradition (a language, a culture) to which existence belongs, and which it reformulates in new messages sent to other interlocutors. Ethical life and historicality coincide here. . . . But how? Principally, by [hermeneutics] thinking of itself not as an ultimately metaphysical descriptive theory of the hermeneutic constitution of existence, but rather as an event of destiny. Hermeneutics must recognize itself as the thought belonging to the epoch of the end of metaphysics,

and nothing more. . . . It is the philosophical thought of secularized Europe.[3]

The vulnerable phrase here is "event of destiny" (although for the Anglo-American tradition of conversational criticism the entire paragraph is vulnerable). Too heroic for the occasion, the phrase alludes to Heidegger, who posits a fateful event, a turn in human history that produced a disconnection of words and things, and consequently a veiling of things by words. A heroic note enters because Heidegger holds that what was fateful is reversible: The past is open to be undone by a courageous understanding, an existential hermeneutics whose potential return to the origin—to refound the truth—is described in Heidegger's early chef-d'oeuvre, *Being and Time*. The etymon of the German word for "event" (*Ereignis*) suggests, according to Heidegger, an "appropriation" of destiny.

Yet Heidegger's strength lies more in a sensitive conceptualization of everyday life, one that expands our vocabulary for what is *inauthentic*, than in making mouths at an event that could usher in a new heroic era characterized by soldierly virtue and national dignity. His expansion of hermeneutics does not result in a clearing away of the veil between words and things but in an illumination of that veil.

Part of the problem, then, is his language—a wordplay applied indifferently to explaining life and explicating poetry. World and text converge. Such phrases as "event of destiny" are unresolvably ambiguous in a specific way: They sound portentous yet are meant to point to the unconscious or forgotten depth of *everyday* existence. This double register allows Vattimo (as I hope to show) to develop a concept, characterized by him as ethical, of *pensiero debole*, "weak thought" or "weak theory." In Heidegger, however, a steady, heroic drumbeat persists that endows intensely contemplative thinking with virtues of the *vita activa* by depicting it in terms of risk, danger, decisiveness. Among those terms is *Destruktion*, a precursor of "deconstruction" that describes the necessity to dismantle Western metaphysics. The more usual German word *Abbau* may have appeared too tame.

Thus Heidegger embarks on an explication of certain great poets who sense that a moment of radical change is near. "Because the destiny of language is grounded in a nation's *relation to being*, the question of being will involve us deeply in the question of language."[4] And, since that destined moment is always imminent, we get an inkling of how a thinker of such stature could be seduced by national socialism's claim to be a spiritual revolution: both a quasi-apocalyptic New Departure (*Aufbruch*) and a totally secular intervention in and against the homogenous course of time.

□   □   □

A Heideggerian intensity of interpretation remains attractive. Understanding the great poets is no longer a missed encounter with—because of—language. Poetic words undo the ideologized, preworded world. But that negative finding or deconstruction is then put in the service of a quasi-religious, this-worldly expectation. The risk of blankness or hermeneutic perplexity is not sustained.

Even if Heidegger is right in postulating "events of destiny"—defining moments, as we now say, in intellectual and political history—these should not usurp the task of doing daily justice to the life of the mind, to the work of naming and interpretation by which we decide what an event is. This task, moreover, can never entirely resolve a questioning discourse into an affirmative one, for two reasons. The first is concisely stated by Maurice Blanchot when he says in *The Writing of the Disaster* that "it would be wrong to speak of the Messiah in Hegelian language." An event called Auschwitz has put a period to all periodization: The very fact that it happened disables our historical or chronological attempts to limit the time of sufferance by positing the relief of an ending. If we wish to speak of a Messiah, another language—not involved in time-honored terms about time—will have to be found.

The second reason, although related, is not dependent on a contemporary catastrophe. To interpret the world is often to change it into a still un-interpreted world, to respect a phenomenological blankness or indeterminacy at the heart of things. From this blankness arise, if only to cover it up, utopian thought, messianic politics, and ideologies that impose an identity or telos on history.

My personal experience of the great poets is that they pass through that moment of blankness or perplexity without erasing it. So William Wordsworth on July 13, 1798, stands doubtful before the mirror of a landscape. His sense of belonging, of how this prospect of Tintern Abbey intertwines with his life, generates a subvisionary intensity of interpretation. Against the background of the French Revolution and the charged date of July 14, a heightened awareness of *this* place and *this* moment makes him ponder future as well as past. He is reading the landscape, its vital relation to the development of his own sensibility; but the "language of the sense" he honors, and introduced to poetry, expands his argument beyond personal or idiosyncratic. This "cultured" valley comes to represent the *English* way of life as a whole. Wordsworth fears it may already be fading, already becoming a memory.[5] Can the poet as culture bearer retain his love of this scene, or will his imagination be alienated from rural nature by disruptive and remarkable changes: the political upheaval across the channel and the ecological transformation of rural life initiated by the Industrial Revolution?

Wordsworth avoids messianic politics and evades apocalyptic premonition. Affirming the power of imagination, he directs it away from grand or sublime topics, including history as the story of life-renewing cataclysms. He wants to include nature in "the event of destiny": nature as we know it, everyday concerns in everyday language. At the beginning of *this* linguistic turn, then, a vernacular is partly recovered and partly created, one that returns us to "things," to the depth of unheroic life in ordinary surroundings.

◻   ◻   ◻

We may still be within that turn. In Vattimo's hermeneutics—as in ordinary language philosophy, in Saussure's semiotics, or in a literary-dialogic perspective like Bahktin's—words are a shadow on truth that cannot be removed. Not only the heaviness of truth is threatened when the prose of the world enters consciousness integrally. Poetry itself, as an alternate (prophetic or weighty) revelation, also suffers. Full awareness of the *weak* substantiality of words—they always retain a trace of alphabetic magic, however—incites a sense of loss, as if an ancient glory had passed.

However illusory this sense of loss may be, it is now part of modern life and the so-called event of destiny.[6] Indeed, one way of distinguishing postmodern from modern is to suggest, with Lyotard, that while modernism has not given up on the glory or its restitution, postmodernism seems more indifferent to what is lost, or holds that our sense of bereavement remains infected by an older mythology. So Eric Santner, dealing with the topic "Postwar/Post-Holocaust/Postmodern," notes the recurrence in contemporary discourses of "a metaphorics of loss and impoverishment."[7]

These discourses, according to Santner, not only criticize the project of modernity and the Enlightenment's faith in progress. They "propose a kind of perpetual leave-taking from fantasies of plenitude, purity, centrality, totality, unity, and mastery." The Third Reich becomes "only the most extreme example in a long historical series." As survivors of modernity, we are invited "to creatively, and even playfully inhabit the heterogeneous language games that constitute the modest forms of community which mark the postmodern landscape." If postmodern critics mourn anything, it is the fantasy—the shattered fantasy—"of the (always already) lost organic society that has haunted the Western imagination." We are asked to tolerate complex, hybrid concepts of personal and political identity.[8]

Thus in terms of intellectual history, postmodern critics battle the idea of contemporary decadence once more, attacking specifically its origin in retrospectively gilded fantasies of total social cohesion. But can we manage without a vocabulary of rise and fall? Can epochalism—the division of history into discrete, well-shaped epochs—be avoided? Vattimo, although a postmodernist, saves hermeneutics, once a theological tool, for an epoch whose "destiny" is, so he alleges, a maximum of secularization.

It remains unclear, nevertheless, whether this epoch is an epoch. For a secularized culture, in Vattimo's view, "is not one that has simply left the religious elements of its tradition behind, but one that continues to live them as traces, as hidden and distorted models that are nonetheless profoundly present." Hence there is an "indivisible confluence of conquest and loss. Modernization does not come about as tradition is abandoned, but as it is interpreted ironically, 'distorted' in such a way (Heidegger, in a not unrelated fashion, talks of *Verwindung*) that it is conserved, but also in part emptied."[9]

❏   ❏   ❏

I will come back to the theme of religious residues or messianic tensions within secularism. It is important to stress, however, that the very notion of style—its ineradicably linguistic or artistic base—is drawn into this conflict. Various theories arise to insist that the truth content of an enunciation cannot be attained by subtracting its style or assigning to that a marginal value. The "style" of philosophizing, in particular, becomes as considerable a feature as in more literary pursuits. Sometimes the linguistic experimentation is quite pronounced, as in Heidegger or Derrida. Even in Vattimo, who is less ambitious on this score, a syncretistic style supports the enunciated position by weaving into its texture allusions to major thinkers. Heidegger, Gadamer, Ricoeur, Habermas, Hegel, and Adorno, among others, are present in fluid, attenuated form. They constitute a collective that historicizes individual thought.

Most of the time Vattimo's argument is not overwhelmed by these references; rather, they provide the pleasures of recognition and intertextual density. (Sometimes his syncretistic vein, the fusion of different discourses, leads to opaqueness rather than a new and defiant density.) His argument is, in effect, that having tried so hard to demystify religion and its empire over thought, *we now have to find ourselves a new darkness:* a principle of non-transparency that would limit the totalitarian temptation to use language and reason only instrumentally, as if communication—like society itself—could and should be totally rationalized.[10]

By now messianic politics are no longer associated exclusively with Nazism and Stalinism, or even a vista of messianic seductions stretching back, as the intellectual historian Norman Cohn has shown, throughout recorded history. What has come to the fore— at least in the West—is the dream of total communication itself. Could anything be more desirable and innocent than the superconductivity of electronic media as they arouse the illusion of complete transparency and universal access? In the revolution of the Information Age, openness, communicability, transparency, have become slogans as inspiring as Kant's "Dare to know" used to be. Or his famous precept, in *The Critique of Judgment,* on a "regard to universal communicability," which he describes as an original social contract "dictated by humanity itself." We begin to believe in a "society of communication," in which the medium is the message, and it tricks us into merging truth and transmissibility.

In this context, the palimpsest of art and the necessity of a new type of reading, one that does not aim exclusively at harmonizing new and old or making texts transparent, plays a critical role in recalling the irreducibility of figural and linguistic elements. Ezra Pound's *Cantos* already acted as a container for a sublime intertextual detritus, radioactive poetic leftovers—the stellar junk for which Wallace Stevens still fashioned twilight words. Poets like John Berryman are in the dumps as well as on the dump, *bricoleurs* of the day's residue, creating a salon of refuse. Derrida's *Glas*, at once exuberant and melancholic, is a glass in which we see darkly "what remains" rather than "what abides": that which cannot be integrated or harmonized, precisely the materiality of the signifier as well as of the signified. The shadow cast by truth on words—the failure of the Enlightenment project of cognitive transparency—adds itself to the shadow of words on truth. The influential French thinker Georges Bataille suggested, not without irony, that there could be a science devoting itself to what systems leave out or leave over, and he proposed to name it "heterology."

Vattimo's darkness is a l-i-t-e version of all this. When he uses the ponderous word "destiny," he means the pressure on us of the turn to metaphysics, complete consciousness, self-presence, or of the will to power, notions without which human existence might seem unbearably light-weight. Yet what may confuse is his optimistic merging of the "ethics of communication" and the "ethics of interpretation." Because hermeneutics belongs, despite itself, to high culture, he seeks to assign an ethical and resistant value to popular culture as a communicative action.

It is here that his concept of "weak" or postfoundational thought enters. *The Transparent Society* as a critique of metaphysical residues presents the two modernities of mass culture and multiculturalism as positive symptoms: "weaker" than previous notions of culture yet consonant with a postmodern understanding of gain and loss. Vattimo's attempt to found a sociology at once critical and redemptive—not only after (against) Heidegger and a restrictive Greek-German high culture canon but also after (against) Adorno and Critical Theory generally—requires a closer look.

◻   ◻   ◻

Vattimo postulates that "the mass media play a decisive role in the birth of a postmodern society," further, that "they do not make this postmodern society more 'transparent,' but more complex, even chaotic" and that our hope for emancipation now lies in the erosion of an older principle of conceptualization as well as a related contemporary principle of "unrestricted communication." From Descartes through Hegel, Marx, and Habermas, an underlying, potentially transpicuous objectivity was presupposed, to be discovered and communicated by an increasingly lucid self-consciousness. But for us, in late modernity, "reality is rather the result of the intersection and 'contamination' (in the Latin sense) of a multiplicity of images, interpretations, and reconstructions circulated by the media in competition with one another and without any 'central' coordination." In a still more enthusiastic passage, Vattimo envisions the "central rationality of history" disappearing, so that "the world of generalized communication explodes like a multiplicity of 'local' rationalities— ethnic, sexual, religious, cultural and aesthetic minorities—that finally speak up for themselves."

This emancipation does not necessarily guarantee every "local rationality" recognition or authenticity: The "emancipatory significance of the liberation of differences and dialects consists rather in the general *disorientation* accompanying their initial identification." In a multicultural world, then, "if . . . I set out my system of religious, aesthetic, political and ethnic values, I shall be acutely conscious of the historicity, contingency and finiteness of these systems, starting with my own."[11]

Can we take seriously this view of knowledge (with its unlimited global "exchange of cultural as well as political information"), after what we know about markets, or the ease with which dictatorial or reactionary regimes manipulate public opinion through the media?

I doubt that a media-disseminated multiculturalism favors the kind of saving historical consciousness Vattimo describes. It is not true that via the mass media every local (decentralized) rationality finds its voice, so that there is a liberation of diversity, of difference, of what Vattimo likes to call "dialect." These "voices" are often little more than a *fait divers*. Pierre Bourdieu has observed that competition in the area of journalism leads to everyone trying to scoop everyone else and so to conformity rather than diversity. Moreover, because there are so many of these cultures or subcultures, and because what is (thought to be) suppressed may be reclaimed as a fabulous origin, no single culture will be secure enough to give up identity politics and blandly think of itself as a piece of determinate historical humanity—just another voice (to use Herder's metaphor of over two centuries ago) in the choral symphony of nations.

There is a further obstacle to Vattimo's utopia, or—as he and Michel Foucault prefer to rename it—heterotopia (to indicate the necessary recognition, within any utopia, of the plurality of such communities). It comes from the very rise of a society of communication and the weakening of cultural exclusivity. Surely this weakening of exclusivist claims, which Vattimo would like to think of as an ethical development, can be true only *in principle*.

As Walter Benjamin first suggested, it derives *in fact* from the increasing mechanical reproducibility of sacred objects or cultural artifacts. And, in line with this, *one reason why the sacred won't go away is that it has become the refuge of the very nontransparence of which Vattimo speaks.* A dumbing-down of cultural life, the shadow side of its diffusion by media-saturated societies, makes us cling to mystery and ritual, even though we should—according to Vattimo—appreciate more thoroughly the aesthetic qualities of oscillation, disorientation, and play. It is difficult to accept Vattimo's version of postmodern "weakness," his "fortunate fall" apology for the media: "The advent of the media enhances the inconstancy and superficiality of experience. In so doing, it runs counter to the generalization of domination, insofar as it allows a kind of 'weakening' of the very notion of reality, and thus a weakening of its persuasive force."[12]

I find this description of a "weakening," a *pensiero debole*[13] difficult, not because it is wrong—for it describes an ominous symptom—but because it tells exactly half the story. We cannot interpret "weakness" as an "event of destiny" without being reminded of a totally different and longtime dominant system of belief, namely Christianity. (The fact that Christian "weakness" became a foil for a bloody history—that the cross as a symbol of suffering joined spiritual to temporal power and was as militant as the crescent—is not in dispute.) Is there here a residual trace, after all, of Christian ideology? I don't mean just personally, in Vattimo, but in a general principle basic to multiculturalism as it tries to respond to every manifestation of human difference. Perhaps we are in the presence of a post-Christian doctrine of charity.[14]

◻ ◻ ◻

I want to focus now on the struggle between the "weak thought" of postmodernist discourse and the assertive rhetoric of fundamentalism. It is a mistake to erect these alternatives into sheer opposites. The "darkness" of fundamentalism is often supported by a claim that Scripture has a univocal kind of transparency, and the "lightness" of postmodern thought, while promoting a maximum of political openness,[15] insists on the darkness (nontransparency) of texts.

Secular discourse, moreover, may carry within it an unacknowledged religious demand—so Nazism and Stalinism were, or degenerated into, political religions. The one task that may not be neglected today is a scrutiny of the persistence and recrudescence of religious politics—even as information technology and global systems of communication tempt us with the promise of world harmony. Religious politics designates here not only the rise of fundamentalism but also of a secular version that has been called *intégrisme* (best translated as "integralism" to distinguish it from the opposing, or liberal, ethos of "integration"). The word seems to have migrated from ideological battles within the Catholic church in Europe, which pitted "integralists" (supporting the Pope, the curia, and strict establishment policies) against "modernists."

There is no need to seek a single explanation for contemporary religious politics in some general formula, such as "a reaction to the complexities of modern life." But the question can be put why so few in Western democracies consider fundamentalism a serious solution to existential and political dilemmas. Not fundamentalism of a nationalist and often terrorist kind, as it has existed and still exists, but fundamentalism as a position capable of development: the dynamic, diverse revival of a religious intuition, of a sense of belonging that seeks adherence to a fixed order of things, a form of embodiment either this-worldly or other-worldly.

❐   ❐   ❐

To understand what spiritual alternatives there are to fundamentalist tendencies, rather than to reject them instinctively as the fool does the seductive figure of Death in Ingmar Bergman's *The Seventh Seal* (1957), I suggest we distinguish between sacred and religious. For precisely what we often name the Enlightenment includes the attempt to separate the sacred as such, and then to find a new political framework for it. Without defining the sacred—or sovereign—as more than an absolute point of orientation, whether based in natural or in divine law, I will assume that some such motive, whether we would like to evade it or not, continues to stir up tensions in the period concept of postmodernity when it is described as "the end of metaphysics" or a version of nihilism.

Periodization itself, unless it is purely heuristic and academic, is an Enlightenment move uncomfortably close to restoring sacred time: close to the B.C./A.D. caesura or to the renewal of the calendar during the French Revolution.[16] It reflects a messianic ideology that decrees endings and new beginnings. In a move against the fluidity of language and the endlessness of interpretation, or in an attempt to create a *saeculum*, even a millennium—a spacious temporality significantly larger than the span of individual existence—time's mathematical sublime is rejected. We seem always to be searching for a divide, a definitive break based on an "event of destiny." That divide is often seen as a crucial intervention, a stroke recalling us to an *exalted* sense of finitude, one that might lead out of abstractness into a new, potentially global, *religio loci*.

The separation of church and state in the United States Constitution, moreover, arguably the single most important political revision of modern times—while it limits the tyranny of particular cults and prevents the state from establishing itself as a political religion, has hardly weakened religious feelings as they search for embodiment in a sacred community. If car stickers are evidence, then together with Gallup's researches they suggest that "God loves you" is believed by many more Americans than by Europeans, who do not always enjoy the same degree of state/church separation. From John Smith, the founder of the Latter-Day Saints, to Elijah Muhammad of the Black

Muslims, there are more cults and epiphanies in the United States than in countries with fewer constitutional safeguards against the church. (Yet it boggles the mind if, as has been reported, there are a thousand cults in Vietnam devoted to Victor Hugo.) Those safeguards protect rather than limit the influence of religion, as all kinds of sects pursue their First Amendment rights.

If the American Revolution was, as Walter Lippmann claimed, the decisive expression of a secular philosophy, then the French Revolution, in its popular upsurge, came closer to *altering* religion: not denying the sacred or sovereign but giving it a fresh political form. The generalizations I want to venture are, first, that religion in modernity is often regarded as a corruption of the sacred, so that retrieving the sacred from its fall into religion—purging it of false mediations—becomes the principal form of *revolutionary romance;* then that the sacred is conflated with the revolutionary, because the latter has the structure of an interruption, a *tremendum*, although what is actually transmitted is always like a new religion; third, that this new religion as an ideal entity is not satisfied with the state apparatus established in the wake of the French Revolution and haunts to the verge of madness some of the greatest writers; and, last, that against modern scientific and technological modes of transparency, to which Vattimo alludes, the ritual part of religion, together with its accompaniment of myth and symbol, resists that transparency in a spectacular manner. One should add, of course, that poetry has always resisted it, or proposes, instead of an absolute demystification, "The immaculate disclosure of the secret no more obscured."[17]

❏   ❏   ❏

Let me take up, in quick succession, and suggestively rather than systematically, William Blake and Gerard de Nerval, and add some remarks on Walter Benjamin. My purpose will be to show not only how they seek to value the sacred in distinction from the religious but also how close the modern mind is in this respect to the postmodern—even if the latter seems to have abandoned the attempt to save, like Vattimo's hermeneutics, the gravamen of critical discourse in a multicultural, media-mediated world, where no one form of discourse has a special legitimacy.

Blake, in the decades following the French Revolution, elaborates in quasi-scriptural poetry (his "Bible of Hell" or Prophetic Books) a genealogy of priestly religion that demystifies it and anticipates Anselm Feuerbach's critique. Priestly religion, according to Blake, originated in powers that used to belong to mankind. The powers of Adam Kadmon (Primal Man) are at once alienated and reified by astonishment at, then recoil from, the faculty of imagination. Established religion, for Blake, is the misprision of our imaginative powers, the exploitation and institutionalization of human fears about them. Mankind, a self-bound Prometheus, exudes the "net of religion" from the guts of his own imagination and, taking the gods literally, worshiping these invented giants, becomes entangled in the net. (The following passage, which is Plate 10 of Blake's *Marriage of Heaven and Hell*, uses the word "realize" where we say "reify.")

The ancient Poets animated all sensible objects with Gods or Geniuses, calling them by their names and adorning them with the properties of woods, rivers, mountains, lakes cities, nations, and whatever their enlarged & numerous senses could percieve [*sic*].
And particularly they studied the genius of each city & country placing it under its mental deity.
Till a system was formed, which some took advantage of & enslaved the vulgar by attempting to realize or abstract the mental deities from their objects; thus began Priesthood.
Choosing forms of worship from poetic tales.
And at length they pronounced that the Gods had ordered such things.
Thus men forgot that All deities reside in the human breast.[18]

A reversal of primal error, however, is not to be achieved by intellectual process alone, by exposing a false consciousness and so recovering an occulted truth. For, as Blake's overflowing and self-revising epics make clear, the historical consequences of this retreat from imagination—interpreted as the Fall of Man from divine plenitude into his present diminished shape, and depicted obsessively as a series of recessionary transformations—can be undone only through a liberation of imagination by imagination. The poetic genius is primary, is humankind itself; Blake insists that priest must become poet again, that a poetry must be found to cleanse the doors of perception and recover a pure deposit of the sacred.

The gods or any strong figuration, therefore, cannot be given up and dismissed in the Enlightenment manner as an error of the Dark Ages. To recover the sacred requires mental fight, an exertion of the most extraordinary kind. It separates us from customary conceptions of body and mind and induces, because of that, the same terror and recoil that caused the original fall, an event interpreted by Blake as mankind's astonishment at its own imaginative powers, followed by a mutilating self-diminishment of the "human form divine" or a panic-stricken withdrawal from vision into the uniformities of nature. Thus Blake's *Vala*, a sequence of nine books called Nine Nights, describes an imagination caught in the nightmare of history and laboring toward dawn. This dawn, when it comes, will have purged a gigantic pile of superstitions in religion and politics that must burn up before we can waken from history. A brilliantly inventive poetry depicts those mystifications as the very fuel that, in burning up, energizes Blake's verse and serves to provide the *son et lumière* leading toward a new day.

There is a further subversive aspect to Blake's revisionary separation of sacred and religious. Although his final emphasis remains on the unity of Adam Kadmon, whom he renames Albion (a grand, spirit-of-place name for England), the imagination in its original, unrepressed state resembles the polytheism of the ancients and sets itself against the censorious monotheism of Christian and Jewish traditions. Recent scholarship has questioned the assumption that ethical monotheism is a spiritual advance over what Jan Assmann calls cosmotheism.[19] Blake's poetic theology is at least imaginatively polytheistic in its multiplication of gigantic or godlike powers—even if it claims to restore and liberate Christianity—and it views all religions as derivations or "different receptions of the Poetic Genius ["the true Man"] which is everywhere call'd the Spirit of Prophecy."[20]

Consider next Gerard de Nerval's *Chimères* (a title that can be translated as either "Nightmares" or "Delusions"). Mainly a sonnet sequence dating from toward the middle of the nineteenth century, the *Chimères* syncretize, in a faithless age, classical and Christian hopes: "Ils reviennent les dieux que tu pleures toujours" (They will return, the gods for whom you weep so constantly). The nostalgia suffusing these poems is common in post-Romanticism, while their resonance helped to found the symbolist movement in art: T. S. Eliot's *The Waste Land* incorporates a line from *Chimères* that represents the conquest of loss, or dispossession as a possession ("Le Prince d'Acquitaine à la tour abolie"). A hint of the heraldic and heroic persists within an inconsolable sense of eclipse.[21]

Nerval's "They will return, the gods for whom you weep . . ." is addressed to a young woman met by chance in Italy, whom the poet sees as a priestess from Apollo's shrine living in the pagan diaspora. Every spot in Italy appears to Nerval's visionary tourism as a potential shrine of Aollo's, a Delfica. It demands a "Know thyself," or a transfiguration of person and place: so the weeping girl is not a weeping girl but, unbeknownst to herself, a mourner for the death of the gods.

Something of that pattern also haunts Wilhelm Jensen's novel *Gradiva*, a "Pompeian fantasy" analyzed by Freud in *Delusion and Dream* (1907). Jensen's protagonist undertakes a journey from North to South that repeats, although with an ironic outcome, Nerval's search for a total, deep, and passionate myth—a myth of destiny that would merge what Vattimo names "historicality" (or even accidentality) and "belonging." A girl glimpsed among the ruins of Pompeii, who is taken to be a classical goddess, a sort of spirit of that place, turns out to be the deluded seeker's home-town neighbor whose image he had totally repressed during his studies of antiquity.

Nerval's delusional and curiously gallant quest for a reawakening of the sacred is not the ordinary neoclassical masquerade pretending that the names of the gods can still be evoked; it is *theurgy* underwritten by orphic tradition; and it makes us aware of a bereavement. There is a distance, beyond redemption but not beyond the memory of art, that separates both girl and poet from their divine archetypes. "It is precisely modernity," Walter Benjamin remarked about Nerval's contemporary, Baudelaire, "that is always quoting primeval history."[22] And Thomas Mann, in a famous essay "Freud and the Future" (1936), proposed that psychoanalysis took its model of psychic fatality from ancient pagan religion in which royal actors shaped their career as an *imitatio dei*, and died by merging with a divine archetype.[23] Cleopatra holding an asp to her breast mimics the Egyptian Isis. The reemergence of a sacred drama of this kind in his own life also entraps Nerval.

To seek a personal encounter or unmediated experience of the sacred suggests, as Blake once confessed, that one has become "mad as a refuge from unbelief."[24] Unable to forgo the ancient symbols, Blake, Hölderlin, Nerval, then Nietzsche, among others, embark on their private crucifixion.

◻   ◻   ◻

Thus what we have come to call the religion of art, and, more recently still, aesthetic ideology, has little to do with religion and almost everything with the sacred. The sacred emerges from its fall into religion, and there are many anticlerical attempts to find new frameworks for it—to build it a shrine, as Keats in a famous ode wishes to do for Psyche, invoked as a belated Olympian god. In nineteenth-century France, a veritable army of intellectuals—Frank Manuel dubs Saint-Simon, Fourier, and Comte the "Prophets of Paris"—seek to create new religions of "reason" or "humanity." They want to substitute culture for cult, rational enchantment for mystery, and technology in the service of social improvement for nature's realm of terror and unfreedom. It will need Benjamin's understanding of technology to give a near-fatal blow to the idea that progress can be achieved in this form or that the sacred is transmitted by art in a purer form than by religion.

Benjamin realized that art was itself at risk because of technology. In an era of mechanical reproduction, of printing and photography that enable translation from place to place and culture to culture, the sacred is vulgarized and loses its "aura." Benjamin meant by aura the prestige and testimonial power that come from originating in a particular time and place, from the concrete mystery—rather than arbitrariness—of that localization. "The here and now of the original constitutes the concept of its authenticity [*Echtheit*]. . . . The entire realm of the authentic withdraws from that of mechanical (and of course not only mechanical) reproduction. . . . The authenticity of thing or fact [*Sache*] is the exemplary aspect [*Inbegriff*] of all its qualities from its origin to its material persistence and historical testimony."[25] Bibles have this prestige, and so do classical works to which we attribute something close to real presence: They embody the sacred as spirit of place. It is the sacred within a religion that remains stubbornly literal, insisting on point of origin, on

Moriah or Mecca, on a shepherd or the child of a carpenter; while the liturgical and collective memory too canonizes certain realistic details. The sacred is counterconceptual to "transparency."

Whether revolutionary romance on the European model has any bearing on Islam or developments in the Middle East is a question I am not competent to explore.[26] In Europe, it seems to me, if modernism is defined as the attempt to discover an authentic political form of the sacred, modernism is certainly waning. Has the revolutionary romance played itself out in Europe? Is it only beginning in the Muslim world? In Europe, efforts to romance a New Order, which would meld a sacred embodiment of authority and technological economism have failed, despite an aestheticizing of technology (and even war) first promulgated by the Futurists and living on, even now, in science fiction and computer games.

For both Benjamin and Heidegger, technique itself, so purifying and exhilarating for modernist art, has been tainted by technology. Technique was once viewed as a mode of discovery and repristination; it helped to expose the "bourgeois" or "metaphysical" myth of depth and countered the ideology of *Innerlichkeit* and any such pseudo mystical way of writing. It seemed to promise a stylistic purification as powerful as that of an outmoded classicism. Carl Schmitt, a legal and political philosopher who supported the Nazi regime, also understood the limitation of the utopian view of technique. He charged that it fostered the illusion of a spiritually and politically neutral sphere. To believe in the possibility of moral through material progress, and of a significant increase in mutual understanding between nations on the basis of technological advances, was merely wishful.[27]

The realization has now sunk in how murderous and amoral technique can become. It proves to be more than a servomechanism or scaffolding. The machine mentality penetrates eyes and ears, invades entire spheres of feeling and cognition. Worse, it can lend itself to any purpose and elide all questions except that of efficiency. *Hier ist kein Warum*, "Here there is no Why," was the brutal warning of a guard to Primo Levi in Auschwitz. Methodically killing off the Why, the possibility of questioning or dialogue, was basic to the concentration camp universe that spread spiritual as well as physical death and stripped inmates of every vestige of personal autonomy.

Because of that repression, we are now forever stuck with the Why as well as with a suspicious linkage of technique and inhumanity. A writer like Kafka may have anticipated our dilemma and depicted it in hallucinatory form: the unabated presence of routinized, often bureaucratic, violence, and the absence of any answering mode of justification. The Why disappears—or becomes an impotent cry, banished to the private realm. Art still represents that cry, brings it to the ears of the public, however distorted or stifled it is. *Hier ist kein Warum* is the premise of Kafka's, then of Beckett's world—an estranged world, irreconcilable with ours, and yet our world too.

In Jean-Luc Godard's film *Alphaville* (1965), with its icy, tranquilized, sci-fi heterocosm, its Orwellian nightmare of total planification, semantics is perverted into a science that freezes the meaning of words, so that they become univocal and controllable entities. People as well as words disappear if they do not adapt. Death, not poetry, infiltrates conversation, and such forbidden vocables as "why" and "conscience" become the faintest of memories. Against this danger, Edmond Jabès's *Book of Questions* evokes, like Godard's film, a return of the repressed. A multivocal Why develops, a questioning with ethical as well as skeptical force. But it remains a precarious development, since questioning, to be forceful, must be more than rhetorical, more than deferring a known answer or inciting an obscurantist "Here there is nothing but Why." Heidegger's effort to retrieve a revelatory mode of questioning—that makes the object of inquiry, including the object-language, emerge as worthy of being questioned, and even the source of the call that questions the questioner—is a fascinating if bedeviled response to this issue.

It will come as no surprise that I end with a question. What constitutes the critical mode par excellence, for which we are still seeking a style, one expressive enough to rival the passion and conviction of messianic, or fundamentalist, or technological dreamers?

PART IV

CHAPTER 10

WHO NEEDS GOETHE?

Eulogy is often more dangerous to artistic reputation than invective or studied indifference. This made Walter Benjamin say on the centenary of Goethe's death: "Every word about Goethe spared us this year is a blessing."[1] It certainly is uncomfortable to read the sincere suggestions of a great historian, Friedrich Meinecke, after the Nazi catastrophe:

> In every German city and large village . . . we should welcome in the future a community of like-minded friends of culture, best called Goethe communities. To the Goethe communities would fall the task of conveying into the heart of listeners through sound [i.e., oral delivery] the most vital evidences of the great German spirit, always offering the noblest music and poetry together. . . . Besides poems, anthologies of German prose must also be read in these festive hours. There might be a *Handbook for Goethe Communities* guiding readers to the right kind of prose.[2]

"As if a Goethe-Youth movement could make us forget the Hitler-Youth," to quote from philosopher Peter Sloterdijk's recent broadside. Targeting what he describes as a failed humanism, but which Meinecke praised as the liberal classicism exemplified by Goethe, Sloterdijk continues: "This despairing neohumanism, looking back to Rome through Weimar, was the dream of the salvation of the European soul through a radicalized bibliophilia."[3]

While it is easy to mock Meinecke's idea—he himself calls it wishful—of communal study cells that would renew and purify, through Goethe, the spiritual strength of a devastated country, at least there is no scapegoating mentality toward the German cultural heritage, as if it had been responsible for, rather than itself the victim of, the catastrophe. Meinecke's visionary scheme is a way of asking: Goethe, do we need you at this hour?

❑   ❑   ❑

As a twentieth-century leftover, I have my anxieties. They center primarily on the progress of insensibility, or future *nonshock*. Much has been made, partly through Benjamin, of the obverse: how the physical as well as culture shock of the great city, the industrial metropolis, began to affect our sense of the world; and how the wastage of life in the trench warfare of the Great War and the literal shellshock that played an important role in Freud's thinking affected Europe between the wars. The horror of civilian suffering, too, that penetrated public awareness with Germany's invasion of Belgium in 1914 has increased immeasurably because of the Holocaust and later genocides—and because of atrocities brought into the home visually, daily, unavoidably, by the mass media.

Given these realities, I understand why Goethe and Wordsworth still appeal. Toward the beginning of an era recognizably ours, both maintain an enviable faith in art as an antidote to the growth of insensibility. The Enlightenment did not shake their trust that thought and feeling could be mutually reinforcing. The dissociation of thought from feeling, while always a danger, was not a historical fatality threatening their work. So Wordsworth explicitly links "Poetry and Geometric Truth," praising in the fifth book of his verse autobiography *The Prelude* "their high privilege of lasting life,/From all internal injury exempt."

By "internal injury" he meant that geometry (which stands for mathematic logic) is exempt from contradiction; but can that claim hold for poetry? Contemporary literary theories in their very diversity agree only on one thing: that literary language is marked by a tough kind of tonal or structural tension, variously named irony, paradox, ambiguity, multivocality, dramatic or dialogic patterning, and so on. Wordsworth's juxtaposition does not make sense unless "poetry" is shorthand for the ideal result of individual maturation. Instead of "internal injury," then, we could say "trauma." For trauma's integration, never complete yet holding the promise of furthering rather than blocking personal growth, is indeed the subject of *The Prelude*. How did the poet survive a complex series of political shocks during the French Revolution?

The greater part of Wordsworth's autobiography is actually about infantile rather than adult trauma. His childhood wounds have to be inferred, however, since he barely records the early loss of parents except by noting the indelible mark that certain scenes from rural nature left on his mind. Wordsworth as a boy is haunted by an unknown agency; he wakes to the "incumbent mystery of sense and soul"; he comes to believe that his sensuous, ecstatic, but also lonely and terrifying feelings single him out. Identity here involves not only learning about the power of imagination—imagination working through a natural scenery that inspires terror as well as pleasure—but also discovering a destined vocation. Genius is linked to *genius loci:* The poet is called by the spirit of place to perpetuate it. He fears the waning of that binding local influence not only in itself but also as a symptom of a future diminution of mankind's sensitivity to rural nature.

Wordsworth's premonition, then, to which his poetry will be dedicated, is that rural nature and the ethos it fosters can no longer be taken for granted. An industrialized society's intensified warfare, massively crowded cities, an escalating demand for new sensations, the proliferation of journalism and "frantic novels"—all these are alienating imagination from its earthly habitat more thoroughly and perniciously than otherworldly religions had done. In response the poet proclaims a new, antiapocalyptic ecology, a "wedding" of earth and mind. On the threshold of what I venture to call the 1800 millennium, he devotes himself to that ecological vision in a prothalamic poetry, a "spousal verse."

A virtuous rural compact is also evoked by Goethe's verse epic *Hermann und Dorothea* (1797). Harmonizing mind and nature, that compact is in good part an imaginary construct. But taken as literal fact, as a vanished utopia, it exerts a virulent influence. By the end of the nineteenth century, it will conjure up a lost organic community, a pastoral patria or political arcadia destroyed by industrialization, urban overdevelopment, and the economic ravages of early capitalism. Yet neither Goethe nor Wordsworth is a naive ideologist. They are diagnostic visionaries.

❑   ❑   ❑

The task that fell to Goethe in the literary history of his country differs from Wordsworth's. The English poet can look back on a glorious literary heritage, that of the Renaissance in England. True, that moment of vernacular potency was attenuated, in Wordsworth's opinion and that of the other Romantics (with the exception of Byron and Landor), by a neoclassical poetics of refinement still dominant in his younger days. But enough rough power remained, even in that master refiner Alexander Pope, to give Wordsworth his traction, and so he goes beyond pruning and taming Spenser, Milton, and Shakespeare, their extraordinary fertility. He produces, in fact, a second harvest by a remarkable modernization. In Goethe's literary past there was no German Renaissance—indeed, strictly speaking, no German nation either. Goethe starts without the burden of the past but also without its embarrassment of riches. He had to create a first, not a second, Renaissance from shadowy Nordic remnants and a Frenchified neoclassicism.

Wordsworth's understanding of poetic development emphasizes the influence of nature rather than art. He claims to have been tutored by nature's indwelling spirit and therefore minimizes book learning. But Goethe, lacking a strong, indigenous literary heritage, had to apprentice himself to nonnative traditions, both ancient and modern: His mission was to appropriate and transform them (the German expressions are "aneignen" or "zueignen") through an adventurous program of self-education. "We should have written and made our own," writes Novalis, alluding to Goethe's novel, *Wilhelm Meister's Apprentice Years* [*Lehrjahre*], "as many *Lehrjahre* as possible, the *Lehrjahre* of everyone who has ever lived."[4] He recognizes in Goethe a belated Renaissancer who enriches his country's literature—and so its sense of identity—by a belated *translatio studii* (a transmission of humanistic and scientific learning from one culture to another) based on both classical studies and a cosmopolitan's knowledge of world literature.

Goethe's enrichment of his native tongue, therefore, his panoramic cultivation of literary forms, is as varied as the chaotic and colorful life that threatens to breach as well as invigorate the morals and manners (*Sittlichkeit*) of a civil society that has only began to take shape. This society, gradually identified with Weimar, prefigures the possibility of Germany becoming a "Kulturnation," a nation unified by culture rather than territory. Playing catch-up with England and France as well as the Italy he loved ("Wir Deutschen sind von gestern," We Germans were born yesterday), Goethe fashions as his alter ego the character of Faust, a would-be magus who seeks to call up life through learning. The Faustian artist in Germany, to fulfill his creative role, had to become a magician, had to find a way of resurrecting classical and medieval literary hauntings, to take them out of the study and give them an alive, contemporary existence. This was a progressive rather than a nostalgic move, meant to stimulate a "gesittete weltliche Gesellschaft" (a well-mannered, worldly society).[5]

While the figure of Faust, the "hochgelahrte" Doctor, is mocked—as we still mock pedantic or abstruse academics—such healthy fun never obscures a fundamental pathos. The "two souls" competing in Faust reflect Goethe's own artistic striving ("Streben") or his wish to develop fully ("Werdelust"). He cannot easily reconcile learning (the decorum of traditional devices) and life (a more passionate, intimate, vernacular relation to them). The forms stand in the way yet the forms are vitally necessary. They are needed not just as vessels to catch an always-evanescent experience or the nuances of a psyche engaged in a perpetual bildungsroman; for Goethe they are *socially* indispensable.

❒   ❒   ❒

The prefatory stanzas to *Faust* entitled "Zueignung" (dedication) portray Goethe's dilemma from the perspective of a writer looking at his own, as well as Germany's, literary past. I suspect that by this time (composed ca. 1797, these verses were not published until 1808, with Goethe approaching sixty), the two biographies, national and personal, are identified in the poet's mind. Remarkably, he intimates his alienation from the play he is about to publish, a play that itself depicts an alienation. Faust bets against his eudemonic desire to possess or dwell with beauty: His opening monologue is a suicidal cry of desire and despair that he cannot achieve a *participation mystique*. Truth and beauty in their immediacy are passing him by. The author's "Zueignung" is therefore an attempted self-dedication, for he already feels at a distance from the drama he is now—finally—giving to the public as a mature rather than fragmentary work.

The microdrama, then, of this prefatory poem deals with the author's changed relation to his own personae dramatis, the floating, unstable figures ("schwankende Gestalten") that rise up before him. He reluctantly acknowledges their magical aura ("Zauberhauch") that brings back youthful emotions ("Mein Busen fühlt sich jugendlich erschüttert"). His creations ("Gestalten") crowd him: They seem to be as jealous of the living writer as ghosts in the underworld swarming around Odysseus or Aeneas ("Ihr drängt euch zu!"). But he hesitates to utter the fateful words, the "Verweile doch" that would ask them to stay awhile ("Versuch ich wohl, euch diesmal festzuhalten?"). He knows too well by now what Ottilie's diary records in *Elective Affinities:* "A person can least appropriate [*zueignen*] that which belongs most uniquely to him."[6] He is caught between "Zueignung" and "Enteignung," between possession and dispossession.

Goethe stops short of suggesting that "Enteignung" might lead to failure of his larger cultural project. (The modern word "project" is deceptive here; it overstates the control of the artist-creator over his intention.) He deepens our sense of his unease by emphasizing that the figures from his play revive other shadows ("manche liebe Schatten," stanza 2), memories of earliest friends and loves. These also renew his pain, for the companions of his youth have died or scattered and are likewise phantoms.

So far, Goethe's elegy is affecting, if sentimental. The two stanzas that follow, however, are remarkable in thought and feeling. The loss of friends and first love-likings evokes a more peculiar, sharper regret: The poet misses his closely knit social circle. In Goethe's own words: "Zerstoben ist das freundliche Gedränge,/Verklungen, ach! Der erste Wiederklang" (Scattered is that crowd of friends/A faded echo their responsive enthusiasm). His friends have turned into figures of, not only in, his mind: This ghosting is suggested by the word "Verklungen," which itself echoes a verse in stanza 2: "Gleich einer alten, halb-verklungene Sage" (Like an ancient legend whose reverberation has faded half away).[7]

Even more striking than Goethe's mental confusion is an avowal that he fears rather than welcomes the applause of a larger, unfamiliar audience. We recognize quite clearly here the social framework neces-sary to his imagination. Without giving up the greater world, it prefers to work within a small circle, a global village before the letter.

The poem's final stanza verges on the mysterious. What identity should we give the still and solemn "realm of spirits" ("Geisterreich") he longs for again, after having weaned himself from feelings of this kind? The vacillating forms ("schwankende Gestalten") of the first stanza, the dear shades ("liebe Schatten") of the second, seem to merge with this ghostly realm. The stanza goes beyond elegy and sen-timentality. A death wish comes to Goethe, or a reminiscence of the state of mind in which he composed his most notorious novel. Are these the "Sorrows of an Aging Werther?"

Goethe's yearning seems to be less for the gothic chimeras or lively witchery ("Hexenwesen") that dominated *Faust: A Fragment* (1790) than for a "stille Grösse," a tranquil greatness associated with the later figure of Helena and Winckelmann's classicism generally. One is reminded of a further remark in Ottilie's diary: "The Ancients entertained a serious and awe-inspiring fantasy. They imagined their ancestors sitting in huge caves, on thrones, all in a ring, conversing mutely with one another. When someone new entered, and he was considered worthy, they would stand up and gesture their welcome."[8] At the horizon of this "Zueignung" is a forbidding as well as intimate circle, that of the noble dead.

Goethe is not so old, however, that he forgets to end with a *pointe*. Loss, nostalgia, and thoughts of death do not shake his sense of deco-rum, his feeling for the formality of poetry. "What I possess, I see as from a distance,/And what has vanished becomes reality."

◻ ◻ ◻

Despite the recrudescence of cultural prophecy in the century just past, we are in a mist that is thickening rather than lifting. The Romantics glimpsed the darkness to come, yet a principle of hope prevailed, perhaps from the fact that, unlike Goethe's fisherman enticed by a mermaid, "Halb zog sie ihn, halb sinkt er hin" (Half she drew him to her, half he lets himself sink down),[9] they did not sympathize with a dionysian or destructive element, except at moments that also played out their resistance to it.

What those writers foresaw, often carried along by the excitement—and betrayals—of the French Revolution, and aware of the gathering storm clouds of a soon-rampant Industrial Revolution, is difficult to respond to at present without the complicity of extreme scenarios. Kenneth Burke talks of Coleridge's "Ancient Mariner" as the author's redemption of his drug. Is that what is going on in the agitated art that has taken over today's literature, movies, and popular music? Rarely, I think. Too many works of fiction return to the vomit of violence for a word like redemption to be valid. Ecstatic fantasies remain the drug as surely as drugs are often what enable such fantasies. When there is nothing to deviate from, when no taboo has a restraining force and no extravagance of style can make an impact that is not immediately absorbed, then Hegel's prophecy of the end of art will have come about, and in a paroxysmic rather than philosophic act of transcendence.

In short, to represent trespass and shock has become nearly impossible. There used to be the expectation that a shift in sensibility—a sensuous expansion or liberation, even approaching Rimbaud's "disorganization of all the senses"[10]—might undo older divisions and dichotomies, such as faith and reason, life and learning, science and art. But serious play toward that end has now been replaced by a spectacular emphasis on technique. Realism itself is no longer a vision to be achieved but something to be trumped by each competitively violent representation. In such a climate Goethe's novels could be an antidote.

❏   ❏   ❏

Typecasting his characters and delimiting the milieu of their action allows Goethe as *moraliste* full play, without losing control to technique. He invents convincingly diverse sensibilities and gives each character enough time to register the pain of unexpected vacillations. He is adept at psychological portraiture, especially in depicting a search for inner freedom in the face of the demands and temptations of the social world. I say this even though it is hard to relish, in *Elective Affinities*, the time spent on exterior decorating, on the genteel effort to cultivate one's garden in retirement. I am not an enthusiastic gardener, I don't have a baronial estate, and I am not subject to quasi-religious forms of social withdrawal.

Yet at times Goethe resembles Kleist. Compare, for example, the *Marquise of O* and the "Confessions of a Pietistic [literally, Beautiful] Soul" (the sixth book of *Wilhelm Meister's Apprentice Years*). Each work has a feminine protest for its subject, and in both the behavior of the woman protagonist remains mysterious. But Kleist's novella takes place in a far more violent setting, and the newspaper notice that asks, in effect, for the demon lover to come forward and marry the marquise is extraordinary and audacious. With Kleist, moreover, a hysterical pace, like that of the fastest ballad, rarely lets up; we are in the sphere less of irreconcilable inner conflict than of trauma's "Würfe und Sprünge" (leaps and bounds). Goethe's portrait of a lady, in contrast, although also disclosing human willfulness or a demonic and self-isolating—perhaps self-punishing—impulsiveness, is steadied by the author's equitable narrative rhythm. All emphatic pathos is distanced into a muted cry for transcendence.

This cry also characterizes Mignon and Ottilie, the most mysterious of Goethe's women. Ottilie's "Letter to my Friends" in *Elective Affinities* parallels Mignon's song addressed to an unnamed friend in *Wilhelm Meister:* "Tell me not to speak, tell me to be silent,/For I am bound to my secret as to a duty" (Heiß mich nicht reden, heiß mich schweigen/Denn mein Geheimnis ist mir Pflicht). In Goethe everywhere there is a resistance to the promiscuous word and a respect for what he calls "Nature's open secret." No force, no haste, can pry what is open open. This is the irony that helps his knowledgeable narratives to escape condescension. At the same time, he relishes his role as national preceptor who transmits every last scrap of personal wisdom and dispenses hope in a providential pregnancy, a "gute Hoffnung" that all human erring will prove redemptive in the end.

Not that Goethe's morality is simplistic. But he seeks, I believe, ideal readers or correspondents as fervently as does the pietistic soul.

Striving to attain the inner beauty of authenticity, it looks for a companionate relation to "the invisible and only faithful friend." God for that soul is the figure of a social absence that no one seems able to fill. It is Goethe's deepest intuition that this very absence motivates a creative restlessness, an intellectual love (in Spinoza's sense) that embraces nature, science, and art.

At some point, however, Goethe's quest for a *larger correspondence*—that is, for culture—comes up against the community-building claims of religion or state. It is no accident, then, that he explores the paradoxes of "Schweigen," of elective silence. "Schweigen" shelters personal autonomy under the cover, usually, of intense piety. The community based on this personal and secret "friend" is bound to compete with another virtual community characterized by worldliness and high culture. The poet remains unsure, therefore, about Germany's reception of his legacy, unsure of its national "Zueignung." Is there not, besides the philistinism we so often find arrayed against art, an unresolvable conflict between religion and culture: between, on the one hand, the journey of the individual soul to God, impelled, as in the case of the "schöne Seele," by the constricting, soft-core atmosphere of Pietistic asceticism, and, on the other, by counselor Goethe's imperative of cultural expansion and societal refinement?

In light of that question, Goethe's distaste for Kleist may actually betray an affinity. The breach of decorum Kleist's marquise commits could signify a deeply antisocial act—*or* still be in pursuit of social convention. In terms, also, of the representation of pain, an important aesthetic issue in the wake of Lessing's *Laocoon*, Goethe, while maintaining a classical stance, finds a "silent" method of depicting trauma that can rival Kleist's. If Goethe's narrator, in *Elective Affinities*, refuses to describe Ottilie's suffering after Eduard leaves his estate—"We do not dare to depict her pain, her tears, she suffered immensely"[11]—it is necessary, while admiring or regretting such discretion, to consider the later, astonishing scene when Ottilie goes, in a few moments, from happiness to absolute despair.

The scene depicts the drowning, while in Ottilie's care, of Eduard and Charlotte's child. The drowning is recorded with a rapidity that disrupts the novel's normal epic rhythm: its delay of denouements, its leisurely deception of the reader, who is often totally enticed by Goethe's moral and descriptive intelligence that constructs what seems like an episodic story with no more of a plan than nature's own. But suddenly ancient myth, minus the anthropomorphism of Water-Sprite ("Nixe") or Waterman ("Wassermann"), invades the plot and threatens our notion of a tamed natural environment. The accident that destroys Ottilie's possibility for happiness—she and Eduard have fallen in love—suggests a fatal plan after all, one that mocks everything the novel had insinuated up to this point, especially the values of "Besitz" (emotional as well as material possession) and "Geschick" (both skill and a bourgeois version of fate, "Schicksal"). "Ottilie," writes Goethe, after she is unsuccessful in saving the child, "separated from everything, floats adrift on the unfaithful, inhospitable element."

Ottilie's complicity in the drowning is unthinkable yet the scene comes on with a speed that reflects imagination's tempo. Surely the operation of an unconscious or secretive desire is evoked, as it is in Kleist. We recall that Goethe had represented the child as illegitimate in a spiritual, albeit not a legal sense. By an uncanny effect of mental adultery its face reflects not its biological father, Charlotte's husband, but the couple's close friend, the Captain. Ottilie, then, because of her symmetrically adulterous situation with Eduard, is now unable to escape a devastating guilt. More exactly, she cannot escape the feeling that a supernatural order working through nature has punished her love of Eduard. The coma in which Kleist's marquise presumably conceived a child parallels, moreover, the comatose sleep into which Ottilie sinks after the death of that other child: It shields her from mental agony while allowing her to overhear everything. Doesn't this sleep resemble the state of mind, at once conscious and unconscious, that enables great writers like Kleist and Goethe to write?

❏   ❏   ❏

The therapeutic action of art, on its creator, on readers, on society itself, is not usually discussed when Goethe is the topic. Yet the more Goethe's artistry is in control, the more aware we are of a contrary, less conscious factor that leads him, by immersion in the messiness of human emotions, beyond equanimity. It is clear, at the same time, that he retained a trust that language can heal as well as wound, and that he depicts what we have learned to recognize as unconscious forces.

The relation of words, on the one hand to natural fact, as in scientific discourse, and, on the other, to human intentions, is already illustrated in a chapter of *Elective Affinities* that lends the novel its title. The conversation about analogies ("Gleichnisreden") found there uses the example of chemical reactions between substances to suggest negative or positive yokings in the interpersonal sphere. At this early point in the plot, the conversation among Charlotte, Eduard, and the Captain remains a high-spirited banter close to a parlor game. Charlotte objects to a metaphorical transfer to the human and social sphere operated by the phrase "Wahlverwandschaften," because the analogy taken from the mechanical operation of nature excludes choice and human freedom. Yet Eduard suspects that Charlotte's intellectual point is an observation directed at him. While not explicitly taking sides through an authorial comment, Goethe does take sides in the way his novel unfolds structurally. His design makes it clear that nothing, even in a casual conversation, is ultimately without intention; while the action of nature, in contrast, however mechanical it may seem to be, draws the human mind beyond conscious intention ("Absicht") toward a deeper principle of order. Thus natural phenomena, whether sublime or demonic, at once humble and exalt the mind. In the catastrophe of *Elective Affinities*, then, which is unexpected although foreshadowed by a gratuitously inserted story (that of the wonderful neighbor children), it is hard to tell whether Nature or novelist deceive the reader. "Nature and art," Goethe once declared, "are too great to aim at ends."

Goethe's interesting habit, moreover, of funneling the overflow of his intelligence into his novels by intruding wondrous stories, ballads, diary maxims, reflections—and, in the case of "Confessions of a Beautiful Soul" an entire autobiographical narrative—has something of an abrupt, accidental feeling to it, even if such interpolations end by strengthening the overall design. Enjoyable in themselves, and as conspicuously irrelevant as nature's overflow, these apparently episodic insertions contribute to that deceptive "epic" narrative rhythm I have mentioned. In a neglected book on Goethe, Benedetto Croce examines Goethe's contradictory technique, whereby the artist "by a reflective method has fashioned a *mechanism*, enclosing and even forcing into it several diverse *living organisms*" (my emphasis). This method is especially evident in the revisions that delayed *Faust* and, according to Croce, left the author feeling that he was "wandering in a 'labyrinth' from which he did not know if he would ever emerge, in spite of the thread handed to him by the 'idea.'"[12]

What this suggests is the coincidence of a maximum of artistic control with a subversion of it. As *Elective Affinities* moves toward an ending, the chance effect of words—how they wound unintentionally—reveals this principle. Words seem unable to escape intentionality, whether our sensitiveness to them comes from the person who speaks or the person who hears. The extraordinary story of the two neighbor children, as told by someone who thinks it cannot but amuse, and has no chance of hurting by coming close to any real-life circumstance, follows an episode in which another storyteller had wounded Ottilie inadvertently by a series of general reflections on his own life. "These confidences affected Ottilie in a terrible way: for a pleasant veil was torn away with force. . . ." That apparently unintentional hurt recurs and takes a tragic turn when Ottilie, near the novel's end, is literally killed by what she overhears. She enters the room at the very moment Mittler is denouncing the inept effect of the commandment "Thou shalt not commit adultery" on a child's imagination. Mittler, of course, is a meddler as well as a mediator, but his role in this particular tragedy is quite accidental and in no way a "demonic" or astonishing intervention.

I doubt Goethe ever settled within himself the issue of the therapeutic effect of words: when therapeutic, are they so *because* disinterested—able to raise us up, like the scientist's contemplation of nature or the craftsman's absorption in the "Geschick" of his material task, beyond guilt and innocence? The theme Goethe shared with Wordsworth, how internal injury or psychic trauma might be overcome, and how a poetic or scientific mode of thought might strengthen personal growth, has not lost its relevance at the present time.

But after World War II and the Shoah, the collapse of symbols, as Julia Kristeva calls it, is more radical than after the French Revolution or even World War I, and affects a German culture grown to maturity, in good part from Goethean foundations. That fact may also help to define Paul Celan's dilemma. Germany has now to face a culture-guilt rather than, as in Goethe's time, a lack of culture. Whether the culture of the West shares in that guilt, as certain postcolonial movements claim, or what revisions might overcome the symbolic collapse is an issue that motivates the anxious search motivating both trauma studies and cultural studies.

EPILOGUE

Only for the sake of those who have no hope is hope given us.

—*Walter Benjamin*, "*Goethes* Wahlverwandtschaften"

Imagine, now, that Goethe, from somewhere in the literary firmament, saw what happened between 1933 and 1945—the murderous assault of the Nazi regime on its Jewish citizens as well as others scorned as ethnically inferior, asocial, or unworthy to live, an assault justified in the name of culture, of a pure Aryan culture. I do not evoke this image because Goethe's temperament was Olympian but, on the contrary, because he understood the extremes of happiness and unhappiness in human nature, the danger of exaltation together with the fall from sublimity into a disenchantment that could lead to savage revenge or endless mourning. "Es fürchte die Götter/Das Menschengeschlecht" (Humankind had better fear the gods): Iphigenia's tribute to the Fates in *Iphigenia in Tauris* is but one of his warnings against identifying with "Herrscher," or mastery mania.

Perhaps you will object to my fantasy because whatever it was that Goethe intuited was exceeded by the enormity of the Holocaust to such an extent that he would have been unable to fathom it, or because the Goethean response, in a poem like Iphigenia's hymn to the Fates, can no longer go to the heart of the matter. Part of me agrees with that assessment. Goethe—who wrote "there are unbeautiful, terrifying things in nature, with which literature, however skillfully it may treat them, ought neither to concern nor to reconcile itself," and who, though recognizing Kleist's genius, was also repelled by it—may not be, if anyone can be, an adequate witness. But as we pass from generation to generation after the Shoah—and by now the third generation has come of age—it is impossible not to include the country from which the destruction came. As the ravage of genocide continues in other parts of the world, it is humanity, Robert Antelme's *l'espèce humaine*, we confront or evade. We should no longer attempt to foresee the lifting of despair only for the victims of the genocide and those of their immediate descendants still affected by its tragic consequences.

It is relatively easy to honor—I do not say understand—Paul Celan, but can the art of a Goethe still move us, can such art prevail despite the disaster? On reading him today, must we simply overlook what happened a hundred years after his death and enjoy his wisdom and virtuosity by limiting the historical context, blinkering the inspiration of a creator who was as important to German literature as Shakespeare was to English?

Even Shakespeare's standing is no longer entirely safe. But he does not come from the perpetrator nation and his plays have proven to be more adaptable to a contemporary world that has "supp'd full of horrors." Akhmatova still invokes him, thinking of Londoners during the Blitz: "Time is writing Shakespeare's twenty-fourth drama." But, she adds, "not this, not this, not this,/this even we aren't capable of reading."[13]

For those devoted to literature, it may be more important to justify art through Goethe. What terror or trauma he knew he rarely portrays directly with the visual force and super-realism of Shakespearean tragedy. Yet it is precisely because of his classical muting of catastrophe, the fact that he can evoke it as if from a distance (e.g., from the position of oral tradition or hearsay, "The ancient song comes to my ears once more," says Iphigenia) that my picture of Goethe in the firmament has relevance. *Iphigenia in Tauris* tries to break a spell of the Fates, the consequences of a fatal misdeed in one of the most horrendous stories ever told, that of Tantalus and his family feud.

Goethe's play exorcising the Furies is a gathering of classical themes handed down and as if heard from the distance of centuries. It is mostly recitation rather than dramatic action. Yet it may be as urgent in its moral focus as anything in Shakespeare. Moreover, for the Berlin audience that attended its revival in 1998, it benefited from a certain topicality, since hospitality to exiles and justice to foreigners are its central themes.

Was it only, though, my ears that responded to the pathos of Iphigenia's refusal to flee with her brother Orestes before the curse of human sacrifice was abolished in Tauris? I cannot vouch for the ears of the audience around me, but I know I thought of the curse the Holocaust brought upon German, when I heard the following words Iphingenia utters:

> Soll dieser Fluch denn ewig walten? Soll
> Nie dies Geschlecht mit einem neuen Segen
> Sich wieder heben?

> (Must this curse then last for ever? Can
> this people never be restored
> by a new blessing?)

CHAPTER 11

THE VIRTUE OF ATTENTIVENESS

Ta forme veille, et mes yeux sont ouverts.
Your form is awake, and my eyes have opened.

— Paul Valéry, *"Sleeping Woman"*

T he problematic of attention, or attentiveness, is situated in a tense area between "looking for" and "waiting for." We are acquainted with this problematic from religion; but scientists, too, often remark on the lucky interplay between an intense period of research, involving the utmost exertion of senses and mind, and a discovery that comes about as if accidentally. No one can say whether patience or impatience is more effective here. A reason that suggests itself for the necessity of this fertile contrariety is that "looking for" tends to be obsessive and that we cannot always tell what motivates this drive. It has to purify or simplify itself, lest it turn into monomania or hypervigilance.

Whatever its psychic cause may be, most of us, on the way to becoming artists or scholars, have experienced a near-libidinous desire for knowledge. Valéry's refined odalisque of a sleeping woman suspends both desire and knowledge lust in a moment many might call "aesthetic." It runs counter to what often shows itself as a fascination with detail, antiquarian or positivistic. Like Nietzsche, we may rebel against this and other types of a wish for intimacy we never sublimate completely. If the novelist spies on us, we return the compliment. We feed on his diaries or intimate correspondence. Every facet, however trivial, of a life or a culture that has disappeared into the past becomes strangely gravid. In a restitutive era like ours, moreover, things that have dropped from sight, or were previously deemed unworthy, take on a special appeal. The very category of "news," basic to journalism, leads to frenetic and sometimes fictional retrievals.

Yet it is not necessarily an anxious or mysterious excitement that makes us attentive. There is also the sense of wishing by acts of attention to give something back, to acknowledge the visible as well as the not yet visible. The modern artist's depiction of the present, Baudelaire says, evidences "a Me greedily hungering for a not-Me."[1] But do we need to periodize this hunger for a world beyond the self by calling it modern? Gothic architecture and its cosmic statuary already reflected the plenitude of creation. They display the world in the all-encompassing light of a Last Judgment; while in the corners of the cathedral's ornamentation curious figures lurk, marginalia, as it were, products of nature's humorous variety or of the human artificer's horror of the void.

John Ruskin in nineteenth-century England is the exemplary artist-scientist, especially in his attention to the gothic as a mentality he wishes to revive. He lovingly sketches a tiny gnome, one of hundreds of figures in the bookseller's portal of Rouen Cathedral. He thereby rouses in Proust a wish to see this gargoyle-like person. Both writers spot a greatness in little things and perform a resurrection not incomparable to what is depicted more majestically elsewhere on the portal.

Michael Maar, in the contemporary period, deduces the right lesson for the literary critic.

> The grotesque little man of the bookseller's portal is a memento for every reader. It depends on the reader whether the cathedrals will become huge tombs or not. Everywhere in literary works these gnomes pullulate, unapparent marginal figures which wait not to be overlooked in the act of reading and to be forcefully rescued from their interim death. Art is nothing without such details. But these

details only live insofar as they are observed and their function is respected.[2]

What saves this lesson from the obvious ("the devil is in the details") is a distinctive pattern: Ruskin's empathic drawings in search of a lost significance, Proust's imitative tracking of Ruskin, finally the reader's *recherche* (a reading and rereading) of a profusion of minor as well as major figures. But repetition as a structure may dull rather than rouse attention, unless we understand it as an activity. Ruskin's sketches or other pictures are constructions that do not elide but enliven perception. Seeing as such is made remarkable. For Wittgenstein, philosophy, insofar as it sets objects and thoughts in motion, or makes them more "perspicuous," is equipment enhancing the convergence of logic and perceptibility.

Maar's frame of reference is interesting for its open quality, specifically its refusal to be hierarchic. The critic generalizes without forfeiting the instance. He argues that the wonder, or naïveté, of our first readings does not have to be destroyed by the deepening knowledge each second reading potentially achieves. Such further readings have no rules except one: not to underestimate the author, his surplus of thought ("das Mehrgedachte").

I would add to this the like-minded rule not to underestimate the reader. Watchful readings may exceed the author's intention—which remains, in any case, difficult to confirm. Such readings are not always subjective or selfish. The mind in the act of finding what will suffice wishes for byways as well as highways and need not end in the cul-de-sac of self-concern.

☐ ☐ ☐

Mind, in short, does not rest content with the single detail, figure, or insight: It suspects that something remains to be found, that something hides from sight, even in the obvious, the very thing that places itself in our way. As in certain detective stories, there are so many clues it is nearly impossible to distinguish the true from the false. Philosophically considered, this points to the fact that beings, in their diversity, can obscure being and incite mere schemes of classification instead of an authentic engagement.

Yet even the schematic can be productive: Think of the poetry enabled by Linnaeus, the great eighteenth-century botanist. Each creature becomes trinomial through his classification: Not only does it gain a Latin name for genus and species, but its vernacular equivalent is enhanced—in compensation for Linnaeus's scientific vocabulary. The butterfly collector treasures "le grand nègre des bois" or "le petit collier d'argent" almost as much as the thing to which they refer.

Another level of inventiveness is shown by Thomas Gray, the English poet, who interleaves his copy of Linnaeus's *Systema Naturae* (10th edition, 1759) with Latin verses elaborating its "Order of Insects," verses that express equal delight in nature's strange variety and the act of naming:

> Occiput Attelabi in posticum vergit acumen.
> Curculio ingenti protendit cornua rostro.
> Silpha leves peltae atque elytrorum exporrigit oras.
> Truncus apex clavae, atque antennula Coccionellae.
>
> (The occiput of the Attelabus comes to a sharp point at the back.
> The Curculio extends horns from a vast beak.
> The Silpha protrudes fine edges of a shield and sheaths.
> The Coccionella has a truncated top to its club and small antennae.)[3]

The unfamiliar, which stands out as such, is less of a challenge than the familiar, which must be estranged to reveal its uncanny aspect. Gray's Latin, its humorous and archaic elegance, has the effect of mock-heroic verse, enlarging and defamiliarizing the object.

❐   ❐   ❐

Thought, however purposive, is not thoughtful unless it remains in dialogue with itself and becomes a *dubito*: a "self-determined indetermination" in Coleridge's redescription of Descartes' *cogito*. Or, as Gaston Bachelard remarks in *La philosophie du non*: "Intuitions are very useful: they serve by dint of being destroyed."[4] The humanities too, it could be argued, not only the sciences, encourage, even while delimiting, this constructive negativity. Yet it is more difficult for them to justify achievements that often remain by-products: unbidden images or verses, conceptions that escape and even undermine the more rigorous *pensum* demanded by religion, science, or philosophy. Here to aim straight may be to miss the mark.

The flip side of this is that marginal inspirations are easily forgotten. We need fixed shapes to keep them vanishing from personal recollection. The arts as a whole constitute a nursery of forms that tolerates imaginings even in their grublike state, where they can mature to emerge some day as part of the collective (we now say cultural) memory.

Art's nursery of forms, then, is a reservoir. Or an archive that allows things to be at once saved and forgotten—forgotten through a benign neglect that permits more time for parturition, or because they seem useless for, removed from, society's purposes. Today oblivion is often a necessity, like an induced power failure, a blackout that saves the whole grid when our attention is overwhelmed. Looking-away-from may therefore become, paradoxically, a mode of looking-for, as when a name has gone and we distract ourselves in the hope it will suddenly reappear. In photography, and more decisively in its evolution as film, the issue of focus becomes all-important, and concentration cannot escape visual distraction. Just as the writing finger moves endlessly toward a narrative or metaphoric containment, so the pupil-like focus of film expands and contracts continually.

The modalities here are many, yet all continue to presuppose a moment of discovery, even of revelation. Light and the knowledge gathered in go out once more to dismay or dazzle. One of the most sustained verbal experiments in this area is Maurice Blanchot's novel—if it is a novel—with the title *L'Attente L'Oubli*.[5]

It is unclear, however, whether discovery as such is the aim of art. Discovery may serve a radical conversion, a turning-around of the mind. Aristotle asserts in the *Poetics* that the moment of discovery in drama ("anagnorisis") works best when accompanied by a reversal ("peripeteia"). But *L'Attente L'Oubli* goes against the grain of this conjuncture. The possibility that words enable us to communicate at a distance, and therefore that an endlessly frustrated desire for intimacy need not trigger a more violent mutation—a *folie à deux*, or a coerced solidarity—is the always-purveyed and deferred "revelation" of Blanchot's prose.

Another way of putting this is that his plotless narrative (he prefers to call it a *récit*, i.e., narrative, rather than *roman*) approaches, always asymptotically, Georges Bataille's ecstatic view of human communication. In the 1940s, Bataille founded an "atheological summa" on the basis of Nietzsche. Communication is deemed impossible by Bataille except where a mutual wounding occurs or is imagined. It is by their very "incompleteness, animal nudity, woundedness, [that] human beings, multiple and separate, *communicate*, and it is through their mutual *communication* that they become alive and lose themselves." About the orgiastic potential in Christianity, he writes graphically: "A night of death, where the Creator and the creatures bleed jointly and tear at each other, and altogether indict themselves—to the extreme point of shame—was necessary for their communion."[6]

□   □   □

As a heightened form of attention, vigilance is spurred by the absence of a presence whose numinous imprints (traces, vestiges, footsteps) remain. Thus the possibility of communication is never completely cut off. As in Baudelaire's famous sonnet, oases of "correspondences" point not only to a residual harmony between phenomena, a mysterious—Swedenborgian—system of analogies (Baudelaire's "forêt de symboles")[7] that watchers tap into emotionally or intellectually, but also to a higher form of communication, an imaginative memory accessible through poetry and dreamlike states. In Saint Paul's definition (Hebrews IX:1), faith is the substance (or assurance) of things hoped for, the evidence of things not seen.

So the fundamental figure here, the epistemic incarnation, is of a watcher in the night, where night can also be a profane, obscuring brightness. It is often impossible to tell whether the darkness to be penetrated, or the delayed dawn, is the effect of (1) a real eclipse, that is, God's radical withdrawal from the world, (2) a pedagogical hide-and-seek, enticing the lover of truth toward union with the absent object of desire, or (3) an obscurity coming from the nature of truth itself, too bright or hazardous for human eyes. "Dark with excessive bright thy skirts appear,"[8] is how Milton describes God's proximity in *Paradise Lost*.

In all these cases, even the first, that of God's withdrawal, the watcher's eyes remain intact: We look for a sign. Learning is not presupposed, necessarily; simple people, that is, are not excluded, for their desire for truth may be as strong as the scholar's. Kafka's "man from the country," who, in *Before the Law*, waits for a sign, for permission to enter, is the rabbis' "am ha'arez," a peasant or simple fellow. Northrop Frye calls such a character an *eiron*, someone whose capacity for attentiveness or understanding is less than ours, and especially less than the reader's, yet who—by a structural irony—reflects our own, unacknowledged condition.

❏   ❏   ❏

From a phenomenological point of view, then, there is a feeling that a lost chance, a lost world, remains present, although hidden and waiting to emerge. This latency is evoked by Gerard de Nerval in his famous sonnet "Delfica." He looks for premonitions of the resurrection of the pagan gods banished after Constantine's conversion to Christianity. An elusively Ovidian Dafné, the girl addressed by the poet, is unknowingly in touch with the gods who will return. "Ils reviendront, ces Dieux que tu pleures toujours!" (They will return, these Gods you are always mourning!) She plays in Nerval's imagination the role of Goethe's mysterious Mignon and anticipates Wilhelm Jensen's (and Freud's) Gradiva.[9] But despite the poet's own "souffle prophétique," nothing stirs:

> Cependant la sybille au visage latin
> Est endormie encore sous l'arc de Constantin:
> —Et rien n'a dérangé le sévère portique.

> (Meanwhile the sybil with her Latin face
> Remains asleep under the Arch of Constantine:
> —And nothing has disturbed that severe portal.)[10]

Expectant yet dumb, such sleepers seem to watch for the right signal: perhaps a still small voice, perhaps a trumpet call. During this "cependant," this interim of hopeful, helpless waiting, and in the very absence of the gods, there arises a collusion, a deep sense of solidarity between creature and creature, between humankind and the nonhuman. Nowhere have I found this portrayed more powerfully than in an autobiographical moment described by Wordsworth—a quintessential experience of intense expectation in ordinary circumstances.

The young poet is on a promontory, straining his eyes to see the horses that, vacation having begun, will take him from school to his home:

> 'twas a day
> Tempestuous, dark, and wild, and on the grass
> I sate half-sheltered by a naked wall;
> Upon my right hand couched a single sheep,
> Upon my left a blasted hawthorne stood;
> With those companions at my side, I sate
> Straining my eyes intensely. . . . [11]

Ten days later his father dies, and this "event" (in the literal sense of outcome) strikes him as a chastisement for his "anxiety of hope."

The episode is named by the poet a "spot of time," an unforgettable marker in consciousness that incites troubling yet vitalizing flashbacks. Place ("spot") and that moment in time fuse as an indelible memory. The forward-looking, natural intensity of a childish hope turns into a moment of terror: "in the deepest passion, I bowed low/To God, Who thus corrected my desires."[12] The assumption of a causal link between his impatient hope and the father's death has induced an illogical guilt in the boy. Seen through Freudian eyes, strength of imagination in this premature mode is an instance of the omnipotence of thoughts. Yet the event's traumatic effect, as it reaches through time, consoles the poet because it evokes a power he once experienced more purely. "[H]ow awful is the might of souls,/And what they do within themselves while yet/The yoke of earth is new to them. . . ."[13] The scene, as Wordsworth says in the episode's continuation, becomes a fountain with a refreshing, reparative effect on his relation to rural nature.

Such incidents of loneliness and feelings of terror akin to the sublime render Wordsworth's nature poetry quite different from verses in the georgic tradition or those based on scientific observation. In particular, calling sheep, hawthorn, and naked wall his "companions" suggests empathy with their own mute hope, with the "expectation" of the creature, as Romans 8:19 expresses it, so that the episode opens onto an eschatological backdrop in which the boy's innocent and impatient longing for home anticipates a not-so-innocent burden: the poet's orphic mission.

❑   ❑   ❑

It may be, however, that nothing is required, a nothing that is a purer form of waiting or a still deeper passivity. Simone Weil approaches this *attente*. We are said to lie in wait in an anguished temporality. She equates "extreme grief" with "a nonoriented sense of time." In the realm of intellect, therefore, "the virtue of humility is nothing else than the power of attention." And, she adds, modifying Malebranche, "L'attention absolument sans mélange est prière" (Absolute, unadulterated attention is prayer).[14]

But what if spirituality demands the opposite: a provocation, even a profanation as egregious as "the duty to trespass" advocated by the false seventeenth-century Jewish Messiah Shavtai Zwi? And how is the Messiah to be identified, the date, or gate he will enter from, a gate—of ivory or horn—reserved for any one among us? It is magic, if not religion, that seeks to keep us on the *qui vive* as to exactly when revelation will occur or what precise words, sounds, acts bring it about.

❑   ❑   ❑

I want to turn to writing as such by considering the implications of a watchword from Maurice Blanchot's *The Writing of the Disaster*: "Veiller sur le sens absent" (Watch over absent meaning). We ordinarily think of writing as an act, and an affirmative act, even when its purpose is denial or negation. But Blanchot's aphorism is strongly linked to a protest against what he calls, in the same book and in reference to Hegel, "l'imposture du Sens achevé" (the imposture of finalized meaning). He wishes to dissociate, or put some distance between, meaningfulness and eventfulness. He may also have been influenced toward this by the decisionism of fascist modes of speech, indeed by any form of triumphalism. He moves away from arrogant uses of the logos and begins to construct a new spiritual yet everyday kind of discourse (*sermo humilis*). The "veille" or watchfulness he counsels had its exemplary ritual in deathbed dramas no longer all that present to the contemporary mind. Especially in Protestantism, to see how a person dies, to watch for signs of that person's election or salvation, was once the ultimate parlor game. We understand such attentiveness best from a poem of Emily Dickinson's, as deeply ironic toward revelation in that context as Blanchot is toward revelation in language, or any punctual manifestation of meaning. I quote the poem without further comment:

> I heard a Fly buzz—when I died—
> The Stillness in the Room
> Was like the Stillness in the Air—
> Between the Heaves of Storm—
>
> The Eyes around—had wrung them dry—
> And Breaths were gathering firm
> For that last Onset—when the King
> Be witnessed—in the Room—
>
> I willed my Keepsakes—Signed away
> What portion of me be
> Assignable—and then it was
> There interposed a Fly—
>
> With Blue—uncertain—stumbling Buzz—
> Between the light—and me—
> And then the Windows failed—and then
> I could not see to see—[15]

An important theme throughout intellectual and religious history concerns the proper use of the eyes, as of the senses generally. "[T]he more you look," Thoreau notes, "the less you will observe. I have the habit of attention to such excess that my senses get no rest. . . ."[16]

Thoreau is always concerned with two converging issues. The first, as above, is the balance between thinking (or meditating) and observing. Thoreau's notebooks make us aware not only of his extreme sensitivity to the out-of-doors but his refusal to be a hunter. He wishes to live in the neighborhood of other creatures as one of them. He walks gently with nature, therefore. "Your mind must not perspire," he writes. "True, out of doors my thought is commonly drowned, as it were, and shrunken, pressed down by stupendous piles of light ethereal influences. . . ." Although his gentle tracking does not always harmonize with the stress of sense on soul, he questions "Humboldt, [Erasmus] Darwin, and others," their science. "Do not tread on the heels of your experience," he admonishes himself. "Be impressed without making a minute of it. Poetry puts an interval between the impression and the expression—waits till the seed germinates naturally."[17]

Yet time is not an unlimited commodity, so the tension between observed fact and latent symbol persists. "How much, what infinite leisure it requires, as of a lifetime, to appreciate a single phenomenon! You must camp down beside it as for life. . . ."[18] Here the second issue in Thoreau's subdued but constant battle between science and poetry appears. Thoreau has no use for god terms, yet the pressure of nature on him is like that on the religious watcher. The single phenomenon "must stand for the whole world to you, symbolical of all things. . . . Unless the humming of a gnat is as the music of the spheres, and the music of the spheres as the humming of a gnat, they are naught to me."[19]

The hyperbole is evident, and Thoreau never quite avoids that strain, never quite bridges the gap between fact and symbol. He tells us he keeps one commonplace book for facts and another for poetry, but finds it difficult to "preserve the vague distinction." Facts tend to be beautiful, or, as he says, "They are *translated* from earth to heaven."[20]

Ruskin and Thoreau—Goethe could certainly be added—belong to the same company. The senses are numinous for them, or should be; yet observation, although based on a pristine, unmediated, matitudinal attitude, is inevitably reflective and synthesizing. Science and poetry must reconcile: "every attentive glance into the world," Goethe writes, "is already fraught with theory."[21] This time we *can* use the adjective "modern" to describe the quality of consciousness exhibited. What remains is poetry, however, even when it aspires to be a new science or a new religion. Here is a benevolent, blasphemous Thoreau at his hyperbolic best: "The sound of the crickets at dawn after these first sultry nights seems like the dreaming of the earth still continued into the daylight. . . . While the creak of the cricket has that ambrosial sound, no crime can be committed. It buries Greece and Rome past resurrection. The earth-song of the cricket! Before Christianity was, it is."[22]

◻   ◻   ◻

Thoreau says he is "pressed down by stupendous piles of light ethereal influences." Every artist attentive to appearances as appearances, and who suspends meaning according to what Keats called "negative capability"—that is, who gives impressions their due rather than "irritably reaching after fact and reason"—evinces a pleasure in the very act of perception, which thinking can supplement but not reduce. The aesthetic mimesis of sensory experience resists as a form of antiselfconsciousness the drive for meaning, for coercing the chaos of accidental encounters into unity or reacting to what Milan Kundera calls an intolerable "lightness of being" with an all-encompassing ideology.

The paradox in Thoreau's phrasing points to the fact that the stress of sense on soul, however "light," is never entirely lifted. "Das alles war Auftrag" (All that was a summons) is Rilke's response to images that beseech or haunt him, as he makes sense of sense. "Auf" in "Auftrag" points upward while remaining phenomenal. The poet's "Aufmerksamkeit" (attentiveness) begins in "Augen-merksamkeit" (eye-mark activity). The simple demonstrative "da" is expressive of what affects Rilke mysteriously and demands the transformation of visibility into a more internal sense—"Da stieg ein Baum. O reine Uebersteigung! O Orpheus singt! O hoher Baum im Ohr!"[23] The ear and a kinesthetic factor counter the dominance of the eye and move the poet's attention inward.

This "saving of the phenomena" despite their fugitive impact is too often neglected by literary studies. A commitment to the phenomenality of things is easily derided as self-indulgent, an escape into impressionism. Yet poetry shows that the pressure of sense on soul, exemplified by Wordsworth as well as Thoreau, contributes to spiritual growth. It is Wordsworth's hope, in "Tintern Abbey," that "in after years . . . these wild ecstasies will be matured/Into a sober pleasure," that mind will become "a mansion for all lovely forms." An active element in sense perception reaches by way of poetry through time: Its lasting echo curbs the thinker's teleological bent without diminishing the "purposiveness without purpose" of existence.

The passage from perception to reflection and back again supports, then, antiselfconsciousness, a negative kind of attentiveness, and explains poetry's devotion to thoughts "washed in the cleanliness of a heaven/That has expelled us and our images." So says Wallace Stevens, thinking of painting as well as literature, in the "It must be Abstract" section of "Notes toward a Supreme Fiction."[24] Closer to Robert Frost's "Counter-love, original response" than to a destructive iconoclasm, this disciplining of the eyes (*custodia oculorum*) is (only) the beginning of wisdom. Although the "Lo!" and "Behold!" will never be purged, we become aware of a desire for revelation that, should it be collectivized, damages the human more than any methodical skepticism. Valéry's transformation of an erotic cliché evokes a virtual state of knowledge that is visual without being prehensile.

❐   ❐   ❐

The hardest task, however, is not a dialectical broadening of attentiveness through visual asceticism or a self-forgetfulness that respects the nonanthropocentric dimension of experience. It is whether we can learn from death, especially when it is massive and man-made. The philosopher, according to Plato and Cicero, is one who studies death; but who can study—keep their attention steadily on—the horror of genocide? Attentiveness encounters here a limit. It is one thing to appreciate mutability and say, with Wallace Stevens, "Death is the mother of beauty."[25] It is quite another to extract lessons from the wanton ruthlessness of ethnically motivated killing. Genocide entails a defeat of both beauty and morality. Only ritual could enter as partial solace, drawing attention to itself through a beauty of its own that seeks to appease the wounded eye. As mourning and thinking converge, they renew the scandal of Aristotle's theory of mimesis: "We take pleasure in contemplating the most precise images of things whose sight in itself causes us pain."[26]

CHAPTER 12

DEMOCRACY'S MUSEUM

The millennial "The Lives They Lived" issue of the *New York Times Sunday Magazine*[1] has no compunction in displaying without moral judgment a startling variety. It is devoted to a wildly democratic (Whitman: "I contain multitudes") mix of celebrities, ex-celebrities, forgotten activists, neglected or semi-known artists and *artistes*, as well as an obscure, recently executed murderer (whose inclusion exposes a repressed "The Deaths They Died"). Consider also a not untypical advertisement for a dance performance called *The Secret Club: Floating Angels 2000*. It combines, we are told, "classically inspired balletic precision with industrial-edged Euro-trash sensibility."

Given this variety, hybridity, and hustle, is it possible to maintain any critical perspective except that of an automatic, hence superficial, demystification? For Nietzsche, genuine critique could only arise, like the tragic sense itself, out of the spirit of music—where music stands for the lure of absorption, self-forgetfulness, even Dionysian enticement. He attacks the simplified spectatorial attitude valuing art as an object that gives pleasure of a disinterested sort. His "ideal spectator" is no more detached from the action, from what is being observed, than the Chorus of Greek drama. Wagnerian music-drama challenges, even as spectacle, the half-moral, supercilious auditors who made up Nietzsche's public. Art subjected them to the risk of being born again as "aesthetic listeners."

Today, both art and art criticism seem to have changed all that by reviving the image of the *poète maudit* or *artiste assassiné:* the artist who must suffer in order to produce and is consumed by a passion for self-exposure. In the contemporary Society of the Spectacle, a world of formalized transgressions and conspicuous consumption, where everything becomes "Let's Entertain," art seems bent on consuming itself so that proliferating sounds and images, however unusual and striking, are soon routinized. A continual self-exhibition glorifies the successful (read: marketable) hustler. Art either cannibalizes its own past by pastiche or expends all restrictive economies to the point of self-erasure. Anamnesis, the mark of a new, all-embracing cultural memory, is partnered by amnesia.

Contemporary exhibitions become more and more the equivalent of MTV: extensive, hypnotic Mobiles that defeat an older optic of aesthetic contemplation. Dionysus has at most, as in Jeff Koons, a cute, rococo presence. There is more eye candy than eye-shock (contrast the surrealistic imagery of Luis Buñuel's 1929 film *Chien d'Andalou*). How can we judge this development, especially when artists themselves make so much interesting noise—bombard us with interfering, programmatic, self-justifying comments? Has Nietzsche's ideal public of aesthetic listeners or viewers ever existed, moreover, except as a tiny elite?

I want to explore what is happening to art criticism generally by distinguishing between cultural memory and public memory.[2] Such a distinction may be, I admit, a rearguard effort, open to the charge of culture pessimism. My point of view, however, does not aim to repeat Theodor Adorno or Dwight Macdonald's rejectionist critique of mass culture to provoke a purgative, breakthrough revision. It is questioning and diagnostic rather than assertive and therapeutic: It asks whether criteria remain that allow a reasoned discrimination, a critical choice among what is offered to eyes and ears, especially in the world of art. Is art still the scene of authentic tokens of human creativity?

❒   ❒   ❒

Nietzsche's sense of the public as an expanding, vulgar crowd of newspaper readers and spectacle seekers leads to the concept of public memory, as does Flaubert's more satiric (but equally pessimistic) *Dic-*

tionary of Received Ideas. In our own time, public memory is formed mainly by the mass media through near-endless repetition, and it accumulates as an accessible cache easily retrieved. The intimacy, moreover, of an earlier theater's demimonde is largely displaced by long-distance viewing and surfing. Indeed, whether intimacy is still an ideal is itself in doubt, given the new *democratic* panopticon: the voyeurism of such reality shows as TV's *Big Brother* and *Survivor.*

Powered by the vast, virtual archive of communications technology and a historicism (new or old) close to the field of cultural studies, the art-and-media surplus disarms judgment even while inciting a flood of opinions—Nietzsche already denounced his era's "cult of tendentiousness." As the conflict between the discourses of history and memory grows within an accelerating information boom, history (a specialized kind of narrative working in an infinite field of data retrieval) approaches Kant's mathematical sublime and memory (a very personal or "positional" response) the dynamic sublime.

With memory becoming too full (Borges says "memorious"), the temptation of a self-protective, or ideological, or orgiastic oblivion draws nearer. What is driving all those influential movements in painting we call suprematism, purism, abstract expressionism, constructivism, minimalism, brutalism, action art, conceptual art, pop art, if not a deliberate forgetting, a culture of elision or even erasure?

Pop art might seem to be an exception, a refusal to exclude any gesture that breaks the frame imposed by high culture. It reverts to complicity with superabundance and a conspicuous display of Western prowess in both production and consumption. Compare Erró's foodscapes and the classical *nature morte.* Yet as antiart, pop often elides the distinction between art and life or falls back on a flamboyant stylization.

I would not deny, of course, that these movements leave interesting traces of the tension between what they elide and the process of elision. A strong intellectual element may enter, as when Stuart Davis, according to fellow painter Arshile Gorky, moves us "to the cool and intellectual world where all human emotions are disciplined upon rectangular proportions." (This seems equally relevant to the more radical aspect of Ballanchine's art of the ballet, as in his *Agon's* angled and asyndetic style.) The constructive and abstractive methods of cubism also combine this "esprit de géometrie" with an "esprit de finesse." We find parallel intuitions in Paul Valéry, Gertrude Stein, and Hart Crane. Action painting, Harold Rosenberg has argued, does not fashion an image or imitation of reality but uses the canvas as if it were the mind of the artist, through which it discovers clues of who the artist is. "[For] the Action Painters, the canvas was not a surface upon which to present an image, but a 'mind' through which the artist discovers, by means of manual and mental hypotheses, signs of what he is or might be."[3]

The tension between elision and construction (abstraction and representation) holds for figurative as well as nonfigurative painting. Andy Warhol's serial method of portraiture, his fixed and fixating icons, his visual stutter, seeks to express—by a pictorial form of skepticism—an endlessly divisible temporal fullness, especially that of cinematic photography. The dimension of time enters to challenge the ideal of timelessness presumed by the classical art of portraiture. Therefore it is hard to determine what fullness is being elided: the time-bound character of life or an idealized perennial presence. The constructive elisions of Moshe Kupferman's 1999 series called "The Rift in Time" have a different figurative/non-figurative structure. Although the Holocaust is linked to this rift, or is a heavy sediment in the artist's thought, it does not close off a remarkable dynamic. The paintings open our consciousness to the fact of a survival: This art is a spacious, even joyful, counterweight, a latticework of bold, overlapping strokes and swatches. Spontaneous and delicately massed, Kupferman's paintings never quite lose their artisanal relation to the materiality of building block or page. The painter, haunted by the rift in time, does not tear it further as a sign of mourning but works in the space opened by it. If he elides an identifiable historical content by abstraction, he also builds by the same method.

The overfullness of the contemporary consciousness, its being "distracted from distraction by distraction," leads to the concept of cultural memory as a fresh ideal that has not found an adequate emblem. The cultural memory is clearly more than a vast archive or thesaurus. Our historical overview of the past having expanded, it is now possible to see how many suppressed "narratives" exist that might challenge a best-of-the-West idealism and perhaps any effort to unify the chaos of human aspirations. Given this backlog of what was elided, and the accompanying sense of guilt, is there still a way to alleviate the burden of the past?

Yet guilt itself, in the contemporary art world, becomes part of the show and is separated from its element of shame. Even important moral and legal advances, after the "great convulsion" (Derrida's phrase) that resulted in both the concept of a crime against humanity, and—eventually—the possibility of a formal pardoning procedure, get caught up in the theatricality of the Age of the Spectacle and Simulacrum. "The simulacrum, the automatic ritual, hypocrisy, calculation or aping, invite themselves as parasites to this ceremony of culpability."[4]

❒   ❒   ❒

In order to rejoin the issue of whether a degree of hope can be vested in the concept of cultural memory, I turn from the visual arts to the general problematic of history-writing. A starting point is Oswald Spengler. His *Decline of the West*, stemming from the era leading to the First World War, has intriguing comments on the importation of non-Western art to Europe, accelerating in the early twentieth century (the exoticism of an older Japonaiserie or Far East influence being augmented, for example, by Picasso's discovery ca. 1908 of non-Western art in the *Musée de l'homme*). Spengler sees in that importation not only signs of decadence but also of a necessary rebarbarization. "Culture," in his view, has declined into "civilization" and must be revitalized by archaic sources of energy.[5]

But I prefer to jump a generation and go to the more explicit political vision of Mircea Eliade, whose distinguished American career as a historian of mythology and religious practices was preceded by a fascist culture politics. Eliade, while still in Romania, remarks in 1939 on "the passion of today's elite for protohistory, races, religions, mythologies and symbols. . . . Tradition is not sought in the Middle Ages but in the origins of the race, in the beginnings of nations. . . . The past is valued not because it represents history but because it represents origins. . . . [P]rotohistory grants us equality with the German and Latin people."[6] This is part of an antihistoricist argument for the indigenous and timeless character of Romanian Christianity, an argument at once modified and maintained in Eliade's later, more scholarly, career, where he praises religion for tolerating an unusual weight of historical contingency despite its apocalyptic drive to value prehistory and timelessness. Religious feasts or fasts, he claims, have always been related to cargo cults that periodically jettison all property and obligations. The historical burden on memory triggers an unburdening that is memory's opposite and raises the specter of nihilism.

A contrast to Eliade's complicitous understanding of messianic culture politics (depoliticized after he settled in America) is provided by the German scholar E. R. Curtius, who refuses this regress to speculative or fictitious origins in his *European Literature and the Latin Middle Ages*. Undertaken in 1933, when the Nazis came to power, the book was published in 1948. Curtius's emphasis on the Latin heritage is less the product of an inner emigration during the Nazi era than an engaged scholar's counterattack on the myth of Nordic origins and Aryan genius with which Nazism purged the canon after 1933. He shows how Goethe's virtuoso transmission of classical forms, not just his youthful addiction to Nordic folklore, proved essential to the development in Germany of a modern literary achievement. These forms—as certain of his German contemporaries, Aby Warburg, Erwin Panofsky, and Ernst Cassirer also recognized in their own way—have an architectonic strength or "mnemic energy" that reaches through time in a nonmystical manner. They become intertextual and historical allusions that serve as building blocks affirming the continuity of a later art.

Even at present, however, despite the fascist experience, we have not gained immunity from vicious cycles of cultural accumulation and cultic purging. The poet Charles Olson, in his guise of American Adam (the One without a Past, or who does not wish to have one), denounced the Western canon—invoked by Curtius in his opening chapter on European literature—as "a great shitting from the skies."[7] Yet while tradition is often authoritarian, and in that respect rightly inspires Olson's anxiety attack, the more liberal concept of cultural memory is hardly a cure.

Deriving its momentum from an amalgam of democratic and genius theory, it posits a quasi-divine spark in each person or cultural period. In line with this perspective, the historical record, previously centered on heroic or eventful, now captures the more habitual selffashionings in everyday life. The result is an inspirational populist norm of inclusiveness. That incites, however, a concern about value relativism and national disintegration. A reactive cultural politics, therefore, may try to resimplify the past and tame diversity once more through a moralistic, self-affirming overview of an age or nation. Already two centuries of theorizing have tried to transform this impasse between unity and diversity into a historical dialectics that would allow the critical observer to stand firmly on the shifting ground of modernity.

❏   ❏   ❏

Histories are written to gain a theory of change and so to control, or at least brake, mutability. But histories are themselves subject to an accelerating rate of obsolescence. Our desire for truth, or at least consensus, continues to be confronted by social and cultural change, and because waste—even self-wasting—is too often a way of life. How is waste itself to be wasted? "The waste remains, the waste remains and kills,"[8] are William Empson's bitter and memorable words.

Dump or archive? The stink of decay or the refinery of library collection and museum?

Archie Ammons has written a voluminous poem entitled *Garbage*. In Don DeLillo's *Underworld*—a lengthy sequel, as it were, to Thomas Pynchon's *The Crying of Lot 49*—images, impulses, episodes, words, even when enjoyed for their exuberance or inconsequence, exist from the beginning as waste-products-to-be: a world within the world that threatens to bury it. Everything will disappear into a junkyard or be contaminated by such offal; so everyone turns into a waste manager. The danger is real: If plutonium doesn't get you, Pluto will. The psychopathology of ordinary life in a consumer culture leads to peculiar visions. "Marion and I saw products as garbage even when they sat gleaming on store shelves, yet unbought. We didn't say, What kind of casserole will that make? We said, What kind of garbage will that make?"[9] A German culture critic has talked of ours as a *Wegwerfegesellschaft*, a throw-it-away society.

Change also arrives because of an opposite if strictly correlative motive: to redeem what the *past* threw away, what had been considered insignificant or harmful. The pressure of this infinite task should not be underestimated. Valéry defined modernity as a Universal Exhibition juxtaposing panoramically all intellectual goods, past and present. He alluded to the World's Fair kind of display, one that pretended to tolerate all kinds of cultural artifacts. He saw loss in this as well as gain: Values would tend to become equivalent. Jules Michelet, another great French thinker, had described the phenomenon more enthusiastically. The historian, he declared, resurrects the dead.

Nowadays, what is marginal or heterological, and even junk memorabilia, challenges us to be alchemists: merchants of meaning who could transmute everything into gold—or, through the culture industry, into an inexhaustible cash flow. All the arts converge on this ideal. But the ethos of cultural retrieval that governs contemporary democratic thinking, has, I am suggesting, an unintended, antithetical consequence. On the one hand, our present-day bricoleurs, in mocking fulfillment of Malraux's heroic "Museum Without Walls," where humanity's creative genius is celebrated through the juxtaposition of Western and non-Western (a.k.a. "primitive") art, load that Museum up with "Euro-trash," "arte povero," or other ingeniously recycled, deliberately emphasized "garbage."[10] New movements in music, moreover, like hip-hop, are historicized with all their commercial derivatives (dubbed "material culture") after only two decades. On the other hand, the will to recover submerged voices and suppressed creative possibilities—neglected or despised materials—provokes a purgative, political variant that calls for the restoration of a purer, nobler (now supposedly contaminated) identity.

Recovery, in this reactive and restrictive sense, is a disburdening of historical complexities by way of a risky utopian nostalgia. And, although liberal or multicultural versions of recovery strive for heterotopia[11]—for greater freedom of expression, expansiveness, and joyful expenditure—they too have a shadow side. If in the narrowly political case there is acting out, in the multicultural there is play-acting.

❑   ❑   ❑

How can there be harm in everything tending to spectacle, performance, *divertissement*, cultural transvestism? Repression is abolished;

sublimation reigns. The French playwright Jean Giraudoux exalted the theater as a "radiant confessional" for all joys and agonies. The artist turns an incipient multiple-personality disorder into a histrionic and empathetic gift. Mimetic identification is rescued from the personal or collective unconscious and exposed to principled scrutiny. The unacknowledged role of fictions in daily and national life comes to the fore.

From the Romantics on, moreover, a vernacular energy asserts itself and claims to be a revitalizing, progressive principle. We are made to feel the hand of the artist, its orchestrated spontaneity, the sketchy (sometimes scratchy) freshness of each picture or improvised sound, motifs drawn from local romance or the street rather than from history's pompous narratives (what French philosopher Jean-François Lyotard called the *grands récits*). Or, as in Cézanne, a direct, visual perception, although always defeated by nature, draws a Mont Ste. Victoire out of defeat. The line from impressionism to cubism shows that a modern classicism is possible, despite loss of totality, fragmentation, perspectivism, the everyday plenitude of subject matter, the *pathétique* of comparing art to labor and its products to earth-works. One would have to be a Malvolio not to rejoice in this recent explosion of art as well as acting.

Indeed, for trying to maintain the memory of a perhaps purely ideal authenticity, I could be charged with harboring, like Emmanuel Levinas, an anti-theatrical prejudice. "Are we on stage or are we in the world?" as Levinas asks. He complains of any art that "bewitches our gestures" and conspires with everything that "plays itself out in spite of us."[12] His point is that this kind of play is not characteristic of personal freedom but of compulsion and servitude. Since human empathy is finite, the moral sense may find itself overcharged and therefore tempted by an aesthetic escape route. The line between image (simulacrum) and reality erodes in the era of reproductive technology; so that, in the end, despite an ever-increasing desire for realism, both catharsis and referentiality fail with a consequence the French social historian Henri Lefebvre has described. "A cry of loneliness rises . . . at the heart of everyday life [from] . . . the intolerable loneliness of unceasing communication and information."[13]

Given this situation, can art criticism, even of the hard-edged variety, make an impact and reopen the doors of perception instead of inciting a sterile pathos? An unstable and quasi-infinite variety is bound to weary a mind no longer able to discriminate between cultural and noncultural phenomena, or art and entertainment. Their growing indifference, blamed by Adorno and the Critical Theory movement on American mass culture, is today the normal state of affairs, at least in the West. We might now talk of "a great shitting from below."

It must be acknowledged, at the same time, despite my own generation's wariness of hysterical mass movements and enthusiasms (due to its experience of totalitarianism), that popular music in particular has a religious effect in bringing people together in periods of great stress. So in the "A Prayer for New York" manifestation on September 23, 2001, which took place in Yankee Stadium, the greatest and most emotional reaction came in response to singers like Bette Midler.

The objection to popular culture, then, is not that it comes from the masses but that, whatever its energetic, vernacular source, it promotes the passivity of mere consumption. In that respect, it is no better than snobbishly venerated icons of high culture. Once again the question returns of how to find a basis for cultural criticism, in the hope that it will not dampen the pleasure we take in art but create a more active, discriminating enjoyment.

❑   ❑   ❑

It is possible to specify at least two differences that preserve cultural memory's critical advantage over the more passive public memory, despite some overlap. First, cultural memory is an abstraction that has to be reconceptualized all the time. Striving for a pluralistic kind of unity, it includes a continuous reflection on itself. A dogmatic attitude in this area simply betrays the power play of special interests. The wish to produce or renew a shared cultural capital cannot neglect the dynamic of social construction and deconstruction. The public memory, by contrast, is media-driven and myopic. What the media go for, except the promotion of particular commercial or ideological interests, remains unclear.

Without being intellectual, the media have a way of leveling, in the name of "balance," all opinion by deploying an endless array of spiders called "experts" or "pundits." The result is confusion and indistinctness—a high grade of low-grade anxiety. You can't sharpen criticism with forked tongues like that. And although the hype of tele-vangelism reminds us sporadically of prophesy's disruptive effect, in the United States and increasingly elsewhere, too, public memory is so besieged, so boosterish commercial, that except for a vociferous right-wing establishment, it lacks any reasoned anxiety about the transmission of values.

"Hollywood" and its celebrity culture contribute to this lack of anxiety. They create a parallel universe, simulacra we turn to when we are not as sure as we would like to be about our identity. Morality, as Levinas points out, becomes role-playing. Elvis Presley impersonators and look-alike Madonnas proliferate. We can always mirror and even remake ourselves in the image of "stars" featured daily on TV's *Biography* series. When immortality fades as a believable hope, they provide an ersatz firmament.

Reality shows, in addition, that invade the privacy of ordinary homes or incite deliberate, circuslike spectacles on TV make celebrities of anyone who survives the pitiless lens of webcam cameras. The nonactor trapped into acting becomes a flexible fetish with a predetermined place in the democratic museum or human zoo.[14] Whatever this fickle fun argues—does it serve as an escape from an unwanted identity, or does it ecstatically embrace the tragicomedy of everyday life?—today such transvestism is given the same (amused) tolerance as a fashion statement.

A similar, permissive attitude has long greeted TV show-biz or sit-com routines. In them embarrassment upon embarrassment is cheerfully overcome by (canned) applause or a zany stream of pseudoevents (no quiet moment without telephone or doorbell ringing the next incident in), or an acting method more stylized than in the silent movies. The false continuity of this sort of narrative is accepted, because there seems to be no other. We might as well enjoy it.

This dearth of anxiety is the obverse, however, of a sporadic nervousness about core values or the ability of families and schools to transmit them. The pedagogical issue is far from being settled and keeps roiling the body politic. Correlative problems with political correctness add to the roil. In many countries, moreover, a new and more relaxed public memory has not yet taken hold, and we see quite clearly an anxiety of transmission at work. Here I recall Germany confronting the Holocaust, France its Vichy government, Russia its Stalinism, South Africa its racist past. In the United States, the popular acceptance of black culture, especially in the domain of music, and the emergence of extraordinary novelists and poets as well as such vernacular-collage formalists as Leonard Drew have created a "rememory" (Toni Morrison) that has partly assuaged the anxiety of transmission concerning an oppressed heritage.

A second difference between the two memories, public and cultural, is that the former is global rather than local, in good part the product of a dissemination through the media. Although the media may target specific recipients, what they transmit is always addressed to a virtual audience: "To whom it may concern." This faceless audience is real enough, as pollsters, Nielsen ratings, and other soundings show. Yet even as an influential political factor, it suggests a metapolitical horizon, for communication itself becomes the goal as an ideal seeking the shortest path between sender and receiver. Once the friction of the medium is technologically reduced to near zero and all signals can, in theory, get through, a superconductive, utopian form of dissemination promises (or threatens) universal transparency—a postreligious kind of apocalypse. To put it another way, transparency is valued more than discretion or, as Walter Benjamin observed, transmissibility than truth.

❐   ❐   ❐

Actually, of course, art has become more, not less, opaque. Although it circulates energetically and is reproduced widely, that is not because of its greater intelligibility but because of its exhibition or market value. If the printing press has made books available and cheap, then, paradoxically, photoelectronic processes have made paintings available and expensive: The more replicas, the more the cultural capitalist looks for the original copy, or the unique (mis)print, as when the post office makes an error on its stamps.

While giving up the hierarchic ranking of paintings in terms of subject matter or recognizable mythic-historical content, we value originality all the more, as if postmodernism had not substituted "self-consuming artifacts" for the prestige of a monumental, genealogically productive source. The authenticating mark of the artist's handwork (*touche* or *tâche*) becomes all-important. (Thomas Bewick, the early nineteenth-century English engraver, once superimposed an obliterating thumbprint as a kind of signature, or intentional mark, on one of his engravings. Lichtenstein substitutes, as it were, the flexible sweep of one brush-stroke, creating in that way the portrait as well as imprint of a material signifier.) Picture making often reverts to inscription, graffiti, an intensive form of manu-script adding graphic mixes, cartoonlike figures, and—as in Charlotte Salomon's *Life or Theatre?*—a seriality like that of comic books. Extruding, moreover, beyond the allowable rectangular expanse, pictures may also restore the *idea* of touch by an extrusive, layering technique. The material of the ground penetrates the pictorial surface or produces a similar effect with a multimedia sort of projection from within the flat screen. Francis Bacon's or Lucien Freud's exaggerated fleshly realism also violates that flatness. Contrapuntally, visual art may deliberately, unashamedly, give up three-point perspective, insist on a lithographic, posterlike surface (a color field) as well as "frame" itself by allowing the "page" of the painting to crop or fragment its subject matter at awkward angles. It signals this way its counterfeit relation to the world. A strangely abstract materiality is born.

❏   ❏   ❏

Is that materiality spiritual as well as abstract? With the modern nude, for example, cubed or otherwise dispersed, or whose flesh exudes clashing rather than smoothing colors, does the painter flaunt the body's materiality or alienate it as effectively as in medieval stylization? The contemporary museum works against the possibility of an adjudication.

Curtius complained fifty years ago, in the preface to *European Literature and the Latin Middle Ages*, that greater progress had been made in modernizing railroads than in a system for transmitting tradition. He was thinking of philological and literary studies, but his comment can be extended to the visual arts, even though enormous sums are being disbursed to mount intelligible exhibitions. The change in attitude toward tradition is clarified by a painting from the

Far East depicting the act of writing. It shows a massively arrayed scholar who directs a pen that is like an additional, elongated finger, its slenderness contrasting vividly with his bulk as he transmits "The Book of Documents."[15] The order-in-disorder of the museum, the planned chaos we call an exhibition, rarely fosters the kind of slow, sequential montage that would allow such an understanding of transmission to emerge. The space necessary for withdrawal and reflection—related to Maurice Blanchot's "espace littéraire"—is now more difficult to attain, even as the interior space of museums become architecturally refined.

❐   ❐   ❐

Think of the changed aura in France of the word "espace" itself. Its contemporary usage points to something so elegant that the exhibition value of the goods displayed in that space overwhelms their use value. The commodity turns into an explicit fetish that arouses rather than purges the acquisitive instinct. Space flows around the exhibited artworks or *objets de luxe*; it caresses them, makes love to them, as the camera does to a supermodel.

Space has a spectacular relation, then, to the objects it encompasses, and begins to defeat the inner eye. In principle, the pleasure of a beautiful museum should enhance everything in it. And, yes, it does: As with all good architecture, we feel a physical lightness—a very tolerable lightness of being—in such an expanse. To the point where (perhaps also because the very variety of exhibits cannot be mentally absorbed) we enjoy that space more than its contents.

Are there conditions of display that would enable us to understand the demand made by all these opaque objects, which insist on their thingy, material presence, even when made of next to nothing? Or do we need to withdraw from public space into an empty room, where there is but a desk and a writing machine? A room where interpretation, that still not fully recognized art, can single out, select, focus, resequence the overwhelming heraldry of human creativity—its "galaxy of signifiers" (Roland Barthes)? And why does such a contemplative withdrawal feel like a flight or a renunciation, close to an act of bad faith?

It can be argued that abstract art has already anticipated a withdrawal of this kind. In a Kline, a Rothko, a Motherwell, the final evacuation of subject matter, reaching from the late canvases of Cézanne to cubism, constructivism, the purist transformation of machinery in Léger and of organic forms in Miró, Matisse's cut-outs and glyphs (as in the chapel at Vence), abstract expressionism, the wonderful abbreviations of Klee and whiteboard scribbles of Twombly, seems to have created a spirit matter or a merging of spirit and matter. Visual music takes over and conquers the material sign. Yet the critic's interpretive montages, wrestling with plethora, are not just speculative fugues but true narratives: They seek to explore, if not resolve, the puzzle of why we now place so high a value—including commercial valuation—on works without apparent content. While the search to give meaning to art from within continues, these icons of a spiritual materiality defy systems of descriptive understanding.

Perhaps, then, the problem is with the knowledge drive (Nietzsche's *Wissensdrang*) itself, with how we understand understanding. That drive seems as hard to renounce as the erotic, and may be linked to it. When we compare Wordsworth's Lucy ("She lived unknown, and few could know/When Lucy ceased to be"[16]) with Madonna's Madonna, we perceive how completely an Age of the Spectacle has taken over. This, despite the monumentalism—as it were—of enlarged Brillo box or Campbell soup can, icons of popular consumption; or the massively ironic juxtaposition of clichés from what Alexander Kluge has called "the eternity of yesterday" woven by Anselm Kiefer into the thickened texture of such canvases as "Lot's Wife" and "Dein Goldenes Haar, Margarete."

Popular music, at the same time, becomes *the* performance art where identities are made and remade. Personality as a publicly traded commodity replaces the wish for inwardness and privacy and stages a conspicuous consumption of taboos. Secrets are worn as openly as Madonna's or Victoria's *dessous*.

Among French authors, it is a reclusive and hermetic Blanchot whose notion of literary space resists that trend. He had passed through the fascist temptation and its cult of the mass political spectacle. Later he refuses to yield up the linguistic to the phenomenal, the letter to the image. Amplifying an impersonality theory as radical as

Mallarmé's, he sharpens the paradox whereby the self produced by the work also disappears into it. But it is significant that he expresses this paradox of the writer in terms of an older paradox of the actor. The author, says Blanchot, has no more of an independent existence than the actor does, "that ephemeral personality who is born and dies every evening, having exposed himself excessively to view, killed by the spectacle."[17] How strange that in order to argue for a recession and even renunciation of the self, rather than for a fashionable self-fashioning, Blanchot honors the very tendency he resists. Yet what intellectual historian Martin Jay has characterized as "down-cast eyes" in modernist French thought also makes Blanchot assert that "to speak is not to see" and that the writer has no secrets, no intimacy to espy. All *oeuvres* are said simply to deepen the artist's consciousness of his *désoeuvrement*. There is no career, no legacy, except the momentum of an "infinite conversation."

❑   ❑   ❑

I have suggested that it is possible to look at certain twentieth-century trends—such as concrete art or minimalism or non-figurative painting, or Giacommetti's vanishing-point figurines and even Oldenburg's fatter, anti-monumental monuments—through Blanchotesque spectacles. Yet to do so is indecisive in terms of the conflict between visual desire and its renunciation. In Blanchot's understanding of what he calls Orpheus's gaze, the moment in which the artist looks—looks back—while leading Eurydice into the light of the upper world, is also her vanishing point. Her loss seems not only fatal but fated: It reveals that the artist cannot give up desiring a possessive kind of phenomenality. We are greedy for vision.

To decentralize the eyes and disseminate the sun's fiery semen does not so much get rid of a commanding logos, or poet Stevens's "master folded in his fire,"[18] as create a bad infinity of fetishes. The miracle is that Van Gogh's icons (though not their reproductions) escape this fate. The cosmos as a "strange wheel of fire deprived of its center" (Blanchot: "l'étrange roue ardente privée de centre") reasserts itself as the quasi-mystical determinant of some of the most colorful formalistic art, that of Kandinsky, Delaunay, Gorky, perhaps Avery.

Blanchot's theory presupposes a blind gaze (a sort of Whistler *Nocturne*) rather than a blinded one, but is a gaze nevertheless. It cannot escape complicity in what it denies.

❑   ❑   ❑

We reach here the last step of an argument exploring the possibility of aesthetic criticism in an Age of Spectacular Amusements. These amusements, I have said, are backed by the democratic belief that there is a spark of cultural value in all that achieves popularity. But if such displays have documentary value, then we are back to the early modern era of the virtuosi with their cabinet of curiosities. Except now every artifact, the "Mona Lisa" or a urinal, can be inscribed with a LOOKH (a famous logo of the modernist painter Marcel Duchamp), every phenomenon, not just the phenomenal (the double-headed calf), can be framed and presented as art in the manner of Picasso's "Gas Stove Venus" (*Venus de Gaz*).

The parodic intent to desacralize both the gods and art itself does not get rid of the distinction between high and low or sacred and profane; in fact, it perpetuates that binary opposition, italicizes the wavering line between them. In Malraux's theory, as in Picasso's practice, art saves the sacred in its absolutely human aspects—horrific or humorous, classical or clownish—from defensive religious pieties. Yet a tendency to value everything that can be recuperated, especially in the aftermath of Nazism as a political religion that formulated a doctrine of "life unworthy of life," establishes a trivial as well as nontrivial right to life that results in a state of *surnomie* rather than anomie. By *surnomie* I mean an excess of norms or a perplexity of choice that defeats both the unification of knowledge and the possibility of dogmatically justifying one's own culture.

❑   ❑   ❑

There has been at least one brave attempt, in political theory rather than art criticism, to support this culture of everything (this movement of thought and life into a visible, supposedly transparent, public sphere) by distinguishing between totalitarian intrusiveness and "the democratic concept of politics as a public spectacle regulated by an attestive [referring to the standards of experimental science] rather than a celebratory visual culture."[19] Certainly there is no substitute for public discussion, and therefore exhibition, if we would achieve a qualitative though always provisional consensus that some works are not works of art and some works of art are of greater value than others. And I accept Hannah Arendt's insight, which she was writing about at her death, that Kant in his *Critique of Judgment* wished to bring taste into the public and political domain by showing the importance of imagination for a sympathetic discussion of differing views in a pluralistic society.[20]

Yet to restore the link between aesthetic experience and judgment requires an understanding why art has become parodic, not only toward previous art (which has always been the case, once we see parody as a serious and not only a mocking engagement) but also toward its own encompassing social and cultural milieu. As Adorno often insisted, criticism of society and its cultural goods cannot stand above them, claiming a special distinction ("Vornehmheit"). Like art itself, critics must deal with social reality in a homeopathic manner. Vision can be communicated through a mimetic, Brechtian alienation effect, or through an allusive technique that revives the memory of previous art, but it cannot be achieved through sheer abstraction.

Derrida may be even clearer than Adorno about this pharmaceutical dimension of social critique. The *pharmakon* is both poison and antidote. Citing in his book on Heidegger the many types of nationalist discourse in the 1920s and 1930s, Derrida remarks: "Our only choice is between terrifying contaminations. Even if not all complicities are equivalent, they are irreducible."[21] He also coins the word "paleonymy" to describe the parasitic condition of both discursive and fictional writing. The disorder within the order of art does not point "to an incoherence in language or a contradiction in the system," but comes from "a necessity: that of installing oneself in a traditional concept system in order to destroy it."[22] The very same sentiment is expressed by Roberto Pinto as interviewed by Maurizio Cattelan: "It is good for the artist to insinuate himself into the open mesh of any system—not in a provocative and visible way, but mimetically, using their same mediums."[23] However hard it may be to describe the concept-system of (especially) pictorial works of art, a similar necessity is operative: that of installing oneself critically or playfully in "the ineluctable modality of the visible" (James Joyce in *Ulysses*).

❏   ❏   ❏

I conclude with the following thought: The theater of the visible, even when painting and sculpture were less of a performance art, has always had to find its own antidotes through an iconoclastic *via negativa*. In an Age of the Spectacle, therefore, retreat and portrait ("retrait") seek to forge a new alliance. In some enlarged black-and-white photos, stilled human faces that show the imprint of age in the texture of their furrows seem as durable, despite those signs of mortality, as rocks etched by time. Conscience has to find its image once more amid the assault of distracting or afflicting sights. Blanchot points to this when he revises the assumption that artists seek immortality and create something visible and monumental in order not to die. On the contrary, Blanchot suggests, the writer is one who writes in order to be able to die.[24]

Aesthetic distance, then, or the space we enter by means of image, sound, or word, is more than a flight from reality, the evasion of a powerful seduction. It is also the marshaling of a counterforce. Wallace Stevens defined imagination as a violence from within pressing against a violence from without. Art displays that nonviolent violence: by action-at-a distance it reaches toward the palm at the end of the mind.

CHAPTER 13

AESTHETICIDE

There was a time when thinkers debated whether nature was growing old. I have recently been intrigued by the possibility that the same question may be asked of literary study.

The question should be considered absurd, or merely provocative. After all, modern literary criticism is barely four centuries old and has systematically neglected most of its prior history, because that was deeply mired in theological exegesis. Until we understand once more the figurative vigor of religious language and see theology itself as one of the liberal arts (the strangest of these) rather than necessarily supporting an oppressive religious politics, we cut ourselves off from centuries of textual study. Sacred hermeneutics is part of our heritage, just as theology in the form of concrete poetic speculation, according to F. A. Pottle, a scholar of Romanticism, is "the domain and the duty of imagination."

A global view of the arts, moreover, as well as of competing concepts of culture seems impossible today. There is too much diversity for definitive assessment or prophetic admonition. Which does not mean, of course, that we should remain silent, but a case can be made for less stridency and more analysis, for a more patient conceptualization. Finally, whatever the dilemmas of literary criticism may be, audiences are not enjoying art less, especially the cinematic and performing arts.

◻   ◻   ◻

Although cultural pessimists, then, have little to go on, there is an unease, much of it focused on the universities. We take it for granted that the vitality of a nation is demonstrated by its scholarship and artistic production, in addition to economic well being and democratic integrity. Within the universities, however, the picture often looks bleak. While energy and vitality are as much in evidence as ever, young scholars today are drawn to, seduced by, the immense growth and dynamism of the visual arts as well as by a cryptic, promiscuous, and aggressive style called postmodern. Both factors have taken their toll on the study of literature, which in turn becomes more personal and more of a performance.

Indeed, the line between high and popular culture is eroding. Every moment of Madonna's career is taken to be deliciously exemplary. According to the latest phase, she has been "enlightened," that is, she has found her true spiritual self through a combination of yoga, the Kabbala, and techno music. Among the professors who celebrate her there is itself a celebrity culture.

A prominent new field, moreover, has entered the academic curriculum together with Madonna: cultural studies. Contextually this is to the good; we have become fully aware of popular and social thought, including the hidden or neglected contribution of women. Yet the place of literature has shrunk to only a minor part of a much larger picture, while the demands made by traditional study are often slighted. How many critics can be accused, as Harold Bloom recently was, of a "barnstorming mission to spread the word of bookishness"?

If we compare cultural studies to comparative literature, which entered the American university in the late 1940s, we would expect it to take even more research time and require a familiarity with foreign languages as a basis for studying other cultures. This is not often the case, however. The program of both undergraduates and graduates has become increasingly scattered; and although there is a hunger to get to know other civilizations and to hear silent or silenced voices, the direct object of literary study—the minor or major works that have come down to us—is displaced. There exist, in brief, many reasons for the recession of literary scholarship and a diminishment in its standards and quality.

Crucial to that diminishment is not only the exclusion of religious thinking already mentioned but a current of skepticism. Aggressively pragmatic, cultural studies views the curriculum as Eurocentric or not comprehensive enough, and it casts a cold eye on the link between liberty and the art of the past. A passage from Tacitus's *Agricola* anticipates this skepticism. Tacitus wished to praise Agricola's tenure as Roman governor of Britain. Agrippa combined, Tacitus says, martial tactics with softer means of pacifying the Britons; and those softer means are described as follows:

> He [Agrippa] began to train the sons of the chieftains in a liberal education, and to give a preference to the native talents of the Briton as against the trained abilities of the Gaul. As a result, the nation which used to reject the Latin language began to aspire to rhetoric: further, the wearing of our dress became a distinction, and the toga came into fashion, and little by little the Britons went astray into alluring vices: to the promenade, the bath, the well-appointed dinner table. The simple natives gave the name of "culture" to this factor of their slavery.[1]

The word translated as "culture" is *humanitas* in the original. Tacitus reminds us of what postcolonial political critics have been saying: The colonizers use culture to weaken the resolve of the colonized, to co-opt them, to prevent them finding their own genius and resources. Frantz Fanon, the Algerian anticolonial revolutionary, insisted that the colonized would achieve independence only through recovering, or else innovating, their own culture; to benefit from the colonizer's civilization merely diverts revolutionary action.

In Roman times cultural and martial achievements—Arms and the Arts—were both in demand. The reason for the toleration of literature remained, however, statist and utilitarian. Stoic, soldierly courage was the ideal, and the orator, who might be an artist, was there mainly to satirize human folly, enact civic business, and recall the empire's glory, even in bad times. Although formulated later, the *translatio imperii et studii* principle, that the arts follow empire, already existed in embryo. The idea of a sacred succession or of a canonical order of works guided both scholarly and artistic tradition.

❑   ❑   ❑

Let me proceed here by giant steps and say that the *translatio* ideal, which legitimized the Holy Roman Empire, was appropriated in early modernism by a historicizing view. Political liberty, with the disintegration of that empire, was said to have moved from East to West, first across time to the countries of the Renaissance, then to Britain; and the arts followed liberty's progress. In the eighteenth century, Bishop Berkeley envisaged this *translatio* as a providential drama culminating in a last act: the transplanting of arts and letters from a decadent Europe to America as the New World.

I come, then, to my central concern. Are the universities of the New World—now not so new—weakening in their will to teach and transmit the Western heritage? Even without agreement about how serious the falling off is, a large contingent of teachers and empirical evidence from the type of courses most in demand suggest that we are experiencing a marked change in attitude. The change is recent, and often linked to the new demographics of the university: the attempt to make it truly democratic in its admissions and hiring policy, a process that gained momentum in the 1960s.

I am not prepared to argue that the disincentive for concentrating on Western culture—hardly a small field of study—is a necessary consequence of this demographic upheaval. I prefer to follow Irving Howe's analysis in the wake of the turmoil of the late 1960s. In his essay "What's the Trouble?" Howe diagnosed a crisis of civilization, distinguished from social crisis in that, unlike the latter, it could not be remedied by politics. What he called "residual sentiments of religion and vague but powerful yearnings for transcendence" enter all the more when "the transmission of values is blocked and a lack of belief in the power of education spreads among the educated classes." Howe had no decisive remedy but advocated a "discipline": giving the ballot box its due yet respecting the gap between politics and the imaginative-expressive needs represented and sometimes satisfied by religion and culture.[2]

That a link exists between culture and political thought is not in question. The trouble comes, as Howe explained it, when all cultural aspirations, all transcendent feelings, are expressed in terms of politics, centered on a democratic ideal of liberty or not. Our very awareness of this development should sound an alarm against identity politics: that is, using genealogy or nationality to claim civil advantages, unless these can be shown to improve rather than worsen communal life and social justice.

Despite outward appearances, then, I fear that our situation in the university is not very different from what was noted by Walter Benjamin in a remarkable essay of 1915. Benjamin denounced the falsification of the creative spirit as it turns toward careerism. The overwhelming task, he wrote, "is to found a community of knowledge seekers [*Erkennenden*] instead of a corporation of civil servants [*Beamten*] and university graduates."[3] The equivalent today, *our* careerism, exploits a divisive form of culture politics.

❏   ❏   ❏

The pleasures of imagination are, I have said, very much in evidence; and they cannot be dismissed by saying that art has become entertainment. That would be an obvious untruth, despite the temptations and tendencies I describe in chapter 12, "Democracy's Museum." My concern is primarily with *studium*, the study of art, which includes trained, critical judgment and assumes a motive to maintain what contributed in the past to freedom of expression and imagination. Today an urgent question is whether freedom and the arts still keep company, whether—to phrase it institutionally—political thought does not require, and more urgently than ever, aesthetic education.

Aesthetic education means, at the simplest level, that art is taken to be a serious empirical object of study and a field encouraged to reflect on itself, on its role in human relations. Learning of this kind is not satisfied by a politics centered on the curriculum, if that remains content to introduce unsettling contemporary works or identifies the aesthetic dimension in older ones as a narcissistic emphasis on beauty or a self-deceiving idealism. There is no other way to strengthen aesthetic education than to expose students to art itself and to those who have written passionately and critically about it. Theory, moreover, however obnoxious its vocabulary, plays an important role in pushing the debate about art and its study beyond practical and parochial concerns. The free discussion of differences in judgment and the recognition of genius as a gift that expands the sympathetic imagination or exposes mediocrity are all the more needful when the temptation is to fight only over ideological matters.

A further obstacle to understanding the link between liberty and art is that, when we talk today of freedom of expression, we think mainly of the status of the press. In the United States, the media are unfettered, and almost immune to sanctions. The dark side of this is that the category of "news" can lead to the spread of disinformation, innuendo, or even overt slander, which in turn actually incites civil or ethnic strife. The free production of news, in short, has problems only less serious than the controlled production of news; and this suggests that the very concept of free expression stands to lose some of its value. The amount of cynicism surrounding the media, a readiness to lie or give in to exhibition and publicity, has cheapened words, increased the influence of images and simulacra, stereotyped the idiom of liberation, and forced us back on something opaque celebrated as "character."

◻   ◻   ◻

When we turn, specifically, to the universities, the problem declares itself in a different way. The notion often contested there, as I have said, is of a composite yet relatively homogeneous culture described as "Western." It is claimed that to transmit it as worthy of teaching overlooks a past contaminated by gender and racial bias as well as uncritical nationalisms. Advocacy teaching has therefore increased, although I continue to hope that, whatever exceptions occur, anything entering the classroom of a responsible university will not be transmitted uncritically. If a particular subject matter is used only for the purpose of either ideology critique or identity affirmation, students are cheated; in that case, neither their mind nor their imagination is being educated, and they are not helped with the task of forming types of communal friendship that favor a broader civil society.

The fact is that, in the West, a plurality of cultural worlds has already replaced a unified culture. The real challenge is how to cope with and genuinely absorb this pluralism. Although we are not infinitely flexible in our mental and emotional disposition, when Herder first proposed this pluralism over two centuries ago it invigorated rather than weakened interest in how literature contributes to *Humanität*, to nations of both East and West considered as a family. Despite the naïveté of Herder's family metaphor, his view opened the arts for study, whatever their provenance.

Toward the end of his life, Goethe formulated explicitly the notion of a world literature; and, by the time of André Malraux, art appears as so various and exotic a domain that the very idea of the museum changes. A creative chaos originates, with the help of the printing press, a museum without walls, whose unlimited reproductions are accepted as part of modern life. To this we must add the explosion of libraries and archives. In the era of retrieval, which is our era, everything is considered worthy of a restitutive attention. The ensuing intensified struggle for unity of knowledge yields to the practical task of classification, of how to order and label all this accumulated treasure, or trash. A sterile formalism or lip service to diversity is often the result.

We should not underestimate, in any case, the emotional pressure now exerted on us: the peculiar sadness of the individual confronted by the multicultural supermarket. I feel poor or *désoeuvré* whenever I am more of a consumer than a producer. Nor do I want to be condemned to replicate what already exists, adding marginal differences. Imitation may be a necessary pedagogical ideal—yet the embarrassment of riches before us today simply intensifies a wish for exacting criteria of selection. Or, in reaction, we succumb to the lure of an unmediated vision, often inspired by what the Romantics valued as *the genius loci*, spirit of place. But that spirit or *Geist*, as history has shown, is easily politicized.

Some optimism remains when we remember that Emerson and Whitman still felt themselves to be liberators, opening democratic vistas: The New World had not yet grown old. Henry James may talk darkly about the impossibility of high culture in America, but American studies since his time, although hedged about by junk memorabilia as well as political pressures, continues to be among the vital disciplines. Meanwhile, the "subaltern" complexities of India and Africa challenge the literary scholar to broaden cultural memory and find a place for them.

❑   ❑   ❑

Returning for a moment to the Old World, there is already a tincture of melancholy in Malraux, whose grand style reflects Nietzsche's concept of a heroic struggle for cultural greatness amid a life-displacing historical knowledge and an incomprehensible plethora of artifacts. With Malraux we are close to Dostoevski's Ivan Karamazov, who says before leaving for Europe: "I know, Alyosha, that I am going to a cemetery, but it is the dearest of all, the most cherished cemetery."[4] In our time a similar melancholy is expressed by Harold Bloom.

Bloom, in all his books, celebrates the strong artist as one who has confronted the great yet burdensome legacy of the major writers. The weak artist fails precisely because of a failure to recognize and emulate greatness. Each significant new writer tries to find a new mode of strength. Major writers do not master the past or free themselves of a psychic burden. Then how do they remain creative? It must become an aim of literary theory to evolve a persuasive concept of originality.

Any such concept combines, however, despite Bloom, with a historicizing narrative about material factors that shape this originality—at least, render it more intelligible. A respect for these mediations is one reason why neither Hegel nor Marx will quit the scene. A historicizing reason demystifies art and seems to keep us in touch with extra-aesthetic realities—even if a few thinkers, like Maurice Blanchot, who remains an esoteric presence, have criticized that mode of intelligibility.

The task is to tame rather than give up learning in a historicizing age. Scholars like Peter Szondi engage the historicity of understanding as a fact rather than a problem to be resolved: His focus on maintaining a specifically literary analysis has made us more reflective about the way *Historie* (positivistic historical scholarship) blocks literary appreciation. To understand art means to renew art as well as one's understanding. This is what assures "die unverminderte Gegenwart auch noch der ältesten Texte" (the undiminished presence of even the oldest texts).[5]

Yet confusion rather than theory prevails when originality is attributed to an archaic and jeopardized identity. An ersatz religion arises, largely invented by nationalistic or ethnic motives. Hence a sense of fatality in many teachers about their role: Do what they may, a dominant culture or ethnic ideology preempts patient and intricate processes of study. Slow reading is out. How then can aesthetic education be strengthened: How can the intricacy of art, or the philological complexity—and often unpredictability—of interpretation, improve the quality of public life? Can art give a law to politics? The word "aesthetic" itself, as I will emphasize later, has become suspect.

◻   ◻   ◻

In fact, one reason the will to transmit (*translatio*) has weakened is that a comprehensive humanistic knowledge may undermine the dominant culture or the administered life. It tends to relativize that culture and make it more difficult for individuals to prefer the rightness of their own existence. Television and the media also remove the excuse of ignorance. As Terrence des Pres, gifted cultural observer, said of the modern condition: "What others suffer, we behold."[6] We may not know what to do with those images of violence and wretchedness, but we cannot *not* be aware of them. There is a reservoir of guilt ready to be exploited in almost all who live comfortably in their own skin.

This means that culture cannot be contrasted as urbanely as before to barbarism. From the time of Freud's *Civilization and Its Discontents* (1930), still under the shock of the First World War, to the role the concept of civilization plays in the Nuremberg Trials after the Second World War, where it appears both as a bulwark against barbarity, breached by Nazism, and as an ordering, bureaucratic force unleashing that very barbarity, this most common and stabilizing concept falls into contradiction.

The skepticism I have mentioned becomes more persuasive, therefore: Many accept Walter Benjamin's insight that the real nature of past achievements, built on the sweat and blood of oppressed or anonymous toilers, has been occulted. "One cannot deny," the cultural historian Jacob Burckhardt already noted, "that the quickly and highly developed power of dominant nations and individuals could only have been purchased by the suffering of the many and innumerable." The static and idealizing aspects of art are subjected to an increasingly critical scrutiny. A hermeneutics of suspicion, as Paul Ricoeur has called it, becomes commonplace.

❏   ❏   ❏

Yet, somehow, the affection we have for art and the attention it demands through its intelligent or instinctive precision of word, sound, image, have prevented a foolish iconoclasm. Indeed, a movement against aestheticide (that is, killing off the aesthetic dimension of art or life) may emerge once more out of the ashes of a consensus: that art, in conjunction with our reflections on it, plays a crucial role in broadening communicability. "The changing wisdom of successive generations," Joseph Conrad wrote, "discards ideas, questions facts, demolishes theories. But the artist appeals to that part of our being which is not dependent on wisdom . . . [and appeals] to the solidarity in dreams, in joy, in sorrow, in aspiration, in illusions . . . [that part] which binds men to each other, which binds all humanity."[7] Art continues to address our common nature, felt if unfulfilled possibilities, even the physiological unconscious. It takes us beyond superficial, selfish, overspecialized interests.

Let us recall, in this respect, that until recently Western art was often based on a classical and playful sense of humanization, on fictive embodiments best illustrated by an epigram from the Greek Anthology. It records as Aphrodite's lament the following inscription on her statue: "Alas, alas, where did Praxiteles see me naked?" Although in nonclassical canons it is harder to discern the transformation of an obvious interest—such as sexuality, anthropomorphism, or the passionate desire to communicate—into a sensuous yet nonobsessive object of contemplation, critical appreciation still turns around these issues.

Art itself is not endangered, then, but its contemplative appeal is now harder to maintain. I do not find the same dedication to it, the same sense of assured value that seemed to prevail from the period of the Romantics (with their *sacré du poète*) into the 1960s. This sense of art's value was nourished by many different sources, including Burckhardt's "Sturmlehre": an awareness of the modern, accelerating dynamics of history, a sense of the conflict and interaction of state, religion, and culture. The very pressure of modernity made art more resistant, more zealous about the need to preserve its privacy and autonomy, less ready to consume itself in the "storm" of public affairs.

❏   ❏   ❏

As the study of art moves from the humanities toward sociology, or as the distinction between these disciplines wavers, it becomes more difficult to acknowledge aesthetic education. For sociology can hardly be seen as disinterested. It is often given its direction, as well as funding, by some corporate interest; and even when the social sciences, or *Kulturwissenschaften*, maintain a certain distance from the centers of commerce or state power, they are "coordinated" in times of national crisis. This can happen through a contagious sort of enthusiasm, as when the historian Friederich Meinecke enlists Kant as German culture hero in 1914, or through organized cultural steering, of art as well as scholarship, as in Stalinist Russia and its dependencies, or in Nazi Germany, or when democratic governments impose on the media during times of war. It can also infiltrate through more subtle economic venues, such as state-sponsored cultural subventions or corporate philanthropy.

The question comes down to whether a disinterested knowledge exists. In the heady years of modernism, artists—especially painters, but also poets like Valéry—turned toward scientific analysis to achieve a purer form, based on color theory (as in Robert Delaunay) or some other philosophy of composition. (Edgar Allan Poe's notorious and puzzling popularity among avant-garde artists in later nineteenth-century France was motivated less by his practice than by his self-parodying aspiration toward such a philosophy.) This was classicism's last gasp, or modernism's rivalry with classical objectivity, and it intensified a fundamental question raised by aesthetics. Does the pleasure communicated by art point to a freer type of understanding, merging knowledge and delight—not only in the study of the arts but in the world of scholarship generally?

Freedom here does not mean aloofness or disengagement: It points to the receptive rather than compulsive element in imagination, to an imaginative visiting of other positions, as Hannah Arendt liked to say. I think we could agree that such knowledge would be worth cultivating and transmitting. The question has its own philosophic standing since Kant. It becomes urgent, however, when art, spreading to a larger audience, and open to public criticism, tries to justify itself—perhaps I should say to rationalize or even sell itself.

Here artists themselves are often not responsible enough. In a consumer society, the distinction between art and technique is reduced through the propaganda put out by artists or those hired to merchandise contemporary works. Art's technique, touted as a mystique, sways the market. Our admiration for contemporary works is not unalloyed, therefore, but mixed with perplexity: There is both a genuine respect for the ingenious way materials are used—new materials, any materials—and a distrust of the artist's connivance (close to parody) with a society that loves not just displays bordering on exhibitionism but the very project or claim as such: self-advertisement as a creator of value. The French social critic Jean Baudrillard goes so far as to allege that there is a conspiracy of postmodern art, abetted by frenetic commercial interests, to disable critical judgment through such claims. Having got rid of the desire for the illusion of reality through the hyperreality of the image, art produces the illusion that it has something important to hide, a secret to convey.

It is not easy, then, for scholar-critics of literature to exercise their function. On one side are exotic, sometimes esoteric forms, which abet that very specialization and division of labor that make articulate communication more difficult and diminish the hope for a compensatory sphere of communal values. On the other side is the mediating cultural critic, seduced at times by a technical vocabulary yet increasingly charged with the public function of deciphering a hermetic or specialized style.

The uneasy status of literary study today is also exacerbated by a philosophy of engagement that calls for artists, and still more for university teachers, to be "public intellectuals." This is an attractive ideal, associated in America with the career of Edmund Wilson as a wide-ranging man of letters. Yet in the Europe of the 1920s and 1930s, as literary criticism broadened its scope and moved closer to newspaper and magazine journalism, it also intensified a partisan relationship that had never been entirely absent. The trend toward engagement was, in fact, denounced by Julien Benda in his famous interwar *The Betrayal of the Intellectuals*, but the prolific muse of Jean-Paul Sartre reasserted it after the Second World War, dichotomizing socially useful prose and narcissistic poetry. Can we today still appreciate Hannah Arendt's paradox, that works of art are "the worldliest of things" in their staying power yet "the only things without function in the life of society"?[8]

For students of the arts, there is a further worry. Even should art and aesthetic insight contribute to what is most generous and disinterested in us, can they be articulated and transmitted as knowledge? Or is there not always a gulf between the university (the *tradition savante*) and popular art (the *tradition vernaculaire*)?

It is doubtful that works of art can be sorted out as worthy or corrupting, as lasting or expendable, without the help of criticism; and this criticism cannot be confined to academic experts. We remain unclear, however, about the nature of that indispensable critical activity. Is it comparable to a social or political science? Is it a didactic mode, like ethics, or a skillful mixture of knowledge and publicity, conspiring with the culture industry?

The French wave of Roland Barthes, Tzvetan Todorov, Gerard Gennette, and others, from about 1960 on, tried to convert literary studies into a "science littéraire" modeled on the linguistic turn of structuralism and semiotics. In the United States, refugee scholars like Roman Jacobson and Michael Riffaterre lent authority to this scientific project. I. A. Richards's *Practical Criticism* had begun a similar, if more pragmatic, trend in the 1920s, seeking to find impersonal criteria for the aesthetic judgment and so to diminish the influence of a genteel and impressionistic elite. Northrop Frye's *Anatomy of Criticism* of 1959 extended Richards's effort: Literary knowledge should be saved from don or gentleman scholar and become a pedagogical force with democratic implications.

Today the scientific model, while still contributing to centralized systems of education in Europe, is not taken all that seriously—except when grants are applied for. At the same time, literature is becoming less the object of literary study than of an informal sociology or politology. I say "informal" because so few who approach literature this way have actually worked in sociology or political science. They use socioeconomic categories, particularly class, gender, race, and property relations, to inspect works of art as "products" of a certain form of social life, which Marx—who *is* being read—considered temporary or transitional. The motivation of most of these analyses is social justice, and the field established by them is what we call cultural studies. But where do we find, together with that social awareness, the inventiveness, playfulness, and art-centeredness of a Kenneth Burke?

❒   ❒   ❒

We all share the aim of social justice; the quarrel is about the means to that end. There is a lesson in the fact that our best cultural critics tend to be ethnologists or anthropologists. They do not assume they already know the rules of the game but observe the ritual, legal, symbolic institutions created by *Homo ludens*—or his apparent opposite, *Homo religiosus.* They teach us, back home, to look at our own surroundings and to regret our wasteful glances. They are not afraid to tell a good story, although they face the issue of cultural translation: How much is compatible with our own way of thinking and talking, how much can "travel"? Ironically, many of these scholars (I can mention Clifford Geertz as a well-known instance) have learned something from the New Critics and the Yale School, from text-centered readers, particularly those who do not take the unity of the artifact for granted but reveal conflicting strains in it—competing symbolisms, breaches of style, heteroglossia, and openness or indeterminacy, rather than overformalized structures like paradox, chiasmus, and erudite literary building blocks called topoi. In short, humanists should become the anthropologists of their own culture once more.

The tension, moreover, between historians and literary scholars has not helped the negative mood in literary study. Historians reject what one of their profession, Hayden White, calls metahistory, which tries to view the writing of history in terms of specific rhetorical or narrative structures. Scholars of literature refuse, in turn, the claim of the social sciences that we can gain a direct and more objectively truthful knowledge of human relations through them. (What might validate that knowledge is, in any case, not clear: the concept of validation, or *Anerkennung*, remains vague and is left to natural process, history as Fortuna, or to an often sentimental politics of acknowledgment.) Even though the new historicism has tried to bridge the two largest areas of study in the humanities, the question of what the subject of history may be—the nation or the individual or humanity as such (our philological home is the earth as a whole, not the nation, Erich Auerbach wrote after the Second World War)—is an unending matter of controversy. Trauma studies, a new, comprehensive field under the sign of Philomela, seems a more promising development, for it seeks a way to acknowledge the relation of wounds and words and to integrate biography, psychoanalysis, minority literature, and religious or other experiences of the sublime. The Law and Literature movement too can be a more conceptual way of demonstrating the intersection of those disciplines with the issue of social justice. Seen in that light, the movement exemplifies cultural studies at its best.

□   □   □

I have not mentioned so far the most difficult present obstacle to literary study, which also weakens rather than strengthens the zeal to transmit a heritage that is still taught formally, but not always "received." The memory of Nazism and the Holocaust—and now of other genocides—continues to be subversive. Here I do not think in the first place of Theodor Adorno's notorious strictures, which stimulate, in the way prohibitions do, what they forbid. Adorno's comments bear on art itself rather than the study of art. Such famous essays as "Engagement" hold, as is well known, that Holocaust experience in its extremity cannot be "engaged" with, in the sense that it could be made the subject matter of art. The reason given by Adorno is not that antihuman events cannot be represented, that the attempt necessarily results in a failure of mimesis. Rather, Adorno believes that mimesis produces the wrong effect: It meretriciously stylizes the event or causes us to take pleasure in it, voyeuristically or by an involuntary movement of despicable affirmation ("verruchte Affirmation").

Nonetheless, the Holocaust—and other atrocities, some within the United States itself—cannot be ignored, and the question becomes what cultural factors were responsible for them and whether they are still active: Is culture, in the older sense of an emancipatory progress of ideas and spectrum of sensibilities, so damaged that it cannot be restored? In many thinkers (but not in Adorno), the fatality of ideology shows itself in a contempt associated with the adjective "aesthetic," which bears the brunt of the failure of culture and the educated class: particularly, of their impotence in Germany and continental Europe when faced with the anti-Semitism and hatred of foreigners that preceded genocide. In some quarters "aesthetic" has become a dirty word, rather than describe the system of the arts generally or a collective body of media that share a special quality.

At this juncture, it is difficult to tell whether literary study will recover from the suspicions that subvert it. Even if we find a way to say, yes, art resisted political servitude or took as much as possible the side of personal and political liberty, the study of literature has a hard time defending itself. The attack on aestheticism spills over into an attack on the aesthetic; so that, in effect, literary theory must return to aesthetics as an integral part of life rather than rejecting it as an artificial or socially incorrect mode of "distinction."

There are those, of course, who prefer not to think about theory at all, who see it corroding an older type of solidarity—apparently humanistic, and yet a god that failed. We could indeed be misled if we try to isolate, like a chemical ingredient, the specificity of art or of an aesthetic state. That art cannot be essentialized has, in turn, larger implications. The resistance of the aesthetic to being categorized does not come from its singularity. The aesthetic is marked by immediacy rather than singularity, and this characteristic maintains itself within the mediations (historical, social, linguistic) we may discover. Art, despite its conscious or unconscious embeddedness in historical processes and its obscure physiological provenance, points to an intelligibility we have not understood. How does art convert learning or information into a vital tradition, what Wordsworth called "the breath and finer spirit of all knowledge," unless it is by getting "the closest fix on the mystery of sensation" (Lyotard), and waking a sort of soul in sense, or even sense itself?[9]

❑   ❑   ❑

At the end of this book, Lyotard's comments, part of a reflection on the "minimal soul," return us to a frontier I have not crossed. It is clear that in any contemporary discussion of spirit, authenticity, and aesthetics, difficult philosophical issues enter. My focus has been primarily on a perplexity, not always conscious, triggered by the increase of simulacra, of potentially deceitful imitations. Perhaps there is a link between such a perplexity and a questioning that intends to make the true image or reality appear, a questioning that, like the medieval Ordeal, is tempted to use force.

There has always been violence in the world, together with the paradox that what counters it in the name of the reality of spirit is itself a "transcendental violence." A further paradox is specific to the rise of aesthetics as a formal mode of understanding art. Crudely put: Is art on the side of spirit against materialistic motives, or is it on the side of a materialism that would chasten, reign in, demystify a violence carried out in the name of spirit? When Adorno calls a sequence of his reflections *Minima Moralia*, and when Lyotard approaches the border of metapsychology and metaphysics with remarks on the minimal soul, we know they are rethinking materialism within a crassly materialistic society that claims to be spiritual in its outlook.

Art becomes a crucial battleground for two reasons. It stands at the beginning of mankind's desire to create simulacra, the question always remaining: simulacra of what and for what purpose? Moreover, art does not disappear into what it represents. As a medium with its own mode of being, it maintains a distance between itself and that reality. This very distance, intrinsic to its reflective power, makes art a doubtful agency in any pressing conflict. We often fall back, therefore, on praising art as a special medium among media—something that mimes the rich, neglected materiality of things. As such, it revives traces of a half-forgotten intensity of perception, when the weight of the world was not quite so desiccating and enervating, when what Wordsworth called "the incumbent mystery of sense and soul"[10] was an adventure that had its end in itself. How effective are those intimations when the phase of life that they recall is condemned as infantile, and the wish to purge its nostalgic presence once and for all, or to mobilize its residual ecstasy for a great cause, becomes a further source of coercive imperatives?

No wonder an aesthetic element continues to be felt wherever there is a resistance to teleological meanings, as in the excess of figurative over utilitarian speech, or in simple effects of color, sound, smell, light, and air. A pioneer in appreciating cinema's cultural influence, Siegfried Kracauer views it as an art alerting us to the existence of an optical unconscious, and so helping to redeem physical reality. The media, before they themselves become routinized, make us more aware that there is a knowledge proper to sense perception, which art raises to a kind of consciousness. In a preface to his lyrical drama *Prometheus Unbound*, Shelley says that it was "chiefly written upon the mountainous ruins of the Baths of Caracalla, among the flowery glades, and thickets of odoriferous blossoming trees, which are extended in ever winding labyrinths upon its immense platforms and dizzy arches suspended in air."[11]

But there is another, all-too-human resistance to normative modes of significance: the result of a drive, compulsive in its intensity and perhaps traumatic in its origin, for a devouring intimacy, even an orgiastic bonding. Call it a communication compulsion, one that is basically communitarian, but also so sensitive, so desirous of response, that in its vulnerability it may prefer silent speech to speech. One senses this undertow in the very eloquence of Shakespeare, Kleist, Melville, Dickinson, Dostoevski, Kafka, Celan—in every great writer perhaps. Trauma study as a new awareness deals with the fact that "even in those who still have the power to cry out, the cry hardly ever expresses itself, either inwardly or outwardly, in coherent language." Simone Weil, who wrote this, adds that what is needed is "an attentive silence in which this faint and inept cry can make itself heard; and finally institutions . . . of a sort which will, so far as possible, put power into the hands of those able and anxious to hear and understand it."[12]

Further, whenever social life succumbs to an ideology of the politically and morally correct, art moves into opposition with an anarchic, in-your-face representation of lust and disgust. The raw distaste for the human species we find in Swift, Sade, and Artaud, in Nietzsche quite often, in certain rock bands, and such novels as Nathaniel West's *Day of the Locust*, Saul Bellow's *Mr. Sammler's Planet*, or Philip Roth's at once honest and hilarious depictions of male sexual fantasies—this energetic disgust is more than cathartic. The authors' hyperbole and deliberate bad taste, like ranting in Shakespeare, takes the risk of sickening us—testing our capacity to humor a breach of the euphemistic clichés on which everyday civility depends.

The relation of aesthetics to taste or the limits of representation is an issue so basic to art that it must be pursued as a subject in itself. To return to my opening question—has literary study grown old?—I conclude that it has too many unfinished tasks to allow itself to decay. Not only recent art keeps the critic alert: Older art, too, even when canonized, and perhaps because of that, can haunt us like a revenant. *The Iliad* as a poem about violence in war is more bearable yet no less effective than Steven Spielberg's *Saving Private Ryan*, with its shameless and powerful camera work. Sophocles' *Electra*, its moments of blistering dialogue and relentless convergence on a foreseen act of bloody vengeance, is, in its very brevity, an event that does not leave the modern viewer untouched. The visionariness of the Bible, too, the harsh, violent, unresolved moments in which the Israelites, bearers of the blessing, struggle with man and God alike, still challenges the dominant contemporary discourse of utopian materialism.

In what he calls an "intervention," Adorno explains why philosophical thinking is not yet outmoded. I want to quote, in conclusion, a passage in which he acknowledges the inevitability of the idealism/materialism split but calls for "militant enlightenment" rather than resignation to an impasse. He himself is drawn to aesthetics in pursuit of this aim. In the following, without mentioning art, he briefly and eloquently summarizes a position that I can join: "A fulfilled materialism would mean today the end of materialism—of the blind, unworthy dependence of mankind on its material circumstances. Spirit is not the Absolute any more than its merger with what exists. Only then will spirit recognize itself for what it is, if it does not cancel itself out. The strength of such resistance is the only measure of philosophy today."[13]

EPILOGUE

9/11

O n that day I checked in at LaGuardia for a flight to Logan Airport and a lecture in Boston, a few moments before the first plane struck one of the World Trade Center Towers.

On my way from the check-in to the gate, I saw people crowding around a TV monitor at a bar. I noticed but did not give much thought to it. (The second plane may just have hit, since I had stopped at an airport store around 9 A.M.) Perhaps ten minutes later the PA system announced that the airport was closed. Only then did I go to the bar and see a replay of the disaster.

I assumed it was an unbelievable accident, until another plane near the second tower disappeared, a cloud of smoke and then flares indicating it also had struck. Although alarmed and perplexed, I cannot say a distinct thought of danger invaded me, until the rumor spread a short time later that the Pentagon and White House had been bombed. Even as flames issued from the wounded towers, I thought only of how many casualties there might be and in no way anticipated the scope of the disaster to come.

After another interval—it may have been fifteen or twenty minutes—we were asked to leave the terminal and found ourselves outside without transportation: The bridges had been closed. I made my way (in what may have been a gypsy limo) to a subway station near the

Queensboro Bridge; then, because the subway was not running, streamed with a large crowd to Manhattan, via the pedestrian sidewalk of the bridge. It was a beautiful day; on my left side smoke could be seen near the horizon, which I kept looking at as if it was bound to go away once firefighters had it under control.

I have had several months to think about what happened on that day. What difference did that event make, which put its mark on time as if an epoch had passed, even if one cannot yet fully gauge the hope that was lost or the determination gained? With some reluctance I decided on this short epilogue. My Foreword, written last, was dated August 2001, and the book had been essentially complete a few months before that.

❏   ❏   ❏

A rhetoric of specificity, common to temporal markers, is used these days with exquisite precision: We hear that the self-awareness of the United States and the West changed shortly after 8:46 A.M. that clear September morning. On the one hand, the flow of time seems mechanical, as if perpetual and infinitely divisible, a banal matter of record; on the other, an emotional stopwatch punctuates life with traumatic or near-apocalyptic effect.

The power of a traumatic episode to define an epoch is caught by Freud's "On Transience," which expressed the feeling that the First World War, then barely a year old, "had robbed the world of its beauties . . . shattered pride in the achievements of our civilization, our admiration for many philosophers and artists and our hopes of a final triumph over the differences between nations and races."[1] Even Europe, that "Old World," subtly permeated as in Henry James's novels by a sophisticated corruption and ceremonies of complicity—Europe, it seemed, had still an innocence to lose. As for America today . . . Many times in the last few months the figure of the American Adam has surfaced: of a suddenly vanished and already nostalgically haloed fall from innocence and security.

I wonder whether there is not always a wake-up call in the life of individuals or collectives. John Donne describes that "now" moment when he calls falling in love a "good-morrow to our waking souls." Its other side is a decisive disenchantment affecting basic trust. The demystifying incident, one that precipitates a major turning of mood or mind, could itself be deceptive in the sense of crystallizing previous shocks rather than being unique. As the life of some of the hijackers comes into view, we are often told that they seemed normal enough, even bourgeois, until "something" changed them into radical Muslims.

Did the strain of living with an invasive sense of alienation, of the unreality of society, self, or world feed their contempt of worldliness and particularly of the Western style of life? The yearning for purity, lost or about to be lost, for dedication, for truth that lodges elsewhere—beyond corruption, humiliation, hypocrisy, injustice, materialism, grinding poverty, or poverty of spirit—can lead to the adoption of a transgressive, even outlaw identity. Instead of impassiveness or trivial pursuit, an exalted, visionary sense of purpose takes over; popular fiction is full of avengers and purifiers of that kind.

A spectacular act can give the illusion of agency or self-identity, even at the cost of unleashing disaster. In Coleridge's famous "Ancient Mariner" poem, the consequence (although not the motivation) of the Mariner's killing of the Albatross is clear: The act opens his eyes to a universe filled with spirits. They demand the perpetrator's punishment yet also make him their focus. Everything turns on his (guilty) presence. His trespass in this Eastern tale, as this kind of story was often called, accrues revelatory power: A hidden legion of supernatural enforcers comes into view. The hijackers, by the light fiction throws on history, may have pursued an aim that seemed to them exalted rather than malignant: something akin to the well-known religious temptation to "hasten the end." Did they also seek to redeem the image of the fatalistic Muslim by making themselves instruments of a fatal action?

The quest for authenticity (intending to restore the true Islam, the true Christian faith, or other religious ways of life) exposes an inflammable identity crisis. Perhaps induced by a "call," a crisis of this kind inheres in every formation of the distinctive individual. The impulse to separate from one community (family, home) leads to a second birth within a chosen community. In extreme cases it creates deodands, self-proclaimed messengers of God, or provokes sacrificial deeds to overcome the vanity, impurity, and emptiness of human life—although it would be sheer hubris to enumerate and typify here all the intellectual and emotional malformations that might ensue. What is clear is that evil can have idealistic as well as cynical roots.

The call may ask believers to change their life and "put away childish things." But what does that mean? What model of maturity or authentic existence is implied? I find it impossible to respect a culture that in fact denies childhood, and trains children to grow into warriors or even suicide bombers. Or movements that wound secular time by seeking to end it, inciting Apocalypse by way of a schism that parts "The man to come . . . as by a gulph/From him who had been."[2] (That is how Wordsworth described certain ideologies accompanying the French Revolution.)

Realpolitik, too, as in legal philosopher Carl Schmitt's sheer polarity of friend and foe, is often presented as a spiritual imperative, though it is really a sick outgrowth of the very desire for a paradisal harmony and unity. Genocide, the German philosopher Theodor Adorno remarked, involves the wish for absolute integration.

The Ground Zero left by the collapse of the Twin Towers is literally a scar of the spirit. It testifies to more than an attempt to shatter icons of capitalism and U.S. power. The smoldering devastation of those ruins creates a new icon, a permanent mental image of how violence can cloak itself as spirituality. Wordsworth discerned the religious or pseudoreligious intensity of the passion leading to such acts when he described how, in the era of the French Revolution, he became for a time "A Bigot to a New Idolatry/Like a cowled Monk who hath forsworn the world."[3]

□   □   □

When I finally reached Boston in October and gave my lecture, I took in a show by two famous fashion photographers working in Europe and America from the 1930s on. Because of TV, my head at that time was filled with images of Afghan women veiled completely in burkas according to the strictures of the Taliban. Nothing of their body was visible. They were shapeless statues. In contrast, the Boston exhibition, covering more than thirty years of models and celebrities, contained but a single photo of a totally swathed woman, a famous dancer.

It was a study of her garments' rhythmic, dynamic flow. It projected the image of a second or more glorious body superimposed on the first, a body more abstract or less patently functional, with lines sculpted as lovingly by photography's liquid gradations of light and shade as the beard and draperies of certain Romanesque figures at Vezelay or the Hellenic "Victory" that greets visitors to the Louvre.

Given our own, intensifying visual culture, it may be hard to understand why Taliban iconoclasm, its fear of images, has gone so far. The key, I think, is not found primarily in the concept of a pure monotheistic religion and its zeal to tame the lust of the eyes. Rather, a normative distrust of appearances turns into a species of gnosticism, that very old religious heresy resisted by both Judaism and Christianity. Positing a deceiving demiurge who may be the god of this world but is not the true God, it fostered the quest for deliverance from a deceit that could only be destroyed together with the world itself.

The *real presence* of falsity is a terrifying notion. It supports the idea of an evil empire. What comforted us in the past, when we became aware of social suffering, political oppression, or generally, living in untruth, was that falsity had only an unreal presence: Truth, as the saying goes, is the daughter of time; political, scientific, economic and medical remedies would surely, in time, alleviate global misery; reality was on the side of progress. In the West, this assumption has suffered a shock. Totalitarianism, two world wars, and a post-Holocaust awareness of continuing genocidal episodes have disclosed the extent to which "organized appearance" backed by terror can create for long and murderous periods a consenting populace.

In those parts of the Islamic world in which religion has become extremist and political, it is modernity, its technological power of imitation and simulation, that is held to be in the service of a deceitful demiurge. But elsewhere, too, uneasiness prevails. While augmenting the pleasure of living among beautiful and distracting things, modernity increases almost beyond human discernment the critical burden of distinguishing a merely vicarious from a truly participant and productive form of life.

The sterility of a consumer culture, the difficulty of endowing it with ultimate value, has a multitude of effects, including pernicious ideologies. These do not see a way out of the dominance of the pleasure principle and complicit institutions except by resorting to violence. The devil of technology is turned strategically against the enemy who fathered it. Moreover, when some Muslims pretend to be assimilated Westerners in order to destroy an infidel culture, the fear revives of the *faux semblant*, or enemy within, and threatens a hard-won multiculturalism as well as settled civil liberties.

Democratic institutions cannot afford to self-destruct under such pressure. We have not forgotten what happened in the McCarthy era; nor the immense tragedy inspired in good part by the Manichean ideology of Nazism. It disenfranchised even assimilated Jews (often more German than the Germans in their love of that culture), dooming them to expulsion and destruction. The Nazis could not often profile the assimilated German Jews by discernable marks of difference. Yet the very absence of distinguishing features (except for the disproportionate contribution Jews made to Germany's intellectual and artistic life) was held against that tiny minority and incited a propagandistic caricature viciously exaggerating the slightest physical difference and claiming that assimilation was a deceptive and dangerous mask. Fear of the real presence of falsity created a devil-myth once again.

Historical analogies are risky, but they are what we have to go on. Unlike the relatively small number of pre-Holocaust Jews, who at that time had no nation-state in which they were the majority, over a billion Muslims, the predominant majority in several nation-states, now pose a real challenge to the West. Most of Islam has not passed through a significant Reform movement separating church and state, and in its confrontation with secular modernity is convulsed by a conservative revolution. Whether or not a "clash of civilizations" is now inevitable, the dual temptation of radicalizing the East/West conflict and profiling differences returns in all its crudeness. Blake's "Human Form Divine," his saving concept of a reconciled, this-worldly humanity, is split apart, wounded by a powerful distrust. And, as surely as those planes crashed into the Twin Towers and the Pentagon, the reality behind the word "evil" has penetrated again our moral vocabulary.

A cause, unfortunately in the guise of a *casus belli*, has unified Americans, perhaps for the first time since World War II. I have never seen so many show the flag. The struggle against semblance and inauthenticity continues, entering an especially perilous phase.

NOTES

FOREWORD

1. Mimi Udovitch, "Visible Man," *New York Times Magazine*, February 18, 2001, 9–10; Margo Jefferson, "Authentic American," *New York Times Book Review*, February 18, 2001, 35.

2. John Smith, *Select Discourses* (London: W. Morden, Cambridge, 1660), 430–31.

3. For a perceptive and amusing take on this, see Michael Lewis, "Faking It," *New York Times Magazine*, July 16, 2001, 32ff.

4. Don DeLillo, *Underworld* (New York: Simon & Schuster, 1997), 155–60.

5. DeLillo, *Underworld*.

6. Martin Buber, "The Question to the Single One" in *Between Man and Man* (London: K. Paul, 1947). Compare how a recent entry into the field of moral and theological inquiry defines its "conceptual space": Eric Santner says he will "span the divide between the sciences of symbolic identity and an ethics of singularity." See *The Psychotheology of Everyday Life: Reflections on Freud and Rosenzweig* (Chicago: University of Chicago Press, 2001), 28.

7. Jean Baudrillard, *Simulacres et simulation* (Paris: Galilée, 1981). In my book, "simulacra" is used without that special conceptual baggage but does point to a likeness or second nature strong enough to be taken as nature.

8. Jean Baudrillard, *La transparence du mal: Essai sur les phénomènes extrêmes* (Paris: Galilée, 1990). Baudrillard generalizes what Valéry noted more cheerfully in his "Monsieur Teste" ("Mr. Head"), conceived almost a century earlier: "We accelerate in the void. . . . That is our state of simulation, in which we cannot but rejoice in all scenarios because they have already taken place—really or virtually."

CHAPTER 1

1. Emily Dickinson, "I cannot live with you." Poem 706 in *The Poems of Emily Dickinson, Variorum Edition*, ed. R.W. Franklin (Cambridge and London: The Belknap Press of Harvard University Press, 1998). First published in 1890.

2. This is all the more the case in what has been called a "society of risk" (*Risikogesellschaft*) by the German sociologist Ulrich Beck. See his *Risk Society: Toward a New Modernity*, tr. Mark Ritter (London: Sage Publications, 1992).

3. Heinrich Mann, "Das weiss eigentlich jeder" reprinted in *Das Führerprinzip/Heinrich Mann. Der Typus Hitler: Texte zur Kritik der NS-Diktatur* (Berlin: Aufbau Taschen Verlag, 1993), 19.

4. See D. W. Winnicott's seminal essay, "Transitional Objects and Transitional Phenomena" (1953) in *Playing and Reality* (New York: Routledge, 1971), 1–25.

5. Friedrich Schiller, *Letters On Aesthetic Education* (1796).

6. Ingeborg Bachmann, "Die gestundete Zeit" in *Die Gestundete Zeit* (Munich, 1953), 16.

7. Jane Tompkins, *A Life in School: What the Teacher Learned* (Reading, MA.: Addison-Wesley, 1996).

8. "[T]he matador who seems to risk everything is concerned about his 'line' and relies, in order to overcome danger, on his technical sagacity. Still, for the torero there is real danger of death, which never exists for the artist except outside of his art. . . ." See Leiris's preface (1947) to *Manhood: A Journey from Childhood into the Fierce Order of Virility*, tr. Richard Howard (Chicago: University of Chicago Press, 1984), 3–15. Sartre, similarly, writes that during the war, "each and every individual choice was authentic because it was made in the presence of death." ("The Republic of Silence" in *Situations III* (Paris: Gallimard, 1949).

9. André Aciman, *False Papers: Essays on Exile and Memory* (New York: Farrar, Straus and Giroux, 2000).

10. Lionel Trilling's phrase in *Sincerity and Authenticity* (Cambridge, MA.: Harvard University Press, 1972) describing Joseph Conrad's tale.

11. A recent twist in this development is inserting one's portrait into Holocaust photos that have achieved iconic status, or making Nazi imagery a mock advertisement, even part of an ornamental package, for a commercial icon. See the controversy over the Jewish Museum exhibition "Mirroring Evil: Nazi Imagery/Recent Art" that opened in New York in March 2002. It includes an altered, rephotographed photo, "It's the Real Thing—Self-Portrait at Buchenwald," by Alan Schechner. The "real thing" is the fakery, reflecting one's own sense of unreality: The self here borrows a Holocaust reality-context (or is it unreality-context) to portray itself. The "real thing" could also be—ironically—the exploitative commercialism of our culture, exemplified by a can of diet coke that the interpolated artist-inmate in striped prison garb conspicuously displays. (See also my remarks, below, on Boltanski.)

12. See "The Work of Art in the Age of Mechanical Reproduction" in Hannah Arendt, ed., *Walter Benjamin: Illuminations* (New York: Harcourt, Brace & World, 1968).

13. See Hannah Arendt, *The Human Condition* (Chicago: University of Chicago Press, 1958), and chapter 12, "Democracy's Museum."

14. Production, especially of animated feature films, involves a cast of hundreds: Just look at the credits for Jeffrey Katzenberg's *Moses, Prince of Egypt*. (Literary works too are often viewed today as if edited by an author in an intertextual situation not unlike that of the medieval and often anonymous composer: hence "death-of-the-author" theories that contrast vividly with the rise of autobiography.) Still, there is agreement that the director is an *auteur*, and it is usual to talk of a Spielberg, Fassbinder, Kubrick film etc., despite the dominance of studio manufacture.

15. Ludwig Wittgenstein, *Philosophical Investigations*, #217.

16. Jean Baudrillard, *Simulacres et simulation* (Paris: Galilée, 1981). My translation.

17. Binjamin Wilkomirski, *Fragments: Memories of a Wartime Childhood*, tr. Carol Brown Janeway (New York: Schocken Books, 1996). The latest false witness syndrome centers on fake Vietnam vets (or protesters). See David Oslinsky, "You Had to Be There, Man," *New York Times Magazine*, July 1, 2001, 21–22.

18. Jean Baudrillard, *Simulacres et simulation* (Paris: Galilée, 1981), 12. My translation.

19. On the nearness of imposture and identification, especially when artists seek to understand abhorrent events, see Sidra DeKoven Ezrahi's perceptive essay, "Acts of Impersonation: Barbaric Spaces as Theater," in the catalogue for the Jewish Museum show,

mentioned in note 11. *Mirroring Evil*, ed. Norman L. Kleeblatt (New Brunswick, N.J.: Rutgers University Press, 2002), 17–38.

20. The psychiatric aspect of the debate is discussed in detail by Ruth Leys, *Trauma: A Genealogy* (Chicago: University of Chicago Press, 2000). Concerning the problematic, centering-on-authenticity issues of "discursive space" in autobiographical narratives with ethnographic or anthropological content, see Mary Louise Pratt, "Fieldwork in Common Places" in *Writing Culture: The Poetics and Politics of Ethnography*, ed. James Clifford and George E. Marcus (Berkeley: University of California Press, 1986), 27–50.

21. *International Herald Tribune*, June 1, 2001, 1. This web phantom, named Kaycee Nicole Swenson, was created by Debbie Swenson, who had produced an online diary weblog called "Living Colours," recounting the story of a "sunny blond" and "unyieldingly optimistic" 19-year-old high school basketball star battling leukemia. Cf. the *New York Times*, July 8, 2001 front-page article on Aki Ross, a "versatile young actress" created by digital magic. "Aki is composed only of pixels, and she is created and manipulated by a computer animator who works his mouse like a weaver at his loom."

22. Philip Roth, *The Human Stain* (Boston: Houghton and Mifflin, 2000), 147.

23. Needless to say, a special theory is not necessary for the practicing writer to make that or a similar point. Here is Flannery O'Connor's take on the matter: "The writer has to judge himself with a stranger's eye and a stranger's severity. The prophet in him has to see the freak. No art is sunk in the self, but rather, in art the self becomes self-forgetful in order to meet the demands of the thing seen and the thing being made." *Mystery and Manners*, ed. Sally and Robert Fitzgerald (New York: The Noonday Press, 1961), 81–82.

24. Mikhail Bakhtin, "Forms of Time and Chronotope in the Novel," *The Dialogic Imagination: Four Essays by M. M. Bakhtin*, ed. Michael Holquist, tr. Caryl Emerson and Michael Holquist (Austin: University of Texas Press, 1981), 84–258. The emphasis on the transgressiveness of writing as such, of fiction as the counterfeit, is my own.

25. "As if his whole vocation/Were endless imitation," Wordsworth writes of the child in the famous "Ode: Intimations of Immortality." This points to the innocent form of what becomes, in later public life, a conscious or unconscious attempt to emulate.

26. These concepts overlap but are not identical. Reason is generally understood to be a universal human capacity, a *lumen naturale*, while inner light could also be a private and providential illumination rather than a spark or *ingenium* in everyone. Inner light (see also chapter 3) can challenge reason's horizontal universality and lead to a vertiginous religious "enthusiasm."

27. That is what Celan's peculiar construction "Aber Du" may imply. The "Aber" (But . . .) is either a syntactical device (like "re" in English) intensifying the precarious referent—the "you"—addressed, or is the emerging prefix of a new word "Aberdu," modeled on the German word for superstition, "Aberglaube."

28. Emily Dickinson, "I'm Nobody." Poem 260 in *The Poems of Emily Dickinson, Variorum Edition*, ed. R.W. Franklin (Cambridge and London: The Belknap Press of Harvard University Press, 1998). First published in 1891.

29. Frank Rich, "The Survival of the Fakest," *New York Times*, Op-Ed piece, August 26, 2000, A13.

30. A remarkable, exhaustive analysis of Blanchot's relation to, in particular, the "I" of autobiography, and by extension the relation of testimony (nonliterary depositions) to literature, is found in Blanchot, *The Instant of My Death*, published together with Jacques Derrida, *Demeure: Fiction and Testimony*, tr. Elizabeth Rottenberg (Stanford, CA.: Stanford University Press, 2000). Derrida takes up Blanchot's account of his mock execution during the war.

31.   Stanley Cavell, *The Senses of* Walden (New York: Viking Press, 1972), 27.

CHAPTER 2

1.   Trauma theory, often in the ambit of a discussion of whether a realistic portrayal of the Holocaust's universe of death is possible, adds to the complexity. So Michael Rothberg describes Holocaust literature's "traumatic realism" as "the absence of the real, a real absence, [that] makes itself felt in the familiar plentitude of reality." See *Traumatic Realism: The Demands of Holocaust Representation* (Minneapolis: Minnesota University Press, 2000), 140.

2.   Edmund Morris, *Dutch: A Memoir of Ronald Reagan* (New York: Random House, 1999).

3.   Morris, in fact, justifies his invention of a fictional first-person narrator by comparing its effect to the "black box" that projects film in the movie house. He claims it can be a non-intrusive device.

4.   Henry D. Thoreau, *Walden, or, Life in the Woods* (Boston: Ticknor and Fields, 1854).

5.   Jacobo Timmerman, *Prisoner Without a Name, Cell Without a Number,* tr. Tony Talbot (New York: Vintage Books, 1982), 71.

6.   Jorge Semprun, *L'écriture ou la vie* (Paris: Gallimard, 1994), 34.

7.   Joyce Maynard, *At Home in the World: A Memoir* (New York: Picador, 1998).

8.   For the power of that book to incite extraordinary (and crazy) identifications, see chapter 2, "Explosive Fictions," in Jay Martin, *Who Am I This time? Uncovering the Fictive Personality* (New York: Norton, 1988). The recent film *Finding Forrester* continues the Salinger legend by transposing it to the inner city. Sean Connery plays a reclusive novelist who mentors (but finally does not abandon) an aspiring and challenging black youngster with a literary gift.

9.   Maynard, 343.

10.   Samuel Taylor Coleridge, "Shakespeare's Judgment Equal to His Genius," 1836.

11.   Maynard, 343.

12.   Maynard, 344.

13.   Roth, *The Human Stain,* 359–61.

14.   Phyllis Rose, *The Year of Reading Proust: A Memoir in Real Time* (New York: Scribener, 1997).

15.   Michael Cunningham, *The Hours* (New York: Farrar, Straus and Giroux, 1998).

CHAPTER 3

1.   G. W. F. Hegel, *The Phenomenology of Mind,* tr. J. B. Baillie (New York: Harper Torchbooks, 1967), 679. Some translators prefer to translate the German word *Geist* in Hegel's title as "Spirit." This entire section of the *Phenomenology* has a strong affinity with Goethe's portrait of the "beautiful soul" (discussed in chapter 10, "Who needs Goethe?"). "Beautiful soul" characterizes Pietism and related kinds of enthusiastic, inner light quests for personal authenticity. Lionel Trilling's *Sincerity and Authenticity* saw the importance of both Goethe and Hegel in drawing attention to the concept.

2.   Herman Melville, *White Jacket or The World in a Man-of-War* (Evanston and Chicago: Northwestern University Press and Newberry Library, 1970), 150–51. The book was first published in 1850.

3.   William Wordsworth, *The Prelude: 1799, 1805, 1850,* eds. Jonathan Wordsworth, M. H. Abrams, Stephen Gill (New York: W. W. Norton and Co., 1979). This passage appears in Book 11 (1850), lines 304–5.

4.   From Book One, Chapter One of *The Social Contract and Other later Political Writings,* ed. Victor Gourevitch (New York: Cambridge University Press, 1997), 41.

5. William Blake, "London" and "The Divine Image" in *Blake's Poetry and Designs: A Norton Critical Edition*, ed. Mary Lynn Johnson and John E. Grant (London: W. W. Norton and Co., 1979), 53, 30.

6. Wordsworth, *The Prelude*, Book 12 (1850), lines 59–60.

7. Matthew Arnold, *Culture and Anarchy*, ed. Samuel Lipman (New Haven, CT.: Yale University Press, 1994).

8. Wordsworth, *The Prelude*.

9. An exemplary close reading of "spirit," which encompasses and animates an entire corpus of discourses, is found in Jacques Derrida's *De l'esprit: Heidegger et la question* (Paris: Galilée, 1987).

10. I am indebted to William L. Andrews's fine *To Tell a Free Story: The First Century of Afro-American Autobiography, 1760–1865* (Urbana: University of Illinois Press, 1986), especially chapter 1.

11. Semiology, as practiced by a Roland Barthes, also suggests a type of literacy that lessens the divide between high culture and a more populist "cultural work." Consider the following from Leona Toker's important book on survivor accounts from the Gulag: "The only aspect of camp experience that can be reenacted imaginatively at second hand is a semiotic proficiency. For the prisoners themselves, the acquisition of the sign-reading skill often brought along new shocks, yet the sense of the growth of one's understanding was one of very few compensatory reprieves, and such reprieves are both vicariously and directly re-enacted by the reader." *Return from the Archipelago: Narratives of Gulag Survivors* (Bloomington: Indiana University Press, 2000), 124.

12. *The Letters of Gustave Flaubert, 1830–1857*, selected, edited, and tranlated by Francis Steegmuller (Cambridge, MA.:Harvard University Press, 1988), 154.

13. *The Letters of Gustave Flaubert, 1830–1857*.

14. John Ashbery, "And Ut Pictura Poesis is Her Name" in *Houseboat Days: Poems* (New York: Farrar, Straus and Giroux, 1999).

15. Collected in *Beyond Culture: Essays on Literature and Learning* (New York: Viking Press, 1965).

CHAPTER 4

1. Patrick Modiano, *Dora Bruder* (Paris: Gallimard, 1997), 54–57.

2. An important stimulus for Modiano's book was Serge Klarsfeld's *Mémorial des enfants juifs déportés de France* (Paris: F.F.D.J.F., 1994), which he reviewed in the newspaper *Libération* on November 2, 1994. (I thank Henri Razymow for drawing this fact to my attention and Berthe Burko-Falcman for supplying more detail.) Modiano's interest in the Occupation appears already in his first novel, *La place de l'étoile* (Paris: Gallimard, 1968).

3. This sparseness is supplemented by coincidences that serve to increase a reader's uncertainty as to whether the personal details are factual or fictive. So Modiano claims he learned, supposedly on another December 31st, when he presented his first novel *La place de l'étoile* to a Dr. Ferdière, that he has unwittingly stolen that title from Robert Desnos's book of 1945, said to have been edited by the doctor after Desnos died in the Terezin concentration camp. The play of such coincidences points to the author's preoccupation with surrealism's *hasard objectif*.

4. Doctorow, *City of God* (New York: Random House, 2000).

5. Patrick Modiano, *Rue des Boutiques Obscures* (Paris: Gallimard, 1978), 7.

6. Patrick Modiano, *Voyage de noces: roman* (Paris: Gallimard, 1990).

7. Reviewing Klarsfeld's *Mémorial* in the newspaper *Libération*, Modiano writes about its 1,500 children, whose photos often show them in familiar, everyday play or situations, that "their extermination [*anéantissement*] makes us feel to the very end of our days a terrible feeling of emptiness." Christian Boltanski also uses found photos to suggest a missing child (or childhood).

8. "J'ai employé un processus de mythomanie qui permet de mélanger réalité et fiction. En même temps j'ai l'impression que cette interférence crée une certaine malaise qui n'aurait pas lieu si le lecteur était sûr de se trouver soit dans l'imaginaire pur, soit dans la réalité historique." Quoted in Alan Morris, *Patrick Modiano* (Washington, D.C.: Berg, 1996), 40–41.

9. He adds that it was this contrast that moved him to write his novel *Voyage de Noces:* see *Dora Bruder,* 54.

10. Ellen Fine, Henri Raczymow, and Marianne Hirsch have written sensitively about this "absent" or "post" memory. It can lead to a feeling which would be inexact to call a version of survivor guilt but does incite an empathetic fantasy of substitution. Modiano's example should not be simplified, however. Pressing and crucial as the Occupation was for him, coming to grips with the life or death of a person from the past, unknown or too close to be fully known (his father, his brother) has elements, as Alan Morris suggests, of an exorcism, and is part of a more universal condition. It evoked a attempt to face a "gray zone" (to quote Primo Levi) in cognitive as well as moral terms. The solidity of the contact between persons in Modiano's novels is always spurious or precarious: Relations are fugitive, drifting, on the brink of sudden rapport then dissolution. We also sense a radicalization of the narrative tone made famous by Albert Camus's *The Stranger.* Modiano's many literary debts (his sometimes flaunted intertextuality) point to yet another dimension of that gray zone, an indefeasible *clair-obscur* that may also threaten his identity as artist.

11. It is strange that eliding a given name by reducing it to its initial letter (Kafka's K., or the W. for Sebald's birthplace Wertach) allows that name to retain its real-life aura, yet glide effortlessly into the fictional atmosphere. The foregrounding of the name also becomes, after the Holocaust and the rise of a photojournalism that portrays masses of people (alive or dead), a minimal gesture of redemptive identification.

12. As in *Double Game*, by Sophie Calle with the participation of Paul Auster (New York: Violette Editions/D.A.P., 2000). This tendency is often characterized by the term "metafiction."

13. "J'ai douté de la littérature," Modiano writes in *Libération,* about his initial response to Klarsfeld's *Mémorial.*

14. This again makes Modiano's procedure so apt: He does not violate a personal and temporal distance, and instead of usurping the role of historian suggests how close that role is to that of private eye—the detective-protagonist of the most popular type of fiction around. Modiano helps to reinvent the detective as *public* eye.

15. From Rousseau to the novels and journals of André Gide, the decision as to what should be directly revealed of private life had a seductive and potentially transgressive aspect. Already with Rousseau, Pascal's "Le moi est haïssable," or the shame leading to such a dictum, stimulates autobiography and so loops back to Augustine's conversion narrative.

16. The critical movement called New Historicism only intensifies this confusion by looking at fiction as if it could be translated back into a socioeconomic context. A move that thinks of itself as expansive vis-à-vis literary interpretation may be reductive in its understanding of the fictive. Within the discipline of history itself, the problem is not only how to value a perhaps distracting personalism but how to respond to the charge that

historians are less objective than they claim: that they are not exempt from psychological processes such as transference or projection.

17. See John Hersey's essay "To Invent a Memory," published by Baltimore Hebrew University in 1989.

18. Tompkins, *A Life in School: What the Teacher Learned*.

19. Or as subtle as in contemporary speech-act theory, scrupulously vetted in another academic memoir, Stanley Cavell's "autobiographical exercises" entitled *A Pitch of Philosophy* (Cambridge, MA.: Harvard University Press, 1994).

20. Wallace Stevens, "Phosphor Reading by His Own Light" in *The Palm at the End of the Mind: Selected Poems and a Play*, ed. Holly Stevens (New York: Vintage, 1990), 195.

21. Lionel Trilling, in his remarkable *Sincerity and Authenticity*, which distills a lifetime of literary reflections, rescues "authenticity" from what he calls "moral slang." His distinctions are too finely explored to be summarized here, but it is clear from his historical account that the novel exposes, in its characters' search for an indisputable sentiment of being, whatever in their milieu is antagonistic to that sentiment. Or what in their own selves is felt to be fraudulent, shameful, inauthentic. The new biographical culture, then, insofar as it sidesteps the novel's polyphonic realism, suggests a lessening of trust in fiction's truth or its kind of sophistication.

22. Henry Louis Gates, Jr., "The Passing of Anatole Broyard," in *Thirteen Ways of Looking at a Black Man* (New York: Random House, 1997), 180–214.

CHAPTER 5

1. Norman Manea, "Blasphemy and Carnival" in *World Policy Journal*, Spring 1996.

2. Siegfried Kracauer, *Theory of Film: The Redemption of Physical Reality* (New York: Oxford University Press, 1960), 300.

3. Kracauer, *Theory of Film*, ix. Kracauer quotes here a journalist commenting on Louis Lumière's films.

4. Emily Dickinson, "I heard as if I had no ear." Poem 996 in *The Poems of Emily Dickinson, Variorum Edition*, ed. R.W. Franklin (Cambridge and London: The Belknap Press of Harvard University Press, 1998). First published in 1945.

5. Sarah Kofman, *Paroles Suffoquées* (Paris: Galilée, 1997), 16.

6. Terrence des Pres, *Praises and Dispraises: Poetry and Politics, the 20th Century* (New York: Viking, 1988).

7. Primo Levi, *The Drowned and the Saved*, tr. Raymond Rosenthal (New York: Summit Books, 1988).

8. Binjamin Wilkomirski, *Fragments: Memories of a Wartime Childhood*, tr. Carol Brown Janeway (New York: Schocken Books, 1996).

9. The tentativeness of my phrasing reflects the fact that the present chapter was written before most of the disclosures were brought together and augmented in Stefan Maechler's *The Wilkomirski Affair: A Study in Biographical Truth*, tr. John E. Woods (New York: Schocken Books, 2001).

10. Harold Pinter, *Ashes to Ashes* (London: Faber and Faber, 1996). The American edition was published in 1997 by Grove Press.

11. See Bessie K., Holocaust Testimony (HVT 205), Fortunoff Video Archive for Holocaust Testimonies, Yale University.

12. Blanchot, *The Writing of the Disaster*, tr. Ann Smock (Lincoln: Nebraska University Press, 1986), 41, 42, 145.

13. Kracauer, *Theory of Film*.

CHAPTER 6

1. Victor Klemperer, *I Will Bear Witness: A Diary of the Nazi Years 1942–1945*, tr. Martin Chalmers (New York: Random House, 1999), 61. A second volume of the diaries has been made available in translation since this essay was written.

2. Primo Levi, *The Drowned and the Saved*, especially "Preface" and "The Gray Zone."

3. David Rousset, *The Other Kingdom*, translated and with an introduction by Ramon Guthrie (New York: Reynal and Hitchcock, 1947).

4. Jean-François Lyotard, *The Differend: Phrases in Dispute*, tr. Georges van den Abbeele (Minneapolis: University of Minnesota Press, 1988), 8 (section 9).

5. In addition to his description of the muselmänner in *The Drowned and the Saved*, Levi has an earlier and very influential passage in *Survival in Auschwitz* (New York: Orion Press, 1960), 90: "They crowd my memory with their faceless presences, and if I could enclose all the evil of our time in one image, I would choose this image which is familiar to me: an emaciated man, with head dropped and shoulders curved, on whose face and in whose eyes not a trace of thought is to be seen." The muselman type was also known from the Gulag, where they are sometimes called "goners" (*dokhodiagi*).

6. Giorgio Agamben, *Ce qui reste d'Auschwitz*, tr. Pierre Alferi (Paris: Bibliothèque Rivages, 1999), 79. All English versions of Agamben are my own, except when I cite explicitly David Heller-Roazen's translation as *Remnants*, i.e., *Remnants of Auschwitz: The Witness and the Archive* (New York: Zone Books, 1999).

7. Agamben, *Ce qui reste d'Auschwitz*.

8. See Laub's contributions to Shoshana Felman and Dori Laub, *Testimony: Crises of Witnessing in Literature, History, and Psychoanalysis* (New York: Routledge, 1992).

9. I borrow the phrase from Maurice Halbwachs's *The Collective Memory* (1949), tr. Francis J. Ditter and Y. D. Ditter (New York: Harper and Row, 1980), but change its meaning somewhat. According to Halbwachs, memory can only be *formed* within such a community; I suggest that the past can only be *recalled* within such a community—not the same, necessarily, in which it was formed, but one with the felt power to integrate the survivor-narrator.

10. The word "integral" in this context is strangely ironic if it retains a nuance of "complete."

11. Cf. Geoffrey Hartman, *The Fateful Question of Culture* (New York: Columbia University Press, 1997), 102–3.

12. Agamben, *Ce qui reste d'Auschwitz*.

13. On silence, in particular that of the survivors, see also sections 14–27 in Lyotard, *The Differend*. The issue implicitly raised by Agamben's entire project, as it seeks to subsume speech after Auschwitz, is the intelligibility of the human condition in its extremity, i.e., whether we can encompass suffering by a philosophic or intellectual operation.

14. The issue of "what remains," in its multiple connotations, is also discussed by Jacques Derrida, especially with respect to testimony's first-person mode of affirmation. See *Demeure: Maurice Blanchot* (Paris: Galilée, 1998).

15. Cf. "This almost infinite capacity to suffer that is inhuman," Agamben, *Remnants*, 77.

16. In Agamben's *Homo Sacer: Sovereign Power and Bare Life*, this appropriation of camp and muselman as biopolitical paradigm of the modern is explicit. Especially problematic is that Agamben involuntarily drives a wedge between the heroism of some extraordinary personalities in the Shoah who sacrificed themselves, and deserve the name of martyr, and the doubtful heroism (though Agamben would not use the word) of this symbolic construction.

17. Jorge Semprun, *Le mort qu'il faut* (The Required Dead Man) (Paris: Gallimard, 2001), my translation.

18. The most forceful statement of this position I know is by Serge Klarsfeld, "À la recherche du témoignage authentique," in *La Shoah: témoignages, savoirs, oeuvres,* ed. Annette Wieviorka and Claude Mouchard (Vincennes: Presses Universitaires de Vincennes, 1999), 41–53.

19. One useful by-product of Agamben's concept of authentic testimony is that he has no problem showing the irrelevance of Heidegger's notion of authenticity (*Eigentlichkeit*). The German philosopher's description of authenticity as a mode of living-toward-death that accepts—by way of an active, even heroic consent—the nothingness or impropriety of death is not applicable because Holocaust death was not something the victims *chose*.

20. Agamben, *Ce qui reste d'Auschwitz.* This despite Agamben's exaggerated emphasis on the "gens obscurs." "One of the lessons of Auschwitz," according to him, "is that it is infinitely more exacting to understand the mind of an ordinary person than that of Spinoza or Dante." But in the body of his text these "gens obscurs," precisely the rank and file of those who have given testimony, are displaced by another kind of "gens obscurs," the muselmänner. Agamben's arduous attempt to testify on behalf of the latter does show that philosophy and ethical thought have entered the camps, but at the cost of what we can learn from actual testimonies about the ordinary, often not particularly literate, people whose stories have been collected. Except that, at the very end of the book, he reproduces excerpts of testimony by muselmänner who survived.

21. Josette Zarka, "Comparaison entre les témoignages recueillis en France et aux États-Unis," *Bulletin Trimestriel de la Fondation Auschwitz* 49 (1995) (special number on *Histoire et mémoire des crimes et génocides nazis*): 7–15.

22. Pierre Nora, "Between Memory and History: Les lieux de mémoire," *Representations* 26 (1989), 17.

23. Ibid., 13.

24. Binjamin Wilkomirski, *Fragments: Memories of a Wartime Childhood,* tr. Carol Brown Janeway (New York: Schoken Books, 1996). Cases exist where the identity of a dead companion is absorbed by, and so lives on within, the one who survives. In other cases the false claim of being a survivor is probably caused by what I have elsewhere described as memory envy.

25. Quoted from Jonas Barish's superb discussion of this surprising linkage in *The Antitheatrical Prejudice* (Berkeley: University of California Press, 1981), 464–69. Wagner's charges are made in his notorious *Judaism in the World of Music* (*Das Judentum in der Musik*).

26. Friedrich Nietzsche, *The Gay Science,* ed. Bernard Williams, tr. Josefine Nauckhoff (Cambridge: Cambridge University Press, 2001), 226. Translation slightly modified.

27. Niklas Luhmann, *Die Realität der Massemedien,* 2nd ed. (Opladen: Westdeutscher Verlag, 1996).

28. Editorial, "Embassy Row: Bombing of the Chinese Embassy in Belgrade," *New Republic,* May 31, 1999, 12.

29. Tony Judt, "Writing History, Facts Optional," *New York Times* (Op-Ed), April 13, 2000, A31.

CHAPTER 7

1. Jean-François Lyotard, *The Inhuman: Reflections on Time,* tr. Geoffrey Bennington and Rachel Bowlby (Stanford, CA.: Stanford University Press, 1991), 141–43.

2. Michel Leiris, *Francis Bacon ou la brutalité du fait* (Paris: Seuil, 1996), 77. My translation.

3. For "paleonymy," a strategic necessity "that requires the occasional maintenance of an old name in order to launch a new concept," and Derrida's discussion of the materialist text, see his *Positions*, tr. Alan Bass (Chicago: University of Chicago Press, 1981), esp. 64–71.

4. See Paul de Man, *The Resistance to Theory* (Minneapolis: University of Minnesota Press, 1986). An ambiguity remains as to the meaning itself of the material base from which the meaning-content of inscriptions emerges. The inscribed letters are already a division in or of the medium: Their spacing, and the semiotic differentiation of marked and unmarked, form the basis of most types of interpretation.

5. Maurice Blanchot, *The Writing of the Disaster*, 17.

6. Emmanuel Levinas, *Beyond the Verse: Talmudic Readings and Lectures* (1982), tr. Gary D. Mole (London: Athlone Press, 1994), 109. It might be observed that typological (figural) interpretation, founded by Paul and which saved the "Old" Testament for Christianity, displays the same plenitude. The difference has to do with a respect for the literalism of the letter: not only for the historical reality of the "figures" (that was recognized by Patristic interpreters) but also for a certain attitude toward the divinely endowed reality of each letter, or combination of letters.

7. "Dans cette écriture qui est la difficulté du poète, de l'homme qui veut parler juste, mais qui est aussi la justice difficile, celle de la loi juive, la parole inscrite avec laquelle on ne joue pas, et qui est l'esprit parce ce qu'elle est le fardeau et la fatigue de la lettre." *L'Amitié* (Paris: Gallimard, 1971), 252.

8. Saint Augustine, *On Christian Teaching*, tr. R. P. H. Green (New York: Oxford University Press, 1977), 93–94.

9. Saint Augustine, *On Christian Teaching*, 72–76.

10. For a painstaking, historical sorting out of different attitudes toward the *pshat*, see David Weiss Halivni, *Peshat and Derash: Plain and Applied Meaning in Rabbinic Exegesis* (New York: Oxford University Press, 1991). For an account of "the radical fluctuation of the 'literal' sense since the Middle Ages" and from the eighteenth century to the present, see John Whitman's "A Retrospective Foreword" to his important edition of materials, *Interpretation and Allegory: Antiquity to the Modern Period* (Leiden: Brill, 2000).

11. There is a vast literature on this. I have been helped, among others, by the work of Saul Lieberman, Judah Goldin, David Weiss Halivni, Moshe Idel, Jacob Neusner, Steven Fraade, Michael Fishbane, and David Stern. The simplifications, needless to say, are my own.

12. See, e.g., Steven Fraade, "Literary Composition and Oral Performance in Early Midrash," *Oral Tradition* 14/1 (1999), 33–51.

13. See Thoreau's chapter on "Reading" in *Walden*.

14. See Jacques Lacan, "The Agency of the Letter in the Unconscious or Reason since Freud," *Ecrits: A Selection*, tr. Alan Sheridan (New York: Norton, 1977), 166.

15. See, e.g., Cathy Caruth on Paul de Man, *Unclaimed Experience: Trauma, Narrative, and History* (Baltimore: Johns Hopkins University Press, 1996), 87.

16. On this literality, cf. Paul de Man, "The Resistance to Theory," in his *The Resistance to Theory*; on "lettrism," see the perceptive essay by Shira Wolosky, "Pharisaic," *Common Knowledge*, 2 (1993), 66–80. Needless to say, lettrism can incite rather than restrain such letter-mysticism as is developed in the Kabbala.

17. The strongest statement bearing on this is found in Nietzsche's *Anti-Christ*. See also Zeev Sternhell on how fascism appropriated the Christian idea, in *Neither Right nor Left: Fascist Ideology in France*, tr. David Maisel (Berkeley, University of California Press, 1986).

18. John Donne, "Twicknam Garden" in *Metaphysical Lyrics and Poems of the Seventeenth Century*, ed. Herbert J. C. Grierson (Oxford: The Clarendon Press, 1921).

19. Gershom Scholem, ed., *The Correspondence of Walter Benjamin and Gershom Scholem, 1932–1940* (New York: Schocken, 1989), 181.

20. Maurice Blanchot, *Thomas the Obscure*, tr. Robert Lamberton in *The Station Hill Blanchot Reader: Fiction and Literary Essays* (Barrytown, NY: Station Hill Press, 1999), 51–123, 60.

21. Maurice Blanchot, *L'entretien infini* (Paris: Gallimard, 1969), 189. I should add that Levinas does not share Blanchot's view of art, since he deems it to gratify "the essential violence of action." See *Totality and Infinity. An Essay on Exteriority*, trans. Alphonso Lingis (Pittsburgh: Duquesne University Press, 1969), 298.

22. " . . . la parole, celle qui invite l'homme à ne plus identifier avec son pouvoir." Blanchot, *L'Amitié*, 253.

23. See Blanchot's postface to *Vicious Circles: Two Fictions & "After the Fact"* (Barrytown, N.Y.: Stationhill Press, 1985), 68. On passivity, see also *The Writing of the Disaster*, 17ff.

24. I have modified slightly Ann Smock's translation found in Maurice Blanchot, *The Writing of the Disaster*, 141.

CHAPTER 8

1. Harold Bloom, *The American Religion: The Emergence of the Post-Christian Nation* (New York: Simon and Shuster, 1992), 15, 256–57.

2. *The Varieties of Religious Experience : A Study in Human Nature* (New York: Longmans, Green, 1902).

3. George Eliot, *Adam Bede* (London: Oxford University Press, 1996), 33.

4. Saul Lieberman, *Hellenism in Jewish Palestine: Studies in the Literary Transmission, Beliefs and Manners of Palestine in the I Century B.C.E.-IV Century C.E.* (New York: Jewish Theological Seminary of America, 1950), Appendix I, "Bath Kol," 194–99.

5. Baudelaire, "L'homme dieu" in *Paradis Artificiels* in *Oeuvres Complètes*, ed. Y. G. le Dantec (Paris: Gallimard, 1964), 376.

6. Emily Dickinson, "The soul selects her own society." Poem 409 in *The Poems of Emily Dickinson, Variorum Edition*, ed. R.W. Franklin (Cambridge and London: The Belknap Press of Harvard University Press, 1998). First published in 1890.

7. Ibid.

8. John Henry Newman, *The Dream of Gerontius* (London: Burns, Lambert, and Oates, 1866), 115–16, 118–20. "As though I bent" corrected in the 1904 edition to "as though I went."

9. The Keats quotation comes from a letter of March 19, 1819 to George and Georgiana Keats. See *The Letters of John Keats 1814–1821*, ed. Hyder E. Rollins (Cambridge, MA.: Harvard University Press, 1958), 2:80.

10. D. H. Lawrence: "Bavarian Genetians" in *Selected Poems*, ed. Jan Todd (Oxford: Oxford University Press, 1993), 97–98. Originally printed in Lawrence's *Last Poems* of 1932.

11. William James, *The Varieties of Religious Experience*, Lecture IX, "Conversion."

12. William Wordsworth, Ode: Intimations of Immortality" in *Selected Poems*, ed. John O. Hayden (New York: Penguin, 1994), 144.

13. Rainer Maria Rilke, "Archaic Bust of Apollo" from *Der Neuen Gedichte Anderer Teil* (*New Poems: Second Part*), first published in 1908.

14. Brooke Hopkins, "A Question of Child Abuse," *Raritan Review*, Winter 1993, 35.

15. Robert Frost, "The Most of It" in *A Witness Tree* (New York: Henry Holt, 1942).

16. The opposite is true of the Kabbalah, which often "relativizes" the letters in Scripture, claiming the Torah was originally, as one mystic claimed, "a heap of unarranged letters" combining in different forms according to the state of the world. See Gershom Scholem, *On the Kabbalah and its Symbolism*, tr. Ralph Mannheim (New York: Schocken,1977),74–83.

17. John Hollander, *The Work of Poetry* (New York: Columbia University Press, 1997), 27.

18. See I Samuel 9:9, perhaps interpolated; but Saul's name in the Hebrew suggests "asking," most clearly after Saul's death in Samuel 1:28:6: "When Saul inquired of the Lord [*vajish'al Shaul beadonai*], the Lord answered him not, neither by dreams, nor by Urim, nor by prophets," which leads into the episode of the ghost-seer of Endor.

19. A good account of this development is found in Moshe Halbertal, *People of the Book: Canon, Meaning, and Authority* (Cambridge, MA.: Harvard University Press, 1997).

20. *Lamentations Rabbah: An Analytical Translation*, Jacob Neusner (Atlanta: Scholars Press, 1989), 14, in Petihta Two (II.i.5.B).

21. See Scholem, *Walter Benjamin: The Story of a Friendship*, tr. Harry Zohn (Philadelphia: Jewish Publication Society, 1981), 107.

22. "Meditation Twenty-Eight" in *The Poetical Works of Edward Taylor*, ed. Thomas H. Johnson (Princeton, N.J.: Princeton University Press, 1971), 139.

23. I am indebted for this example to Herbert Marks. See his "Writing as Calling," *New Literary History* 29 (1998), 15–37. The Buber episode is available in Martin Buber and Franz Rosenzweig's *Scripture and Translation*, tr. Lawrence Rosenwald and Everett Fox (Bloomington: Indiana University Press, 1994), 205–19.

24. Buber and Rosenzweig, *Scripture and Translation*, 208.

25. Buber and Rosenzweig, 211.

26. Elisha tears his clothes at the passing of Elijah (2:12), as does the King of Israel after having read Naaman's letter (5:7) which might portend a disaster. To this day the *q'ria* is a ritual tearing of clothing following the death of a close relative or a public calamity.

27. Emmanuel Levinas, *Éthique et Infini: Dialogues avec Philippe Nemo* (Paris: Fayard, 1982), 15. See also his *Beyond the Verse: Talmudic Readings and Lectures* (London: Athlone, 1994) and *Nouvelles Lectures Talmudiques* (Paris: Éditions de Minuit,1996), passim.

CHAPTER 9

1. See Benjamin's well-known reflections, generally known as "Theses on the Philosophy of History." Concerning the relation between fictions and apocalyptic thinking, the most profound book remains that of Frank Kermode, *The Sense of an Ending: Studies in the Theory of Fiction* (New York: Oxford University Press, 1968).

2. Gianni Vattimo, *The Transparent Society*, tr. David Webb (Baltimore, MD.: Johns Hopkins University Press, 1992), 85, 91.

3. Vattimo, *The Transparent Society*, 112–13.

4. Martin Heidegger, *An Introduction to Metaphysics* (1935), tr. Ralph Manheim (New Haven, CT.: Yale University Press, 1959), 51.

5. See Wordsworth's poem, "Lines Written a Few Miles Above Tintern Abbey, on Revisiting the Banks of the Wye During a Tour, July 13, 1798" in *Lyrical Ballads* of 1798.

6. On the level of social history, the myth of the noble and taciturn peasant, a myth that partly compensates for this loss and reacts to the ravages of the Industrial Revolution, creates its own false aura and becomes—after Wordsworth, who at his best gives it a modern and distinctively local embodiment—a politically vicious form of nostalgia.

7. Eric L. Santner, *Stranded Objects: Mourning, Memory, and Film in Postwar Germany* (Ithaca, N.Y.: Cornell University Press, 1990), 7.

8. Philippe Lacoue-Labarthe and Jean-Luc Nancy are right in pointing out that it is not so much the loss of a particular mythology that troubles the extreme identity politics of Nazism than the weakening of the mythic function itself as capable of concentrating in

one leader/racial type the forces of a collectivity. A cultic, participatory imitation is essential to achieve that mythic and unified embodiment; but postmodernism rejects or at least weakens that kind of identification. For a concise statement of their thesis (which has its relevance to contemporary Arab nationalism after the fall of the Ottoman empire) see the two authors' *Le mythe nazi* (Paris: Éditions de l'Aube, 1996).

9. *The Transparent Society*, 40–41.

10. It can be objected that we don't have to "find" that darkness, that there is plenty of it around. But accepting partial knowledge, opaqueness of event and character, and a degree of *Unwissenheit* or aporia, without sacrificing either hope or intellect, is what a provocative messianic politics combined with a positivistic social science have failed to do. An informed and subtle—yet always lucid—treatment of the challenge of what has been named situatedness, and the likelihood of literature's importance to that condicion, is found in David Simpson, *Situatedness: or, Why We Keep Saying Where We Are Coming From* (Durham, N.C. and London: Duke University Press, 2002).

11. Vattimo, *The Transparent Society*, chapter 1.

12. Ibid., 59.

13. Vattimo also talks of a (tolerable) "lightening of being" (*The Transparent Society*, 71) and sketches a peculiar aesthetic as the ornamental in chapter 5. There seems to be, again, something unresolved in the way he transforms heavy into light when it comes to Heidegger. For an effort to criticize "weak thought" as well as the Heideggerian influence on Vattimo, see Renate Holub, "Italian Heideggerian Affairs," in *Tainted Greatness: Antisemitism and Cultural Heroes*, ed. Nancy A. Harrowitz (Philadelphia: Temple University Press, 1994), chapter 9.

14. A confirmation of this hunch may be found in Vattimo's *Beyond Interpretation: The Meaning of Hermeneutics for Philosophy*, tr. David Webb (Stanford, CA.: Stanford University Press, 1997), chapter 4 ("Religion").

15. For the importance of "transparency" as a political term, at least in post-Glasnost Europe, see, e.g., Peter Zajac's ironic comment: "After scandals with tenders, Russian debt repayment, contests and public competitions smelling of corruption, the word transparency became a magic formula and the organization *Transparency International* its badge. For now, one of the few things we can say with certainty about this region [Eastern Europe] is that the most transparent thing in it is corruption." "Language of the Time Ten Years After," in *Scepticism and Hope: Sixteen Contmporary Slovak Essays*, ed. Miro Kollar (Bratislava: Kalligram, 1999), 303.

16. I do not mean to suggest that periodization began in the Enlightenment, only that this self-conscious "period" makes use of a temporal distinction and historical marker that retains, despite its rejection of a superstitious past, the aura of a religiously inspired break. For an overview of the concept of modernity, see especially Hans-Robert Jauss, "Literarische Tradition und gegenwärtiges Bewusstsein der Modernität," in *Literaturgeschichte als Provokation* (Frankfurt am Main: Suhrkamp, 1970).

17. Wallace Stevens, "A Discovery of Thought" in *The Palm at the End of the Mind*, 366.

18. *The Poetry and Prose of William Blake*, eds. David V. Erdman and Harold Bloom (Garden City, N.Y.: Doubleday, 1965), 37.

19. Jan Assmann, *Moses the Egyptian: The Memory of Egypt in Western Monotheism* (Cambridge, MA.: Harvard University Press, 1997). He traces monotheism back to the fourteenth-century B.C.E. reign of Akhenaten, a traumatic episode in Egyptian history. Akhenaten's iconoclasm provoked a religious counter-revolution that restored the old gods and erased all traces of him and his reform—Aton worship—from Egyptian history. It is only through Moses, a figure in what Assmann has baptized mnemohistory, that the

monotheistic revolution became known, and ironically through an anti-pagan, anti-Egyptian religion.

20. "All Religions Are One" in *The Poetry and Prose of William Blake*, 2.

21. Gerald de Nerval, *Les Chimères* in *Oeuvres*, ed. H. Lemaitre (Paris: Garnier, 1958).

22. Walter Benjamin, "Paris, Capital of the Nineteenth Century" in *Reflections: Essays, Aphorisms, Autobiographical Writings*, edited and with an introduction by Peter Demetz, tr. Edmund Jephcott (New York: Schocken Books, 1978), 146–162, 157.

23. Thomas Mann, "Freud and the Future" (1936) in *Essays of Three Decades*, tr. H. T. Lowe-Porter (New York: A. A. Knopf, 1947).

24. The Blake quotation is found in his *Marginalia*, "Annotations to Spurzheim's *Observations on the Manifestations of the Mind, or Insanity*" (ca. 1819).

25. Benjamin, "The Work of Art in the Era of Its Mechanical Reproduction" (1936). My translation. This essay can also be found in *Illuminations: Essays and Reflections*, edited and with an introduction by Hannah Arendt, tr. Harry Zohn (New York: Schocken books, 1968), 217–52, 220–21. Its complex publishing history is aptly summarized by Richard Wolin, *Walter Benjamin: An Aesthetic of Redemption* (New York: Columbia University Press, 1982).

26. In an as yet unpublished book, Anne Marie Oliver, studying the Islamic movement Hamas, and particularly its suicide-bombers, suggests that an "ecstatic literalism" plays a crucial role in the more fanatical wing of Islam.

27. See esp. Carl Schmitt's "The Age of Neutralizations and of Depoliticization," originally published in 1929, added to his 1927 essay on "The Concept of the Political," revised and taken up into *The Concept of the Political* (1932). Schmitt attacks an "aestheticizing" of technology that builds on a previous ("nineteenth-century") economist illusion that the conflict between nations can be resolved by a improvement in shared wealth and the material conditions of life. He posits two necessary revisions to our view of the "liberal state." The first concerns the priority of the concept of the political to that of nation or state, the political being based on an indefeasible distinction between friend and foe. This dismantles the ideal of neutrality on both national and international levels. The second concerns all "spiritual concepts including that of spirit itself." They are said to be pluralistic, but in the sense that they can be understood only existentially rather than normatively, that is, only from the concrete political situation of the state.

CHAPTER 10

1. Walter Benjamin, "Hundert Jahre Schrifttum um Goethe" in *Gesammelte Schriften* (Frankfurt am Main: Suhrkamp Verlag), 1972–1989.

2. Friedrich Meinecke, *Die Deutsche Katastrophe: Betrachtungen und Erinnerungen* (*The German Catastrophe: Observations and Reminiscences*) (Zürich: Aero Verlag, 1946), 174–176. My translation.

3. Peter Sloterdijk, *Regeln für den Menschenpark* (*Regulations for a Zoological Garden of the Human Species*)(Frankfurt am Main: Suhrkamp, 1999), 15. My translation.

4. The Novalis quotation comes from his "Dialogues" and reads in the German: "Wir sollen so viele Lehrjahre, in demselben Geist geschrieben, besitzen, als nur möglich wäre, die sämtlichen Lehrjahre aller Menschen, die jeh gelebt hätten." See *Novalis Gedichten* (Frankfurt am Main: Insel Verlag, 1987), 147.

5. I quote from "Bekenntnisse einer Schönen Seele" in *Wilhelm Meisters Lehrjahre*, Sechstes Buch.

6. *Die Wahlverwandtschaften*, chapter 3 of the second part. The context is a reflection on the artist, especially the architect or "bildende Künstler": "... am bildenden Künstler kann man auf das deutlichste gewahr werden, daß der Mensch sich das am wenigsten zueignen vermag, was ihm ganz eigens angehört." Albrecht Schöne, whose fine commentary on the poem is found in *Johann Wolfgang Goethes Faust: Kommentare* (Frankfurt am Main: Deutscher Klassiker Verlag, 1994), cites another relevant sentence: "Vom eigentlich Produktiven ist niemand Herr, und sie müssen es alle nur so gewähren lassen" (No one can be the master of what is truly productive; one must accustom oneself to letting it do its work). Goethe's conception is close to Hölderlin's "das Eigene" in the letter to Böhlendorff of December 4, 1801. I quote Ottilie's diary entry from the following edition: *Die Wahlverwandtschaften* (Leipzig: Bernhard Tauchnitz Verlag, 1943), 135 (Drittes Kapitel, Zweiter Teil).

7. Goethe, "Zueignung."

8. Goethe, *Die Wahlverwandtschaften* (Leipzig: Bernhard Tauchnitz Verlag, 1943), 135 (Drittes Kapitel, Zweiter Teil).

9. Goethe, "The Fisher."

10. From the "Lettre du voyant" to Paul Demeny, May 15, 1871 in *Arthur Rimbaud: Complete Works*, tr. Paul Schmidt (New York: Harper and Row, 1967), 102.

11. Goethe, *Die Wahlverwandtschaften*, 104 (Siebzehntes Kapitel, Erster Teil).

12. Benedetto Croce, *Goethe*, with an introduction by Douglas Ainslie (London: Methuen, 1923), 82, 92.

13. Anna Akhmatova, "Fragments" in *Poetry of the Second World War*, ed. Desmond Graham, tr. by Clive Wilmer and George Gömöri (London: Pimlico, 1998), 17.

CHAPTER 11

1. Baudelaire, "The Painter of Modern Life."

2. My translation of "Das grimmige Männchen des Buchhändler-Portals ist ein Memento für jeden Leser. Von ihm, dem Leser, hängt es ab, ob die Kathedralen zu grossen Gräbern werden oder nicht. Überall in den Werken der Literatur wimmelt es von Gnomen, von unscheinbaren Randfiguren, die darauf warten, nicht überlesen und aus ihrem Interimstod gerissen zu werden. Die Kunst ist nichts ohne ihre Details. Diese Details aber leben nur, solange sie wahrgenommen und in ihrer Funktion gewürdigt werden." Michael Maar, *Die Feuer- und die Wasserprobe: Essays zur Literatur* (Frankfurt am Main: Suhrkamp, 1997), 12.

3. *The Poems of Thomas Gray, William Collins, and Oliver Goldsmith*, ed. Roger Lonsdale (New York: Norton, 1969), 338. The editor gives the translation on p. 340.

4. *La philosophie du non. Essai d'une philosophie du nouvel esprit scientifique* (Paris: Presses Universitaires de France, 1940), 139.

5. A very approximate—and awkward—translation of Blanchot's title would be *The Waiting-For: The Forgetting*. The book was published by Gallimard in 1962.

6. Georges Bataille, "Sur Nietzsche," *Oeuvres Complètes*, VI, Tome 2 (Paris: Gallimard, 1973), 43. See also "Annexe 3," 292–99, passim, on the themes of defect, incompleteness, wounds.

7. See "Correspondences" in *Fleurs du mal*.

8. John Milton, *Paradise Lost, Paradise Regained*, ed. Christopher Ricks (New York: Penguin Books, 1968), Book III, line 380.

9. For "Gradiva," see Freud's treatment of Wilhelm Jensen's novel in *Delusion and Dream* (1907) and cf. my remarks on Nerval in chap. 9, "Transparency Reconsidered."

10. Nerval, *Les Chimères*.

11. Wordsworth, *The Prelude*, 12.297 ff.
12. Ibid., 12.315–16.
13. Ibid., 3.180 ff.
14. I quote from Simone Weil, *La pesanteur et la grace* (Gravity and Grace), with an introduction by Gustave Thibon (Paris: Plon, 1948), 96, 148, 135.
15. Emily Dickinson, "I heard a Fly buzz when I died." Poem 591 in *The Poems of Emily Dickinson, Variorum Edition*, ed. R.W. Franklin (Cambridge and London: The Belknap Press of Harvard University Press, 1998). First published in 1890.
16. Odell Shepard, ed., *The Heart of Thoreau's Journals* (New York: Dover Publications, 1961), 99.
17. Ibid., 51.
18. Ibid., 101.
19. Ibid.
20. Ibid., 80.
21. Goethe, *Zur Farbenlehre* (Zurich: Aero Verlag, 1974), 61: "... so kann man sagen dass wir schon bei jedem aufmerksamen Blick in die Welt theoretisieren." But he adds that this admixture of theory must be accompanied by self-knowledge, flexibility, even irony.
22. "A tree rose there. O sheer transcendence! O Orpheus sings! O high tree in the ear!" See the second of Rilke's *Sonnets to Orpheus*.
23. Shepard, 91.
24. Stevens, "Notes Toward a Supreme Fiction" in *The Palm at the End of the Mind: Selected Poems and a Play*, ed. Holly Stevens (New York: Vintage, 1990), 207.
25. Stevens, "Sunday Morning" in *The Collected Poems of Wallace Stevens* (New York: Vintage, 1990).
26. *The Poetics of Aristotle*, translated and with commentary by Stephen Halliwell (Chapel Hill: University of North Carolina Press, 1987), 34.

CHAPTER 12

1. Tom Wolfe, "The Lives They Lived" in the *New York Times Sunday Magazine*, January 2, 2000 (section 6, page 5).
2. See the many books of Jan and Aleida Assmann for an analysis of the concept of cultural memory. Their distinction between the cultural and what they call the "communicative" memory runs parallel to mine between cultural and public memory, without entirely coinciding.
3. Harold Rosenberg, *Arshile Gorky: The Man, The Times, The Idea* (New York: Sheepmeadow Press/Flying Point Books, 1962), 127,118.
4. Jacques Derrida, "Le siècle et le pardon," in *Foi et Savoir* (Paris: Éditions du Seuil, 2000), 105. My translation.
5. Oswald Spengler, *Decline of the West* (New York: A. A. Knopf, 1932).
6. Quoted by Adriana Berger, "Mircea Eliade: Romanian Fascism and the History of Religion in the United States," in *Tainted Greatness: Antisemitism and Cultural Heroes*, ed. Nancy A. Harrowitz (Philadelphia: Temple University Press: 1994), 57.
7. Charles Olson, "Ernst Robert Curtius," in *The Human Universe and Other Essays*, ed. Donald Allen (New York: Grove Press, 1967), 155–59.
8. William Empson, "Missing Dates" in *The Complete Poems of William Empson*, edited and with an introduction and notes by John Haffenden (New York: Penguin Books, 2000), 79.
9. De Lillo, *Underworld*, 121.

10. For Hannah Arendt, artists-writers-historians are *Homo Faber* in the highest degree. They counter mutability and seek something permanent within an "economy that has become a waste economy, in which things must be almost as quickly devoured and discarded as they have appeared in the world." See chapters 3 and 4 of *The Human Condition*. On waste products, see "Jenseits der Archive," in Aleida Assmann, *Erinnerungsräume: Formen und Wandlungen des kulturellen Gedächtnisses* (Munich: C. H. Beck, 1999), 389–408.

11. Gianni Vattimo, in many publications, has championed this concept of heterotopia, claiming that "the only criterion of value now available is that of a *conscious multiplicity*, of the memory [of alternate historical worldviews] exerted to the utmost." Forgetfulness is no longer a dionysian or life-affirming or (as in classical art) harmonizing necessity. His anti-Nietzschean position sees the historical, or rather sociological, memory as resisting an oblivion imposed by the finiteness (Hannah Arendt would say futility) of the human condition.

12. Emmanuel Levinas, *Difficult Freedom* (Baltimore: Johns Hopkins University Press, 1992), 121–22. I have slightly modified Seán Hand's translation. For this aspect of Levinas, see Jill Robbins, *Altered Reading: Levinas and Literature* (Chicago: University of Chicago Press, 1999), 47–54. While Robert Jay Lifton, in *Boundaries: Psychological Man in Revolution* (New York: Vintage Books, 1970) places this identity fragmentation and protean role-playing in a specific modern—revolutionary and multicultural—context, Jonas Barish, in *The Antitheatrical Prejudice* (Berkeley: University of California Press, 1981), has documented the long- standing history of antitheatrical suspicion that accuses the theater of undermining both social and personal integrity.

13. Henri Lefebvre, *Critique of Everyday Life*, translated by John Moore with a preface by Michel Trebitsch (New York:Verso, 1991).

14. Cf. Peter Sloterdijk, *Regeln für den Menschenpark* (*Regulations for a Zoological Garden of the Human Species*) (Frankfurt am Main: Suhrkamp, 1999).

15. "The Scholar Fu Sheng Transmitting the *Book of Documents*." Du Jin, Chinese (Ming dynasty), active ca. 1465–1509, detail from a hanging scroll, ink and color on silk, in the Metropolitan Museum of Art. The "sixth finger" of the scribe's writing hand suggests a delicate reproductive instrument.

16. Wordsworth, "She dwelt beside th'untrodden ways" in *Lyrical Ballads*.

17. Maurice Blanchot, *Après coup, précédé par Le ressassement éternel* (Paris: Éditions de Minuit, 1983), 86. My translation.

18. Stevens, "Notes Toward a Supreme Fiction" in *The Palm at the End of the Mind: Selected Poems and a Play*.

19. Yaron Ezrahi, *The Descent of Icarus: Science and the Transformation of Contemporary Democracy* (Cambridge, MA.: Harvard University Press, 1990), 94.

20. Hannah Arendt, *Lectures on Kant's Philosophy*, ed., and with an interpretive essay by Ronald Beiner (Chicago: University of Chicago Press, 1982).

21. Derrida, *De l'esprit*, 66.

22. Derrida, *Positions*, tr. Alan Bass (Chicago: University of Chicago Press, 1981), 64–71.

23. From literature for the exhibit "Let's Entertain" at the Centre Georges Pompidou, February 12-April 30, 2000.

24. See "After the Fact," in *The Station Hill Blanchot Reader*, op. cit., 127.

CHAPTER 13

1. The Loeb Classical Library *Tacitus* 1. *Agricola*, tr. M. Hutton, rev. R.M. Olgivie (Cambridge, MA.: 1930), 67.

2. Irving Howe, *The Critical Point: On Literature and Culture* (New York: Horizon Press, 1973).

3. Walter Benjamin, "The Life of Students," published originally in *Der Neue Merkur.* See *Walter Benjamin: Selected Writings*, eds. Marcus Bollock and Michael W. Jennings (Cambridge, MA.: Harvard University Press, 1996), vol.1 (1913–1926), 37–47. I have modified Rodney Livingstone's translation.

4. Fyodor Dostoevsky, *The Brothers Karamazov*, trs. Richard Pevear and Larissa Bolokhansky (New York: Vintage, 1991), 230.

5. See Szondi's essay translated as "On Textual Understanding" in *On Textual Understanding and Other Essays*, tr. Harvey Mendelsohn (Minneapolis: University of Minnesota Press, 1986), 3–22.

6. Terrence des Pres, *Praises and Dispraises: Poetry and Politics, the 20th Century* (New York: Viking, 1988).

7. Joseph Conrad, "Author's Note" to *The Nigger of the Narcissus* (1897).

8. Hannah Arendt, "The Crisis in Culture" *in Between Past and Future: Six Exercises in Political Thought* (New York: Viking, 1961), 209.

9. I am severely abbreviating Jean-François Lyotard's ambivalence about our dependence on the aesthetic in chapter 15 of "Anima Minima," *Postmodern Fables* (Minneapolis: University of Minnesota Press, 1997). The Wordsworth quotation is from the "Preface" to the *Lyrical Ballads* of 1800.

10. Wordsworth, *The Prelude*, Book 14 (1850), line 286.

11. Percy Bysshe Shelley, preface to *Prometheus Unbound* in *The Norton Critical Edition of Shelley's Poetry and Prose*, selected and edited by Donald H. Reiman and Sharon B. Powers (New York: W. W. Norton and Co., 1977), 133.

12. From Simone Weil's fragment "On Human Personality," quoted in a translation I have slightly modified. See David McLellan, *Utopian Pessimist: The Life and Thought of Simone Weil* (New York: Poseidon Press, 1990), 274.

13. Theodore W. Adorno, "Wozu Noch Philosophie" ("Why Philosophy, Still") in *Eingriffe: Neun kritische Modelle* (Frankfurt am Main: Suhrkamp, 1963), 25. My translation.

EPILOGUE

1. Sigmund Freud, "On Transience" in *Writings on Art and Literature*, with a foreword by Neil Hertz (Stanford, C. A.: Stanford University Press, 1997), 176–179.

2. Wordsworth, *The Prelude*, Book 12 (1850), lines 59–60.

3. Ibid., Book 12 (1850), lines 77–78.

INDEX